*To the Members and Friends of
the First Brethren Church
Clay City, Indiana,
whose fellowship has been our delight,
whose faithfulness has been our inspiration,
for a quarter of a century*

WOMEN IN MINISTRY

FOUR VIEWS

EDITED BY
BONNIDELL CLOUSE
& ROBERT G. CLOUSE

with contributions from

ROBERT D. CULVER
SUSAN FOH
WALTER LIEFELD &
ALVERA MICKELSEN

INTERVARSITY PRESS
DOWNERS GROVE, ILLINOIS 60515

InterVarsity Press is the book-publishing division of InterVarsity Christian Fellowship, a student movement active on campus at hundreds of universities, colleges and schools of nursing. For information about local and regional activities, write Public Relations Dept., InterVarsity Christian Fellowship, 6400 Schroeder Rd., P.O. Box 7895, Madison, WI 53707-7895.

Distributed in Canada through InterVarsity Press, 860 Denison St., Unit 3, Markham, Ontario L3R 4H1, Canada.

Cover illustration: Roberta Polfus

ISBN 0-8308-1284-9

Printed in the United States of America ∞

Library of Congress Cataloging-in-Publication Data

Women in ministry: four views / edited by Bonnidell Clouse and Robert G. Clouse; with contributions from Robert D. Culver . . . [et al.].

    p.   cm.
    Bibliography: p.
    ISBN 0-8308-1284-9
    1. Women clergy.   2. Sex role—Religious aspects—Christianity.
I. Clouse, Bonnidell.   II. Clouse, Robert G., 1931- .
III. Culver, Robert Duncan.
BV676.W548   1989   *89-1773*
262'.14—dc19   *CIP*

17	16	15	14	13	12	11	10	9	8	7	6	5	4	3	2	1
99	98	97	96	95	94	93	92	91	90	89						

INTRODUCTION
Robert G. Clouse

Each generation of Christians faces the task of making the gospel relevant to those who have not accepted Christ. As Jesus commanded, believers are to be "in the world but not of the world." One of the greatest of the Christian poets echoed this thought when he wrote that he would try to "justify the ways of God to men."[1] As Christians take this task seriously in the closing years of the twentieth century, they are faced with the problems associated with giving women a more prominent place in society. Among evangelicals the debate over the role of women usually focuses on whether they should be ordained to the Christian ministry. In most churches ordination is understood to mean the choosing of certain individuals to occupy positions of authority within the congregation. This qualifies them to preach, administer the ordinances and supervise the affairs of the congregation. Because of the special place of preaching in Protestant churches, the issue of ordination is very closely tied to that function.

Since the time of the Reformation (1517-1648), the majority of evangelical Protestants has been reluctant to allow women to serve as ministers. Despite the fact that the New Testament does not present a clear pattern which can be applied at all times and in all places for structuring the Christian community, these individuals feel that they have the biblical approach. In the New Testament texts one finds that ministers are called by various names, including apostles, prophets, teachers, bishops, deacons or elders. Also, the exact description of their duties is not explained. Margaret Howe states, "There was no standard practice of leadership in the early church and . . . initially title and function varied from place to place. The needs of the individual community determined the nature of the leadership function."[2]

The Protestant attitude toward women ministers was based not so much on New Testament texts as on the medieval Catholic approach. In an effort to give a clearer structure to their organization, the leaders of the medieval or Latin Church in the fourth century developed an understanding of ministry that borrowed heavily from the analogy of the Old Testament priesthood. Earlier statements had compared the minister to a priest, but these writers formulated the doctrine that the pastor was no longer like a priest, but was in fact a priest. A theology of ordination was accepted that made the recipient a member of a special class removed from the laity in function and value.

Because there was no precedent for women priests in the Old Testament, they were not appointed to such positions within the Christian church. The major ceremonial functions of the church, such as serving communion, were to be performed only by the priests, and consequently women were not allowed to lead these services. The exclusion of women from a leadership role in the communion was reinforced by the teaching that the service was a re-enactment of the sacrifice of Christ, and ritual purity was demanded of those who offered up the sacrifice. The fact that women were supposedly defiled by menstrual periods made them unfit to be involved in the divine service.

Later the church also demanded that clergymen be celibate, and thus women were forced even further into the background. Christian ministers were to have little contact with women because friendships with the opposite sex might lead to romantic attachment. Consequently, priests were to depend on all-male communities for their encouragement and support. The medieval outlook on women fostered by this view of ministry was ambivalent. On the one hand, women were put on a pedestal and adored as similar to the Virgin Mary, but on the other, they were viewed as scheming descendants of Eve, who would lead men astray with the sins of the flesh.)

The Protestant Reformation brought a shift in the interpretation of ordination. Martin Luther taught that there was no special priestly class but that "every man was his own priest." There were at least two reasons why Luther modified the medieval view of ministry. First, he did not believe that God had set aside a special elite group of individuals who were empowered to keep God's law in a particular way. Second, he argued that no one could merit God's grace by obeying the law. Salvation was bestowed fully and freely on all who trusted in Christ. Denying oneself physical pleasure, doing good deeds or performing religious services did not earn salvation for anyone.

Perhaps if Luther had not been such a reluctant revolutionary, he would have given women a greater role in the church's ministry, but he did not. Following in his steps the Lutheran and Reformed (Calvinist) Protestants did not allow women to serve as ordained ministers. However, both Luther and John Calvin did express some ideas about women and Christian ministry that might have influenced Protestant groups to allow participation of women in positions of leadership.

Luther taught that every Christian had the duty to carry out certain priestly functions and that in unusual circumstances, when no man was available, a woman should be permitted to preach. Calvin believed that matters involving church government and worship, unlike basic doctrine, could change to fit into a particular culture. The church had to be sensitive to the world around it so that it would not be unduly offensive to society on these issues. Among such issues he included the silence of women in the congregation as a matter of human opinion.

Despite the possibilities opened up for women in ministry by the more egalitarian ideas of the Protestant Reformers, women were still generally denied the opportunity to teach in public or assume positions of leadership in the church. Luther taught the subordination of women to men because of the role of Eve in introducing sin into the world. He believed that before the Fall and the consequent divine punishment, male and female were equal in the sight of God, but the introduction of sin into the world led to male leadership. Calvin, with his emphasis on creation rather than redemption, argued that woman

was made after man and as his helper was to be in subjection to him.
Consequently, throughout history women have been forced to obey
men and forbidden to exercise authority over them.

Another group of reformers, sometimes called the Anabaptists, radical reformers or the third force of the Reformation, differed from
Luther and Calvin on baptism, church-state relations and the role of
the Holy Spirit in the church. They also believed that God could
inspire any believer to preach the Word. A minister did not need to
be learned or ordained. The stress that they put on the participation
of lay people in preaching the gospel tended to sidestep the issue of
ordaining women. Also, the emphasis in these groups on a prophetic
role for clergy began a shift in the view of ministry away from an
institutional outlook which tended to use the priesthood as a model.

Two groups of these radical reformers that gave special opportunity
for women to minister were the seventeenth-century Baptists and the
Quakers. As one prominent Quaker points out, "Because everyone is
illumined by the Holy Spirit, the spoken ministry is, of course, not
limited to men. All Friends, men or women, are welcome to stand up
and speak. . . . They were not unique in this position. Baptists and
others had women preachers. The scornful designation of 'she-
preachers' was given to them in a list of errors, heresies, and blasphe-
mies in a seventeenth century anti-Baptist tract. 'An audacious virago'
is an expression used elsewhere."[3]

Other sources support this observation, as they explain that women
preached among the Baptists in the Netherlands, in England and in
Massachusetts. One London congregation had special services in
which women could preach, and these, on occasion, drew crowds of
over 1,000 people. The activity of women ministers among the seventeenth-century sectarians led to the publication of the first book in
English defending the participation of women in Christian ministry.

Written by Margaret Fell, this work asserted that women have the
right to participate in every aspect of Christian life because the Holy
Spirit empowers both men and women. To object to women ministers,
Fell argued, is to ignore Paul's statement that "there is neither Jew nor
Greek, there is neither slave nor free, there is neither male nor female; for you are all one in Christ Jesus" (Gal 3:28 RSV). She believed
that such Pauline statements as "Let a woman learn in silence with

all submissiveness" and "I permit no woman to teach or to have authority over men; she is to keep silent" (1 Tim 2:11, 12 RSV) were directed against the heretical women that Paul describes in the context of the passage.[4]

Encouraged by the example and teaching of individuals such as Margaret Fell, many of the early leaders of the Quaker movement were women. They went from England on missionary journeys to such distant places as North America and Turkey. One of the first to come to the colonies, Elizabeth Hooten, made two missionary trips to New England after she was sixty years old. The Puritans did not tolerate Quakers and persecuted Hooten in a most inhumane way with imprisonment, starvation, beatings and exile to the wilderness. In contrast to the opportunities open for women in the sectarian movements, the major Protestant churches during the seventeenth century remained adamant in their opposition to women being ministers.

Most Protestants were forced by the controversies that arose during the Reformation era to define their doctrines in a more precise manner. They did this by drawing up creedal statements that depended on the philosophy of Aristotle. This produced a period called the Age of Orthodoxy. Although there were those who led lives of deep devotion to Christ during this period, many believers were discouraged by what they considered a dead orthodoxy that emphasized correct doctrinal statements at the expense of a vital Christian faith.

Those who reacted against the emphasis on the official stance of the churches were called Pietists. Such individuals found new sources of strength within the gospel by emphasizing fervent moralism, personal conversion, holiness of life, a concern for human need, and a devotional life reflected in prayers and hymns. Pietism was a call for believers to model Christ in their daily lives. The movement encouraged Christians to internalize religion rather than emphasize external formalities and creeds. Originating in Germany with the work of Philipp Jakob Spener and August Francke, this renewal of Christian faith had an openness toward women that led to new opportunities for women in leadership positions.

Especially in England and America, Pietism associated with the eighteenth-century Methodist revival led by John Wesley, was to have significant consequences for women in ministry. Wesley was in many ways a curious combination of a conservative Anglican and a radical religious innovator. His attitude toward women is certainly an illustration of this.

On the one hand, Wesley wished to take the statements of Paul against women preachers as a general rule for all time; but, on the other, several factors led him to modify these ideas. Among these were his desire to consider Methodism as a movement within the church, rather than as a separate denomination. Consequently he believed it was possible to do things within Methodism that could not be done within an ecclesiastical organization. Also, he felt that God called people to preach in a direct, personal, extraordinary manner. This idea finally led him to allow lay men and women to preach. As a leading Methodist historian explains:

> At first he was startled at the thought that an unordained layman might engage in leadership of a congregation to whom he preached. Wesley squirmed and hedged, allowing witnessing in informal groups but not preaching (that is, from a text). Yet he soon discovered that his lay "helpers" or "assistants" were good preachers, though not ordained. Hence the distinction between "preacher" (Methodism) and "priest" (Church of England). One more step naturally led to the recognition of women as lay preachers. Although Wesley resisted the evidence for a long time, he finally admitted that women too could have an extraordinary call to do that which was traditionally prohibited, to speak in meeting, to testify in faith, to instruct—yes, finally, to preach.[5]

Pietism was also influential in America where it was partially responsible for the Great Awakening (c. 1725-c. 1770). Leading to the conversion of masses of people through evangelistic preaching, this revival began among the Dutch Reformed Churches and then spread to other groups such as the Congregationalists in New England, where it produced the most notable preacher of the age, Jonathan Edwards.

Women played an important role in this movement because the revivalists stressed the need for a personal experience with God. All people, including women who were born again through faith in Christ, were supposed to witness to others. Also, many of the leaders of the awakening were open to experimentation as long as it led more people to Christ, and this could mean that women as well as men would preach. Many believed that the revival was a sign of the end of the age and such extraordinary times meant that exceptions to the customary ways, including women preachers, were acceptable.

One woman who was given an opportunity to exercise a leadership role during the Great Awakening was Sarah Osborn. The revival came to her community, Newport, Rhode Island, during the years 1766-67, and she responded by leading a worship service in her home. Over five hundred people attended these functions, and her activities attracted a great deal of criticism. It was claimed that she was in error because both men and women were present. Furthermore, she was threatening the social order by allowing black people to attend.

She responded to these criticisms by claiming that she had not sought a public ministry but that God had called her to it. She pointed out that she had tried to recruit men from her church to lead the services but that none of them were interested. Also, she said that the people of her community preferred her counsel to that of the men. Finally, she stated that her leadership role gave her meaning and purpose in life that could not be supplied by the ordinary tasks assigned to women in her day.

The Evangelical Awakening of the eighteenth century was followed by a similar revival in the first half of the nineteenth century. Many estimate that two-thirds of the converts during this "Second Great Awakening" were women under the age of thirty. Perhaps due to this influx of women into the church, the nineteenth century became in an even more pronounced way the age of women preachers. This new opportunity for women was more evident in the English-speaking world, especially in America.

The higher percentage of females in the church led to the acceptance of the belief in "true womanhood" or, as it is sometimes called, "the cult of domesticity." According to this teaching the ideal woman was supposed to be morally pure, submissive and pious. She was to be a skilled homemaker who would make the domestic scene a refuge from the outside male world of competition in politics and business. Her duty consisted of encouraging her husband, rearing her children, caring for the sick and managing the home. This view of women, shared by Christians and non-Christians alike, was based on the belief that males and females are radically different. Women are less rational, extremely emotional, and more likely to be physically or mentally ill.

Although the emphasis on "true womanhood" would seem to work against a greater participation of women in ministry, those who presented these ideas also claimed that women were more inclined than men to religious faith and moral righteousness. Consequently, nineteenth-century Americans reversed the view of women as prone to sin after the example of Eve. Rather than being weak, lustful creatures, they were idealized as examples of virtue and piety, while males were cast in the role of sensual, immoral brutes. Women were not only believed to be morally better than men, but they were also felt to be spiritually superior. As one writer explains:

> Religion therefore became an integral part of the domestic sphere over which women were to reign. They were "peculiarly susceptible" to the Christian message. Ministers suggested that women were by nature meek, imaginative, sensitive, and emotional, all qualities that were increasingly coming to be associated with Christian piety. They added that women more readily responded to Christianity out of gratitude for the way in which this faith had elevated their social status. Women were viewed as imitators of Christ. Like Christ, they brought redemption to the world through their moral virtue and religious fervor. Like Christ, they endured the sufferings of this life with patience and in silence.[6]

This new emphasis on the role of women had other effects that encouraged them to assume leadership positions. One of these was an extension of educational opportunities for women beyond the elementary level so that they could be more effective in childrearing and household management. As women became more educated, they read their Bibles and found a message of justice and liberation. Then they began to feel that God gave them leadership and speaking abilities which they could use in numerous Christian causes that extended outside the domestic sphere.

Another result of this new definition of womanhood was a sense of female self-worth and a desire to do something to help shape society. If the assertion that women were spiritually and morally superior to men was true, then why should they be excluded from running the world. Such an attitude led women to form missionary societies to spread the gospel and benevolent associations to care for the sick and the poor.

During the period from 1820 to 1840, many women joined reform societies founded for the purpose of creating a Christian America through social change. These groups were concerned with peace, temperance and prison reform. By the 1840s they were directing their attention to the antislavery movement. As women argued against the defenders of slavery, they were led to reflect upon their own place in society. If Galatians 3:28 meant that slaves should be equal to their masters, then women also ought to be included in the biblical concept of equality.

The more these women pondered on their place in society, the more they came to believe that freedom for blacks ought to be coupled with freedom for all people. Two early leaders in the anti-slavery movement, Sarah and Angelina Grimke, began to behave in a way that reflected this attitude as they spoke in an effective way to audiences that included both men and women. They became role models for other women of their time, and some of their followers succeeded in organizing a conference at Seneca Falls, New York, in 1848 for the purpose of securing women's rights.

While many nineteenth-century women were led to preach through working in movements for social reform, other women became involved in ministry through the more normal channels of church organizations. They were generally in groups that would be considered sectarian. As Ruth Tucker and Walter Liefeld point out:

> In England these groups included the Quakers, Primitive Methodists, and Bible Christians; and in America, the Quakers, Freewill Baptists, Free Methodists, as well as factions connected with the holiness and deeper life movements. All of these movements emphasized direct communion with God, the leading of the Spirit, and the call to ministry over and above clerical counsel, church bylaws, and ordination. As was the case with the Anabaptists and other free church movements in history, the high priority placed on spiritual gifts left the door ajar for women in ministry.[7]

Some of the more well-known of these women include Phoebe Palmer (1807-74), Catherine Booth (1829-90) and Hannah Whitehall Smith (1832-1911). Palmer spent most of her life in New York City where she was married to a physician. She felt called to spread the Methodist doctrine of holiness through revivals and camp meetings in the United States, Canada and Britain. Her publications, including a monthly magazine, *The Guide to Holiness,* and the book *The Way to Holiness* (1851), had a substantial impact on Wesleyan theology. She also established several missions to the poor in the New York slums and was active in the movement for women's rights.

Catherine Booth participated with her husband in the founding of the Salvation Army. The mother of eight children, she not only preached but also worked to reduce the exploitation of women and children. Within the army she established the principle that women have absolute equality with men. In addition to her preaching ministry she published a number of pamphlets on witnessing, popular Christianity, and the relation between church and state. As her son would later write of Catherine:

> She began her public ministry when I, her eldest child, was five years old. But her own home was never neglected for what some would call—I doubt whether she would have so described it—the larger sphere. Both alike had been opened to her by God. She saw His purposes in both. In the humble duties of the kitchen table, her hands busy with the food, or in the nursery when the children were going to bed or at the bedside of a sick child, she was working for God's glory.[8]

The third member of the great triumvirate of nineteenth-century women ministers, Hannah Whitehall Smith, became involved in the deeper life movement and played an important role in founding the Keswick Conference. Despite her husband's affair with a young woman, which caused him to leave the ministry, she continued to teach, preach and write. Her most famous work is a devotional book entitled *The Christian's Secret of a Happy Life.* The holiness movement has proudly claimed her as a popularizer of the doctrine of sanctification as a second work of grace.

These three women—Palmer, Booth and Smith—have common characteristics in their lives: They were all members of husband-wife teams, in each case the woman being more prominent than the man; all had several children and managed to combine homemaking with their ministry; and each was identified with the holiness movement.

Other sectarian groups whose activities led to an increase of women in public ministry throughout the nineteenth century were the Brethren Church, the Christian Missionary and Alliance, the Church of God (Anderson, Ind.) and the Church of God (Cleveland, Tenn.). The Brethren Church is a typical example of these new organizations.

Soon after the progressive wing of the Church of the Brethren organized a separate denomination in the later nineteenth century, it encouraged women to assume leadership roles. By 1894 the General Conference of the Brethren Church had passed a resolution granting women the right to serve as pastors and missionaries. The first ordained woman, Mary M. Sterling, was an energetic evangelist for the Brethren. During one seven-month journey through West Virginia and Pennsylvania, she preached 207 sermons in 187 days, added 27 members to the church and baptized 18. She was such a respected leader that in 1894 she gave one of the main sermons at the General Conference.

During the early years of the movement, many other Brethren women also served as preachers, pastors and evangelists.[9] But after the foundational work of the church had been carried out and the church was better organized, men took over the leadership role. Perhaps small groups such as the Brethren wished to become more acceptable to society, and to do this they imitated the larger denominations in excluding women from positions of authority. Women were allowed to continue to minister on the mission field, but even here they were regarded as second best to men. As the famous pioneer missionary Gladys Aylward confessed:

I wasn't God's first choice for what I've done for China. There was somebody else. . . . I don't know who it was—God's first choice. It must have been a man—a wonderful man. A well-educated man. I don't know what happened. Perhaps he died. Perhaps he wasn't willing. . . . And God looked down . . . and saw Gladys Aylward.[10]

In the twentieth century the growth of the Pentecostal movement resulted in a wider role for women in ministry. However, the same process that caused the decline of female leadership in the nineteenth-century sects was repeated in the later charismatic groups. By this time, however, the mainline Christian churches—such as the Methodists, Lutherans, Episcopalians and Presbyterians—were beginning to ordain women as ministers. In contrast to these denominations, the evangelical movement which developed in the period between 1920 and 1960 discouraged female leadership. Reacting to the social gospel, these conservatives turned back to a literal understanding of the Bible. It is with this tradition that the following essays wish to deal.

Each of the interpretations presented here has devout evangelical Christian adherents. The statements are written by those who hold the view on women and Christian ministry that they express. Robert Culver gives the traditional view that women are not to be involved in Christian ministry. Susan Foh presents the case for a limited involvement of women in ministry as long as they are under the direction of a male senior pastor. Walter Liefeld supports the position that all believers are ministers and that an overemphasis on ordination has caused Christians to argue over women's roles in the church to a greater extent than they should. In the last essay Alvera Mickelsen discusses the egalitarian view that fully supports female ministry. She explains that women should be able to engage in any kind of service for which God has endowed them and to which they feel called. At the conclusion of each essay the other three contributors respond from their respective viewpoints. Final remarks are given by Bonnidell Clouse, followed by a bibliography dealing with women and ministry.

It is our hope that these essays and discussions will help readers to formulate their own views about the role of women in the church. As has been stated, this is one of the most pressing problems facing believers in the closing years of the twentieth century. Those who follow Jesus Christ must seek to understand his will in relation to women's rights. Beyond the need to come to terms with the times, however, is the requirement that Christians deal justly with others regardless of race, social class or gender.[11]

Notes

[1]John Milton, *Paradise Lost* (1667) Book 1, line 22.
[2]E. Margaret Howe, *Women and Church Leadership* (Grand Rapids: Zondervan, 1982), p. 69.
[3]Robert J. Leach, *Women Ministers, A Quaker Contribution* (Wallingford, Penn.: Pendle Hill Publications, 1979), p. 6.
[4]The title of Fell's work is *Women's Speaking Justified, Proved and Allowed of by the Scrip-*

tures. For more information on women preachers in the seventeenth century, see Richard L. Greaves, "Foundation Builders: The Role of Women in Early English Non-Conformity" in *Triumph Over Silence, Women in Protestant History*, ed. Richard L. Greaves (Westport, Conn.: Greenwood Press, 1985), pp. 75-92.

⁵Frederick A. Norwood, "Expanding Horizons: Women in the Methodist Movement" in Greaves, *Triumph Over Silence*, p. 152.

⁶Barbara J. MacHaffie, *Her Story, Women in Christian Tradition* (Philadelphia: Fortress Press, 1986), p. 95.

⁷Ruth A. Tucker and Walter L. Liefeld, *Daughters of the Church: Woman and Ministry from New Testament Times to the Present* (Grand Rapids: Zondervan, 1987), p. 258.

⁸Bramwell Booth, *These Fifth Years* (London: Cassel and Co., 1929), p. 25.

⁹Jerry R. Flora, "Ninety Years of Brethren Women in Ministry," *Ashland Theological Journal* 18 (Fall 1984): 4-21. For the story of the major branches of the Brethren or Dunker movement, see Donald F. Durnbaugh, ed., *Meet the Brethren* (Elgin, Ill.: The Brethren Press, 1984).

¹⁰Gladys Aylward as quoted by Phyllis Thompson, *A Transparent Woman: The Compelling Story of Gladys Aylward* (Grand Rapids: Zondervan, 1971), pp. 182-83.

¹¹As Calvin College philosopher Nicholas Wolterstorff so eloquently states: "People [in the ninetenth century] asked why such and such differences were relevant to the distribution of social benefits and deprivations. 'Why is my being born of a commoner and your being born of a noble relevant to whether we will become educated?' At each point a question of justice was raised, for people are being treated unjustly where benefits and deprivations are distributed on the basis of differences that are not relevant. The question that women in the church are raising is a question of justice. There are, indeed, a good many more dimensions involved than this one of justice, but justice is basic. Women are not asking for handouts of charity from us men. They are asking that in the church—in the church, of all places—they receive their due. They are asking why gender is relevant for assigning tasks and roles and offices and responsibilities and opportunities in the church. The gifts of the Spirit are relevant. But why gender?" ("Hearing the Cry," in *Women, Authority and the Bible*, ed. Alvera Mickelsen [Downers Grove, Ill.: InterVarsity Press], p. 289).

1/A TRADITIONAL VIEW: LET YOUR WOMEN KEEP SILENCE

A TRADITIONAL VIEW:
Let Your Women Keep Silence
Robert D. Culver

There is no question that in many church-sponsored situations, both private and official, Christian women may speak, sing, pray and express questions, perhaps even debate. The question is, Are they, according to biblical teaching, allowed to teach with church authority as pastors or elders and teachers of pastors? May they serve in positions of authority where some adult members exercise "rule over" others? This sort of "rule" is set forth in passages such as 1 Thessalonians 5:12-13 and Hebrews 13:17. Those who thus "rule" also "teach," or at least some of them do. They are called presbyters (or elders) and overseers (or bishops) in the New Testament. Qualifications for the office of elder-overseer uniformly imply wielding of authority of some kind over others (1 Tim 3:1-7, especially 4-6, and Titus 1:5-11). Presiding and liturgical functions will normally be in their charge.

Chief among the questions I wish to address is whether there is an authoritative *tradition* in Scripture regarding women in ministry. Did Paul—apostle to the Gentiles and teacher of the churches, author of almost everything the Bible has to say specifically about church governance and polity—did he leave a *tradition* in his letters limiting the ministry of women? If so, what is it and how was it understood at the time? How permanent and binding is it? Let us further inquire what reasons for this tradition may exist in the constitution of society set forth in the early chapters of Genesis. (Paul claims to build his regulations and reasoning on those early accounts and directs his readers to the law to establish his points—1 Cor 14:34.) Then, after some attention to preservation of what 1 Corinthians calls *ordinances* or *traditions* in the subapostolic age, I shall close with some possible correction or modification of what are sometimes only esteemed to be scriptural traditions and suggest some ways that we may preserve both scriptural order and peace in the churches in unstable times like our own.

Is There a Tradition?

I have chosen to use *tradition* in the biblical sense—not in the popular sense of something that happens regularly in a group or society, or even an alleged statement of Moses or an apostle unrecorded in Scripture but passed on through the generations by other means, as in Jewish or Roman and Greek Orthodox theology. Tradition, in the rather strict sense of the New Testament, is something precious, instituted by authority which has been delivered over for safekeeping, not to be changed or tampered with. In 2 Thessalonians 3:6 Paul speaks of his instructions about behavior as a "tradition received of us" and in the preceding chapter urges the brethren to "stand fast, and hold the traditions which ye have been taught, whether by word, or our epistle" (2 Thess 2:15 KJV). In each case the Greek word is *paradosis*, which means something over, or along, received intact and to be passed on just as it was when received in the first place.

I think nothing could better reflect Paul's feelings about matters of tradition and impart a sense of the importance he attached to them than the opening sally of his first great charge on the public ministry of women: "Now I praise you, brethren, that ye remember me in all things, and keep the *ordinances* [my emphasis], as I delivered them to you" (1 Cor 11:2). If the venerable King James Version's *ordinances* be too strong, then NIV's *teachings* is much too weak, for the Greek word is the plural of *paradosis* ("traditions"), the same as in 2 Thessalonians 2:15 and 3:6. The verb *delivered* in 1 Corinthians 11:2 is parallel to "taught" and "received" in 2 Thessalonians 2 and 3.

Tradition, in this sense, is much more formal and important than casual words or incidental expressions of opinion, but rather "the form of sound words" to be held "fast" (2 Tim 1:13). Some passages suggest Paul required the rote memory of a catechism or liturgical portion, to be passed down the generations (2 Tim 2:2). Many New Testament scholars think they find pieces of such permanent liturgy or catechism—such as Philippians 2:6-11 or 1 Timothy 3:16—embedded in Paul's epistles. Ancient people in general, Asiatics of all times and Jews in particular, have commonly set more value on memorized, set permanent ways of saying and doing things than modern Western people do.

Paul, however, was in some respects quite modern in the words he used to proclaim the gospel message. Consider how many ways he stated the doctrine of justification in Romans 3—11 and Galatians. Think of how various were his illustrations of it and the examples he used—Abraham, David, Hagar, Isaac, Esau, to suggest a few. In doctrine he was no stickler for a certain verbal formula. Yet in some matters he was extremely rigid—chief among these apparently being the ordinances or traditions surrounding preaching, ruling and observance of the Lord's Supper in the Christian assembly (see 1 Cor 11:2, 20-22, 34). In the case of the Lord's Supper he set forth a definite *paradosis* ("ordinance," "tradition") and order (the Greek word is *taxis*, "a prescribed arrangement"—1 Cor 11:34).

What Is the Tradition? 1 Corinthians 11:2-16[1]

[2]Now I praise you, brethren, that ye remember me in all things, and keep the ordinances, as I delivered them to you.

[3]But I would have you know, that the head of every man is Christ; and the head of the woman is the man; and the head of Christ is God.

[4]Every man praying or prophesying, having his head covered, dishonoureth his head.

[5]But every woman that prayeth or prophesieth with her head uncovered dishonoureth her head: for that is even all one as if she were shaven.

[6]For if the woman be not covered, let her also be shorn: but if it be a shame for a woman to be shorn or shaven, let her be covered.

⁷For a man indeed ought not to cover his head, forasmuch as he is the image and glory of God: but the woman is the glory of the man.

⁸For the man is not of the woman; but the woman of the man.

⁹Neither was the man created for the woman; but the woman for the man.

¹⁰For this cause ought the woman to have power on her head because of the angels.

¹¹Nevertheless neither is the man without the woman, neither the woman without the man, in the Lord.

¹²For as the woman is of the man, even so is the man also by the woman; but all things of God.

¹³Judge in yourselves: is it comely that a woman pray unto God uncovered?

¹⁴Doth not even nature itself teach you, that, if a man have long hair, it is a shame unto him?

¹⁵But if a woman have long hair, it is a glory to her: for her hair is given her for a covering.

¹⁶But if any man seem to be contentious, we have no such custom, neither the churches of God.

After discussing moral problems in the Corinthian church, Paul turns his attention to "the Lord's Supper" in chapter 10 and to related aspects of public worship in chapters 11 through 14. The portion of chapter 11 quoted above relates specifically to how women and men should behave themselves when Christians meet together in public worship. It has taught believers of every clime and time, almost without exception of any major group I know of, that:

1. God distinguishes sharply between the sexes as to appearance and activity in formal Christian assemblies. A man's hair is to be short and his head uncovered by hat or shawl, while a woman's hair is to be uncut and, in visible recognition of submission to God's order, she is to wear an additional head covering in order to veil, not her face (as in Muslim practice), but some of the rest of her head.

It is fairly certain that men and women did not sit together in the Jewish synagogue. The Christian churches may have followed the same custom. Jewish men may not yet have adopted the head shawl or cap for worship; in any case the Christian man at worship must not cover his head ("head covered" means something hanging down from the head—the sides, not the top).

2. As nearly as I can determine, the opinion has prevailed through the Christian centuries that women should wear their hair long and should also wear a hat or veil at meetings for worship. There has been a change in practice, if not of Bible interpretation, within the living memory of millions of people; women attend church in bobbed hair of every conceivable feminine style and almost never wear a hat or other head covering. People do not seem to be very troubled at the startling inconsistency.

When we ask for explanations, we are cautiously informed that (a) the Greek words really do not require the extra covering; (b) cultural changes have placed different meanings on short and long hair—if in her heart she honors God's authority through the man (pastor, husband) that is enough[2]; (c) perhaps the usual coiffure for ladies is sufficiently long to meet the requirement; (d) long hair and hats are simply too much trouble to bother with; (e) any other culturally current way of managing the visible distinction between men and women is acceptable; (f) the whole affair is rooted in a patriarchal social culture which, like slavery, Christian society has now outgrown. Christians must therefore abandon every distinction based on sex in the name of a perfected Christian faith.[3]

3. Since Paul would not allow in chapter 11 what he plainly forbids in chapter 14, it must be assumed that the praying of women in verses 4 and 5 means they performed liturgical acts such as group recitation of prayers, amens and the like. Similarly the prophesying is in the singing of psalms, hymns and spiritual songs. Also included is the playing of instruments. Because in the Temple worship the sons of Asaph and Jeduthun "prophesied with a harp, to give thanks and praise to the LORD" (see 1 Chron 25:1-7), it seems quite reasonable that in the context of public worship, to "prophesy" in 1 Corinthians 11 should mean the same as in 1 Chronicles 25.

Another possible approach to the seeming discrepancy between chapters 11 and 14 is given by Nathaniel West: "You must notice that Paul is discussing here in chapters 11 not the question directly as to whether either man or woman has the right to 'pray or prophesy,' but solely the question of costume-decorum, and head-covering. No permission to pray or to prophesy is given to either party. One thing is very clear, the man who does either with his head 'covered' dishonors his head; the woman who does either with her head 'uncovered' commits an offence that is a shame or disgrace to her sex and the Church. Both offences are prohibited."[4]

Still another proposal seems to fit: sometimes a pastor in charge invites a godly woman to speak or pray in the service of worship. In such a case it is proper for the woman to do so under the conditions of this passage. This practice is widespread.

This epistle offers no single line of proof; several are brought to bear. It argues, *in the first place,* from the principle of headship. Headship is a common metaphor for authority. It is the only symbolism that fits (certainly not source, for God is not the source of Christ). The Christian man's head is Christ, and the Christian woman's (not wife's) head is man, as also Christ's head is God (v. 3). In each case *head* means a precedence of authority.[5]

In the order of the Triune Godhead, God the Father God has precedence over Christ the Son. Whether this is to be understood in an *economic* sense (the way things are done, line of operative command) or *ontological* sense (how things are in and of themselves), Paul does not say. At any rate, in his incarnate earthly state the Son said, "I do always the will of him that sent me." The Father stands in relation to Christ the Son where man stands in relation to woman in the church. Paul here is not concerned directly with human relationships in marriage or in political-civil-social relationships. Certainly no hierarchy of men in general over women in general seems to be described.[6]

In the second place, Paul argues specifically from the laws of creation as set forth in the basic document of all biblical religion, the Law of Moses. More than one aspect of creation is brought to bear. Paul treats the first pair, man and woman, as archetypes (or prototypes)—not Platonic forms or some type or antitype in heaven, but as concrete examples of man-ness and woman-ness. The man is not simply Eve's husband, nor she merely Adam's wife, but each as either man-ness or woman-ness forever. This is inescapable.

In that case, two features of the Genesis account bear on the relation of male and female humanity in the church. *First,* female humanity was derived out of male humanity—"for man did not come from woman, but woman from man" (1 Cor 11:9 NIV). True, as the chapter later says, "man is born of woman" (v. 12 NIV), but that is how the race goes on, not how it started. What goes onward through the generations consists of "pieces" that were put together at the start in the archetypal man and woman. In that original "put together," woman was derived from man. Paul cites that as one sufficient reason for some kind of precedence to the man in public church relations, not denying there may be similar precedence in other departments of society. Whether people of our individualistic, self-assertive epoch regard this as adequate or important or not, it is what this particular basic document of our religion plainly asserts.[7]

Second, in the archetypal pair "neither was man created for woman, but woman for man" (v. 9 NIV). Genesis 2, after verse 7, tells us how and why God did just that. Among the beasts there was none suitable as man's helper. So God made a woman for him. God made a woman *for him,* not him for her nor each for one another—pious as that sounds. (Again, no one who forms his views in harmony with the spirit of the age will feel comfortable with this.) Yet, this is the interpretation which this basic document of Christianity places on the creation account, Paul citing it to support his teaching of male precedence in public worship in the church.

There is a *third* argument: "Because of the angels, the woman ought to have a sign of authority on her head" (v. 10 NIV). Now, if one wishes, he may think the authority here is woman's own. But the assertion seems strange in context of man's authority. In a context where God's precedence over the Son, the Son's precedence over the man and man's precedence over the woman are clearly taught, it seems out of place to see here a shift to one's own (the woman's) authority. The covering, whether long hair or veil or both, was to signify woman's subordination to man in a Christian assembly, ordered by Scripture and apostolic regulation.

What do angels have to do with this (v. 10)? If the proper order for worship in Christian assemblies requires that women have the sign of willing acceptance of rightful authority, then angels are interested. Angels are called God's Holy Ones and his Watchers in Scripture. So they "watch" God's special affairs on earth as unseen witnesses, pursuing their interests in every service of Christian worship. The women at Corinth and elsewhere should not offend the angels by offenses against the created order.[8]

There is much more that cries for attention, but I think the main elements in the tradition are plain. Men are to exercise authority and take leadership in the church. Women should acknowledge that authority and support it in every Christian way, including how they dress and adorn themselves when they attend public worship. Whether the sign of recognition must take the form of long hair and some other head covering, as was the case in the sixth or seventh decade of the first century, is a problem we seem to shrink from facing today. It is hard to insist on either long hair or a hat in a day when almost no one, including women missionaries in pulpits on deputation, has either. We have a problem.

1 Corinthians 14:34-37

[34]Let your women keep silence in the churches: for it is not permitted unto them to speak; but they are commanded to be under obedience, as also saith the law.

[35]And if they will learn any thing, let them ask their husbands at home: for it is a shame for women to speak in the church.

[36]What? came the word of God out from you? or came it unto you only?

[37]If any man think himself to be a prophet, or spiritual, let him acknowledge that the things that I write unto you are the commandments of the Lord.

There has been, historically, less unanimity about the meaning of this passage than of 1 Corinthians 11:2-16. Few have felt that the "silence" women are to preserve in the churches is an absolute silence. Likewise, the "obedience" women are to be "under" is not commonly felt to be absolute. There are important exceptions, of course. Verse 35 can hardly mean that Christian wives of unbelieving husbands, widows or single female adults must wait until they get home to ask some man what the pastor meant by an obscure passage in his sermon. Plainly, however, the passage should be applied generally "in all congregations of saints" (v. 34). It would be difficult to make verse 34 work in any assembly where the pastor is a woman appointed by a female bishop or district superintendent—whatever the minimal regulative content.

"Keep silence" ("remain silent" NIV) is *sigaō* in Greek. One could wish that something a bit less uncompromising than this were the meaning of the word. But it is used throughout the New Testament in the sense of "be silent," "stop talking" or "keep [something] secret." The idea seems to be that as far as the *public act of teaching* in the assembly is concerned, women were to keep silent. It has been commonly held that the prohibition is against not only public discourse in sermon or lecture, but also debate or contrary questioning of teachers of the church in public worship. The ancient church had no feature like our Sunday schools, where the teacher, male or female, might invite questions or debate. Evidence, however, suggests that the ancient Christian sermon, unlike the usual monologue of today, was open to discussion and questioning as in the synagogues.

Women are not to interrupt or question the teacher (preacher); the "to speak" is not a pejorative word but is simply the word for talking in the widest possible sense. It does not mean to jabber, babble or the like, though sometimes it means to have conversation *with* someone. Perhaps it is this idea of exchanging words with the speaker that Paul has in mind. Nowadays even the men do not frequently do that either, unless invited by the preacher to do so and seldom even then.

It is clearly stated that women at church "must be in submission" (v. 34 NIV, a much preferred rendering). I cannot help quoting Barth again. After citing not only this verse but many other New Testament passages which employ the two usual Greek words for woman's submission to man, he writes, "What is here expected of women in their relation to men is in no sense to be conceived on the analogy of the relationship between subject and prince, subordinate and superior, or chattel and owner. . . . The authority to which woman bows in her subordination to man is not the latter's [man's] but that of the *taxis* [Greek for order or good order] to which both [woman and man] are subject."[9] Paul is speaking simply of quiet, unprotesting acceptance of God's order of things expressed in Christ's apostolic instruction regarding male leadership in worship and public life of the Church.[10] Paul asserts that "the law" (that is, the Pentateuch or even all the Old Testament) says the same as he is teaching. We shall take up this issue again later in the essay.

The epistle also employs some sarcasm (v. 36). Obviously Paul is addressing impudent and recalcitrant female readers: "Did the word of God originate with you? Or are you the only people it has reached?" (v. 36 NIV). There are some who think the first question is reminding the Corinthian women that no females had ever been channels of scriptural revelation and that God was not about to use women as a means of revelation at that late date. Perhaps so. It is more commonly, and I think correctly, held that the sense is to be related to Paul's assertion in chapter 11 that the custom of a male leadership and ministry was the accepted rule in all churches of God. There is no "alternate leadership style." He is showing them that they of Corinth have no basis for claiming any special or peculiar right to make changes in "the ordinances" or "the tradition." Theirs was not the only church in the world and certainly not the first one, with the privilege of setting the style.

1 Timothy 2:8-15

[8]I want men everywhere to lift up holy hands in prayer, without anger or disputing.

[9]I also want women to dress modestly, with decency and propriety, not with braided hair or gold or pearls or expensive clothes, [10]but with good deeds, appropriate for women who profess to worship God.

[11]A woman should learn in quietness and full submission. [12]I do not permit a woman to teach or to have authority over a man; she must be silent. [13]For Adam was formed first, then Eve. [14]And Adam was not the one deceived; it was the woman who was deceived and became a sinner. [15]But women will be saved through childbearing—if they continue in faith, love and holiness with propriety. (NIV)

This epistle raises the subject of functions, practices and order in public worship in the assembly, as in 1 Corinthians 11 and 14. The prayers of the church are first mentioned—prayers for all men everywhere, but particularly for national leaders and public magistrates (verses 1-7). Paul claims in that connection that he, himself, had been "ordained a preacher, and an apostle . . . a teacher" of those very

"Gentiles [nations]" (v. 7). He continues his thoughts on the subject of prayers and giving of thanks for "kings and all those in authority" (v. 2), saying that the *men* should do the praying (v. 8). The text is very plain. The words are *tous andras*, "the men." The word means "men" in contrast to "women" or "boys". It is not simply the males. Paul wants grown-up, responsible men in the leadership of the local churches.

In the same connection he tells what he wants the women to be and do: "I also want women to dress modestly, with decency and propriety, not with braided hair or gold or pearls or expensive clothes." In this community (Ephesus) both poverty and wealth abounded, and evangelism of all classes had been successful. The fancy hairdos, flashy jewelry and lavish attire to which many women of every age aspire would be worn to church by those who could afford them—to the embarrassment of the gospel and to the humiliation of those who could not afford them. Paul discouraged these excesses. He might have been speechless if he had seen the leading women on current syndicated "Christian" TV talk shows or on the platform of some fully Americanized Christian "crusades," "rallies" or the like.

Women are not to peddle their distinctly female wares at church. Nothing else in public life then or now seems to exclude excessive carnal display, but one ought to be able to escape it at church. I think it is safe to say that by far the majority of Christian teachers of every age of the church has understood this epistle not to forbid any of these things to Christian women but to enjoin restraint, modesty, consideration of others.[11] "The object of the Apostle is not to enjoin a general rule of life for Christian women, but especially for their demeanor at the place of prayer. He does not forbid all ornament, but only the excess which is a mark of frivolity and love of display, and awakens impure passions." With *decency* and *propriety* means "inward aversion from everything unseemly," and "propriety" the "control of the passions."[12]

There is a better way to achieve distinction in the circle of faith. It is something women of the Bible and good women everywhere always excel in. The epistle specifies "good deeds, appropriate for women who profess to worship God" (v. 10). Dorcas, the Christian woman of

Acts 9:36-42, is a New Testament example of what Paul means, though I fear women today might not fit her into their model of "women professing to worship God." At least that is not what most books and articles for and about modern women seem to be telling our women and girls.

The prescription of silence and submission in church, together with the prohibition against women teaching men found in 1 Corinthians 11 and 14, is repeated in verses 11 and 12. Argument from the created order of things is raised again in verse 13.

Paul introduces an important new argument, based on the early chapters of Genesis, as follows: "And Adam was not the one deceived; it was the woman who was deceived and became a sinner" (v. 14 NIV). The verse *seems* to begin by referring to the first human pair simply as individuals, but it only seems to do that. Paul is referring to the *womanhood* of the first woman, the archetypal woman. He supports his Apostolic refusal to let women be ruling authorities in the church or to be the teachers of men by referring to something about woman's nature—something different about woman as woman from man as man. In the temptation incident woman showed herself to be more susceptible to temptation through deceit than was the man. This is the tradition of 1 Timothy 2:14, stated similarly in 1 Corinthians 11:3.

Until getting acquainted with feminist literature and commentators influenced by feminism, I never heard the verse expounded in any other way—and my recollection covers more than half a century, including scholars who taught New Testament courses in theological seminary, humble Sunday-school teachers of long ago, pastors, Bible conference teachers and every older orthodox commentator in my library. Eve was *deceived* by a flashy half-truth; her man was *persuaded* by a tie of affection. She was deceived, but he was not.

I have just consulted again several old standard theology texts such as Alford, Bengel, Lange, Jamieson, Fausset and Brown, Wace, Ellicott, Spence, Meyer and a sermon by H. A. Ironside. With some slight difference of emphasis, H. D. M. Spence in Ellicott's commentary on the whole Bible (one of the most orthodox, dependable and transparently honest of the large grammatical, popular commentaries of a few generations back) speaks well for them all:

The argument here is a singular one—Adam and Eve both sinned, but Adam was not deceived. He sinned quite aware all the while of the magnitude of the sin he was voluntarily committing. Eve on the other hand, was completely, thoroughly deceived (the preposition with which the Greek verb is compounded here conveying the idea of thoroughness); she succumbed to the serpent's deceit. ✓ Both were involved in the sin, but only one (Eve) allowed herself to be deluded. So Bengel, *"Deceptio indicat minus robur in intellectu, atque hic nervus est cur mulieri non liceat docere"* ["The deception indicates a lesser ability in comprehension, and so this limitation is why it is not allowable for a woman to teach"]. . . . This may sound to our ears a farfetched argument, when used to discountenance female usurpation of intellectual supremacy. It was, however, a method current at the time to look for and find in Scriptures the concrete expressions of almost all philosophical judgments. At the present day we could hardly find a more vivid illustration of the essential difference between masculine and feminine nature. If there be this distinction between the sexes, that distinction still furnishes the basis of an argument and a reason for the advice here rendered. The catastrophe of Eden is the beacon for all generations when the sexes repeat the folly of Eve and Adam, and exchange their distinctive position and function.[13]

Is There Support for the Tradition in Other Scripture?
Paul thought so (see 1 Cor. 14:34, "as the Law says" NIV; as also "saith the law" KJV). No one knows for sure what part of the Old Testament Paul was referring to. On a related subject Paul quoted Isaiah 28:11 as "in the Law" (1 Cor 14:21); so we are at liberty to assume that he means the whole Old Testament. He says it supports his requirement that men, not women, will normally be the people's representatives and spokesmen in corporate prayer, ritual sacrifice, liturgical ceremonies and the like. Similarly men, rather than women, will ordinarily be God's agents and spokesmen as in theocratic government (priests, kings, judges) and in revelation (Moses and the prophets). Such has indeed been the case, as everyone knows.

Old Testament history supports the eminence of men over women in every kind of leadership. Genealogical lines are ordinarily traced only through the male line. Women are introduced as the complements and helpers of their men. This is so overwhelming that no special documentation is required. The same was true of all ancient peoples. It might be that a woman named Elissa founded the city of Carthage, but it was by way of loyalty to her husband and uncle Acherbas whom her brother Pygmalion had caused to be assassinated. The same has been true throughout the world to the present day.

In the area of civil affairs there is, of course, the biblical story of Barak and Deborah and of Jael, another heroine of sorts, in the story of Judges 4 and 5. But Deborah set no precedent. The judges before her and after her were men. There were also Athaliah and her mother Jezebel, who were civil leaders, but one was queen of an apostate kingdom of Israel and the other a personal apostate and reprobate who reigned briefly by terror and was removed as quickly as possible by her own people in favor of a grandson. We know the names of a few prophetesses also. They also are exceptional, and no books of scriptural prophecy come from them. The priesthood was wholly composed of the male descendants of Aaron, the brother of Moses. In fact, every official feature of the Old Testament theocratic system was in the charge of men. Perhaps this, in part, is what the epistle to the Corinthians had reference to in the clause "as also saith the law."

Some commentators think "the law" in 1 Corinthians 14:37 is the Pentateuch only and specifically Numbers 30. Perhaps so. The entire chapter of about a full page in the Bible relates to vows and oaths of women. A man's vow or oath was to be binding upon him, not to be nullified by anyone (slaves are not mentioned). A woman's vow was not to be binding unless confirmed by the silence of her husband when he should hear it or, in the case of a minor daughter, "in her father's house in her youth." The vow or oath could be "disallowed" only if the husband or father expressed himself so "in the day that he heareth." In the case of a widow or divorced woman "every vow . . . shall stand." Unattached, single, adult women who never marry are not mentioned. Presumably if there were such they would have come under the rule for widows and divorced. If this were the rule today, Mrs. Thatcher might have some difficulty doing the Queen's business without her husband!

Many commentators suggest that there is an allusion to Genesis 3:16. Some reference Bibles supply that reference, the ASV with a question mark. Whether Paul was thinking specifically of Genesis 3:16 or more generally of the whole Hebrew Bible, that passage is very important to our subject.

The version of 1611 provides a correct literal rendering: "Unto the woman he said, I will greatly multiply thy sorrow and thy conception; in sorrow thou shalt bring forth children; and thy desire shall be to thy husband, and he shall rule over thee." Recent translations, beginning with RSV, invariably change the sense from two things to one thing. The two things of the Hebrew text and of the 1611 version are an increase in pains (sorrows) for woman (again Eve is an archetype) and an increase in the number of children she will conceive and bear. The one thing of the new translations is neither of the two but something else, namely, "I will greatly increase your pains in childbearing."

The two are said to be an *hendiadys*,[14] a Greek word which means one-through-two. As nearly as I can trace it, E. A. Speiser spread this notion many years ago through his influence on a now older generation of scholars. For reasons I find unconvincing, Speiser insisted on *hendiadys* as a strong feature of Genesis. No other author in the Anchor Bible series whom I have read makes such a big deal of *hendiadys*—and the series now runs to nearly thirty volumes.

Hendiadys does exist in the Hebrew Bible, but Genesis 3:16 is not an example of it. Sorrow and conception are not two phases or expressions of one idea. Quite the contrary. The whole human race seems quite agreed that there is a lot of pleasure in connection with conception of babies. The sorrow comes later and lasts for years. As a matter of fact "sorrow" or "pain" appears later in the verse and as a separate member of the four-member address to the woman. Is the whole verse about sorrows for females? I think not! Bible translations are like many other things; improvements may be irregular; and not every new rendering is better than the old. Translators, like department stores, do follow fads. The coming of death for every man ("It is appointed unto man once to die") required "a quantum leap" in the number of conceptions and births if the race were not to end soon. Each married couple must produce more than one or two offspring, or instead of "increase and multiply" we have "decrease and disappear"—as the Swedes are now grudgingly acknowledging of their new contraceptive society.

The pronouncements of Genesis 3:16 are frequently treated as if they were curses. A more careful assessment shows that while the serpent is cursed, and "cursed is the ground" with thorns and thistles, the pronouncements of God on the man and the woman as such are simple statements of fact about the present and future, made necessary by the Fall of man. Man's aggressive impulses and sexual desires will be checked by hard work and the harsh realities of the natural order now partially turned against him. Woman now lives in a partially disordered world. Marriage and family life will not be bliss. Husband-wife-child relationships will be a very distorted mirror of the perfect economy of the Triune Godhead. Now in addition to being created happily after Adam and as a helper *for* him, she will be limited in two ways.

In the first place, woman will have a desire to be a wife to a man. ("Your desire shall be for your husband" NIV). No mere man can know exactly what this is.[15] Karl Barth acknowledges that there is some sort of a feminine "mystique" involved, but declines to define it. Other theologians have tried, with at least some credibility, to say some things about it. If there were no primal urge in a woman to want a man (children and home as well) and, knowing quite well from observing marriages of others what painful burdens multiple conception, children and housekeeping can be, she might remain single. We have to think of the human situation before industrialization took some of the drudgery out of ordinary housework, childbearing and family living. If God wanted the race to continue, female humanity must coexist with this pesky double-feature prospect of the burdens of conceiving many children, together with intense and prolonged desire for a husband.

The last clause, "and he shall rule over thee," seems to be the one Paul had in mind when he wrote "as the Law says" (1 Cor 14:34). How can we avoid connecting this with the tradition or ordinances of 1 Corinthians 11 and 14 and 1 Timothy 2?

Genesis 3:16 ("he shall rule over thee") contains the first occurrence of the word *rule* in the Bible, and it is the same Hebrew word *mashal* which the Bible ordinarily employs of civil rulers throughout.

The text, then, tells us to expect that in areas of life where authority is exercised over adults, men will ordinarily not be ruled by women, but rather, women will be ruled by men. With occasional exceptions, this is the way it has always been and likely always will be. The passage is not a command for men to rule women or for women to accept their rule, prudent as that may be; it is a statement of fact, which neither the Industrial Revolution nor the feminist movement is likely to overturn. When, as now, this bit of social fiber is stretched and bent, there will likely be increasing resistance and a return to what must be regarded as normal. The radical feminists should give up and quit. Normal, universal, female human nature is against them. Most women prefer things the way they are, at least wherever biblical norms have prevailed.

I think it is a mistake to label any and all inversions of this steady state of affairs as a sin. Those caused by the manifold vicissitudes of history are unavoidable, as when illness strikes down a husband and a father; or laws of dynastic succession place an Elizabeth, Anne, Mary or Catherine on a throne; or when male failure of nerve promotes a Margaret Thatcher; or voters simply prefer a Margaret Chase Smith; or the personal genius of a "wise woman of Tekoa" or a Huldah is sought after by kings. They are exceptions to a general rule and do not break any moral law.

Male ascendancy in most affairs is not a legal ordinance to be obeyed; it is a fact to be acknowledged. As far as the churches are concerned and the present-day eagerness of some to open up the "clergy" to women—this too shall pass. All the local, state and federal laws about equal rights, equal access, nondiscrimination on the basis of sex and the like have produced more exceptions but not changed the rule. "The exceptions prove [i.e., test] the rule." In all aspects of life where authority of one over another, among adults, is involved, the ancient facts built into human nature will prevail.

If I am mistaken and the radical feminists prevail, some wise words of Scripture will apply: "As for my people, children are their oppressors, and women rule over them. O my people, they which lead thee cause thee to err, and destroy the way of thy paths" (Is 3:12 KJV). This is the same chapter which denounces youth rebellions that affect the fabric of society: "And I will give children to be their princes, and babes shall rule over them. And the people shall be oppressed, . . . everyone by his neighbor: the child shall behave himself proudly against the ancient, and the base against the honorable" (Is 3:4-5 KJV).[16] Isaiah closes with the lengthy denunciation of feminine preoccupation with cosmetics, costume and luxurious finery cited earlier. The passage ends with a dire prediction: "Thy men shall fall by the sword, and thy mighty in the war. And her gates shall lament and mourn; and she being desolate shall sit upon the ground" (Is 3:25-26 KJV).

I cannot comment on all the teachings of this third chapter of Isaiah. A major thrust is plain: when the people of various natural orders of society (men, women, children—the book of Proverbs mentions wise, prudent, fools and simpletons) are out of place (children or childish adults ruling affairs; women or womanish men directing society; the wise being overruled by fools; prudent people set aside for fools), then that society is on its way to dissolution.

Granted, this is not the whole truth about the relative merits of people. True, the Preacher says, "better is a . . . wise child than a . . . foolish king" (Eccl 4:13 KJV). Some children and some women have remarkable wisdom and leadership qualities. History furnishes many examples. These numerous examples, however, do not affect the general rule of common human feeling and the teaching of Scripture. Ordinarily the authority of adults over other adults *ought* to be by men and almost certainly will be. The scriptural standard for male leadership of churches is even stronger.

The Tradition in the Early Church

The last book of the New Testament—likely written very late in the first century by John, the last living apostle, from his exile on the Isle of Patmos—has a small section which is pertinent. To "the angel of the church in Thyatira" Christ directed John to write: "Nevertheless, I have this against you: You tolerate that woman Jezebel, who calls herself a prophetess. By her teaching she misleads my servants into sexual immorality and the eating of food sacrificed to idols. I have given her time to repent of her immorality, but she is unwilling" (Rev 2:20-21 NIV). It appears that in this one New Testament case where the teaching office was filled by a woman, Jezebel, the results were disastrous. The Lord made dire pronouncements upon her as well as the church which tolerated her. We know of no other women of the

New Testament exalted to be teachers of the church. It can hardly be claimed that the private ministrations of Priscilla or of Philip's daughters are exceptions.

Of greater interest and significance is a Christian epistle from about the same decades, but not a part of Scripture. Paul refers to a certain Clement in his epistle to the Philippians (4:3). He is one whose "name is in the book of life." He was a Gentile and a Roman, associated with both Paul and Peter while they still lived. In the name of the church at Rome he addressed a rather long letter to the church at Corinth at about the same period John wrote Revelation. Though lost for hundreds of years and recovered only about 350 years ago, it is known to have been held in high esteem in the first centuries. Eusebius, the great fourth-century church historian, wrote, "Clement has left us one recognized epistle, long and wonderful, which he composed in the name of the church at Rome and sent to the church at Corinth, where dissension had recently occurred. I have evidence that in many churches this epistle was read aloud to the assembled worshippers in early days, as it is in our own."[17]

A reading of this epistle shows a feud had broken out in the church of Corinth. Presbyters appointed by apostles or their immediate successors had been rudely deposed. A younger generation had rejected the older leaders. As a consequence, disorder and moral laxity prevailed. In addition, recent persecution added to their distress. Clement warms to his themes of rebuke, instruction, exhortation and consolation by a reference to their better days of the past in his first paragraph. Here it is clear that the tradition of male leadership had been well known and acknowledged at Corinth. I quote several lines:

> For who that had sojourned among you did not approve your most virtuous and steadfast faith? your sober and forbearing piety in Christ? . . . hospitality? . . . your perfect and sound knowledge? For ye did all things without respect of persons, and ye walked after the ordinances of God, submitting yourselves to your rulers and rendering to the older men among you the honour which is their due. On the young too ye enjoined modest and seemly thoughts: and the women ye charged to perform all their duties in a blameless and seemly and pure conscience, cherishing their own husbands, as is meet; and ye taught them to keep the rule of obe-

dience, and to manage the affairs of their household in seemliness, with all discretion.[18]

I select a few exhortations from the rest of the epistle to show how thoroughly Clement believed in the Pauline standards for church order and how fervently he exhorted the backslidden Corinthians to return to them. Jealousy at Corinth stirred up "the mean against the honorable . . . the foolish against the wise, the young against the elder" (par. 3, p. 58). Jealousy brought Peter and Paul to their undeserved deaths (par. 5, p. 59). "Let us reverence our rulers; let us honour our elders; let us instruct our young men in the lesson of the fear of God. Let us guide our women toward that which is good: let them show forth their lovely disposition of purity; let them prove their sincere affection of gentleness; let them show their love, not in factious preferences but without partiality towards all them that fear God, in holiness" (par. 21, p. 67). "Let us . . . enlist ourselves . . . in His faultless ordinances." Using Paul's figure of the body, "all the members . . . unite in subjection, that the whole body may be saved" (par. 37, p. 73).

"We ought to do all things in order, as the Master hath commanded us to perform at their appointed seasons" (par. 39, p. 74). "Let each of you, brethren, in his own order [Gr. *idiō tagmati,* that is, own rank, own group in marching order] give thanks unto God, maintaining a good conscience and not transgressing the rule of his service. . . . They therefore [thinking of Lev. 10] who do anything contrary to the seemly ordinance of His will receive death as the penalty" (par. 41, p. 74). He argues that the apostles received from the Lord instructions as to certain "orders" for installing overseers (bishops, presbyters) and deacons. The Corinthians have sinned grievously in turning them out for younger people with new ideas (paragraphs 42-47, pp. 75-77). The church should repent and reverse this "sedition against its presbyters" (par. 47, p. 77). That Clement is not moved by anti-female feelings is certain, for he declares, "Many women being strengthened through the grace of God have performed many manly deeds [Gr. *andreia,* that is, like-the-human-male deeds]. He mentions Judith and Esther and adds that God, "seeing the humility of [Esther's] soul, delivered the people" (par. 53, p. 80).[19] But he cites no women who aspired to rule or teach the Lord's congregation on earth.

When we read comments like these coming from a period only thirty years or so after Paul wrote his First Epistle to the Corinthians, it seems certain that the obvious prima facie meaning of chapters 11 and 14 about the silence of women in church, leadership of men, teaching of adults by men only, is exactly the impression the apostle wished to convey.

The practice of the churches through the centuries and the teaching of the theologians and pastors varied little from what we have already seen. Books and articles appearing over the last generation document the exceptions in practice. Fierce arguments have been spoken, penned and published for opening up the teaching and ruling offices to women, but the tradition has held in the main and up to the present hour.[20]

I would like to issue some possible qualifications and warnings regarding an over-rigid application of the biblical tradition. Popular figures sometimes arise to do wonderful works of great benefit to mankind quite apart from general practice. I have already affirmed that Genesis 3:16 is a statement about what men and women are. It is a prediction of how they will behave on the basis of who and what they are, not specifically what they must be and do. That does not mean that the genius of a Deborah should have been unavailable to Barak and Israel any more than the steady courage and admirable leadership qualities of a Princess Elizabeth should not have been accepted by Protestant Englishmen in their Queen of the sixteenth century or the noble genius of nurse Florence Nightingale by the British military in the nineteenth century. John Knox in 1558 fulminated against the monstrous "regiment of women" in that day, but Providence had already overruled Knox.[21]

Let me quote something I published over fifteen years ago, even though I suppose some will see, wrongfully, a condescending attitude in it: Scripture conditions its teachings "in such a way as to remove most, if not all, feminist objections. . . . The Bible authors understand the familiar lovable difference of woman's nature as something to be cherished and protected. Can a virgin forget her ornaments, or a bride her attire? (Jer 2:32) God, Himself, in an Old Testament parable, is represented as adorning a virgin with jewels, beads, and rings— even including a nose ring! (Ezek 16:1-14). The Mosaic laws protected her rights against unjust fathers, slave masters, brothers, or husbands. She is represented, in spite of some misunderstanding of Paul's dictum ("workers at home," Titus 2:5), as having legitimate and profitable interests outside her husband's home (See "considereth a field and buyeth it. . . . Her merchandise is profitable"—Prov 31:16, 18, cf. 10-31). The . . . service of gifted women is reported with high approval (e.g., Miriam, Ex 15:20; Deborah, Judges 4:4-24; wise woman of Tekoah, 2 Sam 14:2-20; Huldah, 2 Chron 34:22-28; Philip's daughters, Acts 21:8-9; Priscilla, Acts 18:2, 26; 1 Cor 16:19; Phoebe, Romans 16:1)."[22]

The church also has innumerable avenues of service, social expression and of Christian witness for women within the biblical limits of the tradition of male authority. This has always been the case and remains true to the present.

Some Reflections, Cautions and Suggestions
1. I have quoted and provided documentation for only such writings as serve in one way or another to further the immediate goals of this essay. I belong to several scholarly societies whose journals for fifteen or twenty years have been full of the issues related to women's rights. I have read again almost all of these as well as a number of books. Every conceivable interpretation is represented. Much of it, though strident and often angry, is both relevant and irrelevant. For example, a 1985 symposium by twelve female "theologians" proceeds on the premise that it has become abundantly clear that the Scriptures need liberation, not only from existing interpretations, but also from the patriarchal bias of the texts themselves. The more we learn about feminist interpretation, the more we find ourselves asking, "How can feminists use the Bible, if at all?"[23]

2. The ceremony of ordination is not the issue. The early fathers of the Reformation, Luther and Calvin and associates, saw no conferral of divine grace in the laying on of hands. Christ has already conferred the gift on gifted men-apostles, prophets, evangelists, pastor-teachers (Eph 4:8-11). The church acknowledges their Christ-imparted authority by appointing (ordaining) them to offices (or functions). In the New Testament, deacons do not "rule" the church, but elders (presbyters) or bishops (overseers) do. Whether a woman

(Phoebe) was a deacon or not is irrelevant to the question of the ordination of females to "the ministry."

3. The majority who follow the biblical tradition grant a very wide range of ministries for women.[24]

4. Many very large churches which honor the tradition are placing women on their regular paid staffs. The old professions of "Bible woman," the Lutheran "deaconess" and the like are being revived under new names. Proper channels for specialized "professional" services by women are increasing.

It can hardly be doubted that people today expect pastors to perform services they should not perform and which formerly were done by women in other than elder-bishop-pastor capacity. Some of these were simply done by older Christian women; some by "sisters" or "deaconesses" or "wise women" of old, frequently the pastor's wife. Clearly Paul assigned the task of counseling young women to other than Pastor Titus. He was to counsel older men and young men as well. "The older women" were to "train the young women" (Titus 2:1-6).

There are other things the male pastor should pass by. Thomas C. Oden has written: "Women may be equipped physiologically and psychically to do some tasks of ministry better than men. With a different hormonal structure that elicits differently nuanced patterns of responsiveness, women may be more natively gifted in empathy. It may be that some of the nurturing response implied in the pastoral metaphor may come more easily for women. . . . This is all the more probably the case of parishioners faced with miscarriage, childbirth, mastectomy, hysterectomy, and menopause, where men may have less access to the felt dynamics of feminine psychology."[25]

5. Theological seminaries are advised not to encourage women to enroll in programs which ordinarily lead to pastoral appointments. Those who successfully complete the program are unlikely to find openings as pastors. There are other more appropriate programs of study.

6. Frequently heard and often attested: "Put the women in charge and before long you have a women's church; the men simply stop attending," as Paul may be hinting in 1 Timothy 2:8-15.

7. On accommodation to "non-sexist" language: "Why, even chil-

dren know that women are included under the word 'men'!"[26]

8. If someone is convinced Paul means exactly what he seems to say about women's silence, head covering and the like, yet is reluctant to insist on carrying it out in the present culture lest harm be done, he has a sympathetic Reformation counselor of the highest authority.[27] Calvin advocates a sensible freedom in secondary matters. "What? Does religion consist in a woman's shawl? . . . Is that decree of Paul's concerning silence so holy that it cannot be broken without great offense?[28]

9. One of the more insightful books of our century is *Ideas Have Consequences* by Richard M. Weaver.[29] The following brilliant extract on the follies of feminism appears a few paragraphs from the close of the book:

> The rage for equality has so blinded the last hundred years that every effort has been made to obliterate the divergence in role, in conduct, and in dress. It had been assumed, clearly out of this same impiety, that because the mission of women is biological in a broader way, it is less to be admired. Therefore the attempt has been to masculinize women. (Has anyone heard arguments that the male should strive to imitate the female in anything?) A social subversion of the most spectacular kind has resulted. Today, in addition to lost generations, we have a self-pitying, lost sex.
>
> If our society were minded to move resolutely toward an ideal, its women would find little appeal, I am sure, in lives of machine-tending and money-handling. And this is so just because woman will regain her superiority when again she finds privacy in the home and becomes, as it were, a priestess radiating the power of proper sentiment. Her life at its best is a ceremony. When William Butler Yeats in "A Prayer for My Daughter" says, "Let her think opinions are accursed," he indicts the modern displaced female, the nervous, hysterical, frustrated, unhappy female, who has lost all queenliness and obtained nothing.
>
> What has this act of impiety brought us except, in the mordant phrase of Henry James's *The Bostonians,* an era of "long-haired men and short-haired women?"

10. Modern science has known for a generation that the psychobiological differences between human males and females make the

claims of radical feminism doubtful in the extreme. This is apparent even in college textbooks on behavior. Melvin Konner, in a 1983 book *The Tangled Wing: Biological Restraints on the Human Spirit,* lays this out in devastating detail, summarizing hundreds of research reports.[30]

Notes

[1]Even at this late time the ideas involved in the discussion are thought of in terms of the version of 1611. I cite it here to keep the game honest by retaining the language in which the discussion up to now has been phrased. Some recent versions support the view I take better than does the old King James, but in this text and the next (1 Cor 14:34-37) it seems to me to be the base from which to proceed.

[2]A learned turn to this explanation is furnished by J. G. Sigountos and Myron Shank, "Public Roles for Women in the Pauline Church: A Reappraisal of the Evidence." *Journal of the Evangelical Theological Society* 26, no. 3 (Sept. 1983):283-95. They conclude, "We can begin to reconstruct Paul's thinking about women in 'ministry' from the exegetical and historical data presented. Permissible roles seem to have been established on the basis of cultural norms, not abstract theological considerations. How culture viewed a role or activity appears to have determined whether or not it constituted insubordination. Conversely, *any role that was not viewed as inappropriate by the culture* [emphasis mine] was permitted by Paul" (p. 293). G. R. Osborne thinks some "commands" of Scripture "have proven detrimental to the cause of Christ in later cultures" and "must be reinterpreted." The "the loving greeting of the holy kiss is normative, but the particular cultural method is not" (G. R. Osborne, "Hermeneutics and Women in the Church." *Journal of the Evangelical Theological Society* 20, no.4 [Dec. 1977]:337-40). So "it is the subjection of the woman, not the wearing of veils, that was part of the early Church's catechesis [that is, tradition, *paradosis*] (ibid., 343). I heard Harry Ironside say that Paul's "greet ye one another with a holy kiss" should be now equated with "a hearty handshake." Ironside was no advocate of *Redactionsgeschichte* or of cultural relativity, though he employed one of its principles.

[3]These are by no means all the proposed interpretations. An assessment of several other recent proposals with documentation will be found in Osborne's article ("Hermeneutics," pp. 337-52).

[4]*Women and Church Ministry* (n.d., no publisher), p. 11.

[5]Karl Barth, *Church Dogmatics,* trans. H. Knight et al. (Edinburgh: T & T Clark, 1960), devotes about 165 pages to the subject of man-woman issues and comes very close to what I have been calling *the tradition* (III/2, pp. 285-344 and III/4, pp. 116-240). After referring to 1 Corinthians 11:7-9, Barth asserts: "This basic order of the human established by God's creation is not accidental or contingent. It cannot be overlooked or ironed out. We cannot arbitrarily go behind it. It is solidly and necessarily grounded in Christ . . . so solidly grounded in the lordship and service, the divinity and humanity of Christ that there can be no occasion either for the exaltation of the man or the oppression of the woman. . . . It is the life of [the] new creature which Paul describes here with the saying that the head of the woman is the man. Gal 3:28 is still valid, in spite of shortsighted exegetes, like the Corinthians themselves, who shake their heads and think they can claim a contradiction" (III/2, pp. 311-12). Later, "It is quite ridiculous to think that progressiveness should be played off against

conservatism in the matter. . . . Progress beyond it can be only regress to the old eon. It is only in the world of the old eon [outside of Christ] that the feminist question can arise" (ibid.). Barth goes on to say that the distinction might have arisen in a different form in a different culture. He says it is rooted partly in "natural sensibility" as Paul says. Barth concludes, "The decisive point was that enthusiasm for equality which outran the form was not particularly Christian, but that the custom should be accepted in Christ. We cannot say more than that it should be, for Paul was not arguing from the Law, but centrally from the Gospel" (ibid.).

[6]See Barth's telling remarks to this effect. *Dogmatics,* III/2, p. 311.

[7]Barth devotes lengthy discussion of the fact of woman's derivation from the man and approvingly comments on Paul's argument on the basis of it: "Paul tells us plainly enough in vv. 11-12 that he does not retract anything he has said in Gal. 3:28. In the Lord, 'of God,' it is just as true that the woman is of the man and the man by the woman. Both are told us by Genesis 2. Woman is taken out of man, but man is man only by the woman taken out of him. Yet only an inattentive enthusiasm could deduce from this that man and woman are absolutely alike, that there can be no question of super and subordination between them, and that it is both legitimate and obligatory to abolish the distinction between the uncovered and the covered head in divine service. It was the same inattentive enthusiasm which concluded from the fulness of spiritual gifts of which there was evidently no lack at Corinth, that there was no further need for the teaching, exhortation and admonition of an apostle. In both cases, as in many other respects, it was forgotten that God (14:33) is not a God of [confusion] but of peace. But there is peace only if distinctions are observed" *(Dogmatics,* III/2, pp. 309-10).

[8]Most commentators agree. Barth is typical: "The angels are generally the bearers of and representatives of the relative principles necessarily posited with the work of God . . . specifically . . . the divine work of salvation. They cannot, therefore, see these orders violated without sorrow" *(Dogmatics,* III/2, p. 310).

[9]Karl Barth, *Dogmatics,* III/1, p. 172.

[10]I note that in recent times in America a "chain of command" theory is being propagated. The notion is that authority is mediated downward through a definite chain: God, Christ, man, woman, child and the like. Such a ladder or chain is not taught in Scripture, though the Bible has much of approval to say about the principle of authority in many realms. But that is another subject.

[11]A very interesting column in the *Oxford Classical Dictionary,* 2d ed., p. 1081, states that almost every "aid to beauty" known today was "to be found in ancient times on a lady's toilet table." It mentions many of them and goes on to say, "Cosmetics and perfumes were fully used. Athenian wives attached great importance to white cheeks, as distinguishing them from sun-burned working women; they applied white lead, and also used a rouge made from orchids. . . . Greek women usually wore their hair arranged simply in braids, with a parting in the middle drawn into a knot behind. . . . But . . . a fashion arose of raising a structure of hair on the top of the head, painfully arranged by a lady's maid. Blondes were fashionable in Rome, and brunettes could either dye their hair or use the false [Nordic blond] hair which was freely imported from Germany." Is that a bouffant which Nefertiti wears in her famous likeness? Or is it a royal hat? The prophet Isaiah fulminated at length against feminine attachment to gaudy jewelry and excesses of cosmetic decoration. Neither Roman ladies nor the burgeoning jewelry and cosmetic market of today have gone

essentially farther than the "daughters of Zion" (Is 3:16-26).

[12]P. Lange, *Commentary on the Holy Scriptures,* trans. Philip Schaff (New York: Charles Scribners, 1915), p. 33.

[13]Charles John Ellicott, ed., *A Biblical Commentary for English Readers,* (London: Cassell & Co. Ltd., n. d.), vol. 8, p. 188.

[14]E. A. Speiser, *Genesis: Introduction, Translation, and Notes,* Anchor Bible (Garden City, N.Y.: Doubleday & Co., 1964), p. 24.

[15]Evidence that this means that women will all seek to dominate their husbands seems insufficient. I do not find this view defended by critical exegetes, though it has some current popularity.

[16]See Is 3:16-26; 4:1; 19:10, 16; 49:15; 50:37; 51:30; Jer 48:41; 49:22; Neh 3:13; 13:26; Eccles. 7:26-28; Ezek 8:14; Esther 1:17; Prov 31:3; 2 Sam 1:26; Ruth 3:11; 4:12.

[17]Eusebius, *The History of the Church from Christ to Constantine,* trans. G. A. Williamson (New York: Dorset Press, 1965), pp. 124-25.

[18]"I Clement," in *The Apostolic Fathers,* ed. J. B. Lightfoot (London: Macmillan, 1898), p. 57.

[19]I Clement passim.

[20]Space does not allow me to document the doctrines of Roman Catholic, Greek Orthodox, Lutheran, Presbyterian, Congregational, Baptist, Brethren, Anabaptist groups and others. They are in general agreement with the tradition. Methodists are less so, as are also Quakers, Salvation Army, and several Wesleyan, Holiness and Pentecostal denominations.

[21]Knox had published a scorching work against the idea of women in any public office just before Elizabeth came to the throne. It had been published anonymously at Geneva where Calvin was chief pastor and Knox's host—greatly to Calvin's embarrassment. He apologized to a leading Englishman as follows: "Two years ago John Knox asked of me, in a private conversation, what I thought about the Government of Women. I candidly replied, that as it was a deviation from the original and proper order of nature, it was to be ranked, no less than slavery, among the punishments consequent upon the fall of man; but that there were occasionally women so endowed, that the singular good qualities which shone forth in them made it evident that they were raised up by Divine authority; either that God designed by such examples to condemn the inactivity of men, or for the better setting forth of his own glory. I brought forward [the Old Testament examples of Huldah and Deborah] . . . I came . . . to this conclusion, that since . . . by custom, public consent, and long practice, it has been established that realms and principalities may descend to females by hereditary right, it did not appear to me necessary to move the question, not only because the thing would be invidious, but because in my opinion it would not be lawful to unsettle governments which are ordained by the peculiar providence of God" (*The Works of John Knox,* cited by Steven Ozment, *The Age of Reform,* [New Haven: Yale University Press, 1980], p. 430).

[22]Robert D. Culver, *Toward a Biblical View of Civil Government* (Chicago: Moody Press, 1974), p. 23.

[23]Letty M. Russell, ed., *Feminist Interpretation of the Bible* (Philadelphia: Westminster Press, 1985), p. 11. A 1984 book already refers to feminism in the past tense, Megan Marshall, *The Cost of Loving: Women and the New Fear of Intimacy* (New York: Putnam's Sons, 1984). Though not yet departed to join "the Shakers and Prohibition" (D. A. Vicinanzo in *Chronicles of Culture* 9, no. 7, p. 25), the recent surge seems to have passed its

peak. I wish I thought the same to be true of the push toward "ordination of women."

[24]For a surprise, see H. A. Ironside, *Addresses on the First and Second Epistles of Timothy* (Neptune, N.J.: Loizeaux Bros., 1947), ch. 6.

[25]Thomas C. Oden, *Pastoral Theology* (New York: Harper & Row, 1982), p. 46.

[26]Calvin *Institutes* 1.2.13.3.

[27]Calvin *Institutes* 2.4.15-20.

[28]Calvin *Institutes* 2.4.10.31.

[29]Richard M. Weaver, *Ideas Have Consequences* (Chicago: University of Chicago Press, 1948), pp. 177-80.

[30]See also my article, "Does Recent Scientific Research Overturn the Claims of Radical Feminism and Support the Biblical Norms of Human Sexuality?" *Journal of the Evangelical Theological Society* 30, no. 1 (March 1987).

A MALE LEADERSHIP RESPONSE
Susan T. Foh

Culver uses the biblical definition of tradition in presenting the traditional view of women and ministry. That Paul intended the content of our faith to be received, preserved and passed on without change is a helpful observation. However, a distinction must be made between what Paul, inspired by the Holy Spirit, gave as tradition and the tradition of the church, unless it can be shown that they are the same. For example, the fact that many commentators throughout history have thought that 1 Timothy 2:14 teaches that women are by nature more easily deceived does not mean that that interpretation is automatically correct. *If* the Scriptures have been completely and correctly understood from the beginning and that understanding has been transmitted, it would seem that there would be little or no need for further biblical or theological study.

Culver sees the leadership of men in the churches as one of the main elements in the tradition taught in 1 Corinthians 11:2-16. Though I agree with the idea of male leadership in the church (that is, elders), I do not see this point as the main emphasis in 1 Corinthians 11. The passage is relevant because it relates to the different ways men and women are to participate in worship, but Culver's misunderstanding of its main emphasis affects his interpretation of verse

10. Because he thinks the focus is on male leadership, he views *authority* as belonging to the man—a view which disregards the Greek word's natural meaning.

In discussing 1 Corinthians 14:34-35, Culver notes that the order in the church is God's order, an order to which both men and women are subject. This understanding is preferable to the chain-of-command theory, and it acknowledges that authority belongs to the One from whom it originates.

1 Corinthians 14:36 cannot be addressed only to females, as Culver suggests, since the pronoun "only ones" is masculine plural. It would refer to an all-male group or a mixed group.

I disagree with Culver's understanding of Adam and Eve as archetypes expressing man-ness and woman-ness. He sees 1 Timothy 2:14 as teaching about the nature of woman (more easily deceived) as distinguished from the nature of man. This theory does not take into account the aorist tense (completed action) of the word *deceive* and the perfect tense (completed action with present consequences) of the word *become* nor the use of Adam's name and the definite article before *woman*. One might also ask whether women, if they are by nature more easily deceived, should be allowed to teach children or other women.

Culver's interpretation of Genesis 3:16 is also based on his view that Adam and Eve are archetypes. "And he shall rule over thee" is taken as a general statement of male government in all areas (rather than simply as a statement about marriage). According to Culver, Genesis 3:16 establishes the inevitability of patriarchy (as a statement of fact made necessary by the Fall). It is not a moral law but a fact to be acknowledged.

Culver's eighth point under the heading "Some Reflections, Cautions and Suggestions" is confusing. Does he mean to suggest that occasionally it is acceptable to put Paul's commands aside?

Culver's suggestion that the activity of women (like Huldah or the wise woman of Tekoa) was an exception to the rule undermines the significance of their work. The woman's role in the work of the kingdom may be designated *subordinate* (in the sense of "ordered under," in this case, under male elders), but it is essential.

A PLURAL MINISTRY RESPONSE
Walter L. Liefeld

It is helpful that this essay was open and consistent in its espousal of tradition. One can take it at face value. The attempt to identify Paul's teachings on women as permanent tradition stumbles at the outset, however, with 1 Corinthians 11. While Paul's *premise* is tradition, he refers to his specific *teaching* as "custom" (v. 16). The Greek word is *synetheia*. The NIV translates it "practice"; it can also mean "habit." But it definitely does not mean tradition. Paul's use of this word brings the point into focus. Three terms can be applied: (1) The *tradition* may be the relationship of husbands and wives, specifically, in this passage, that the wife should not shame her husband. It may also be the exercise of spiritual gifts, especially prophecy. (2) Woman's ministry in a first-century church is the *circumstance* in which the principle or tradition is to be applied. (3) The covering of women's heads is simply a *custom* by which the Corinthians were to apply the tradition in that particular circumstance.

Before continuing with further remarks on Culver's exegesis, an observation on his concept of authority is in order. He uses the terms "church authority" and "positions of authority." The traditional logic is often as follows: (1) Pastoral ministry means having authority over others. (2) 1 Timothy 2:12 prohibits authority to women. (3) Therefore women cannot exercise pastoral ministry. Although not made explicit, this syllogism seems to underlie Culver's approach. While the various denominations differ on the matter of ministerial authority, in all quarters the stress in recent years has been on ministry as *service*. Also the idea that 1 Timothy 2:12 prohibits ecclesiastical authority has been seriously challenged recently, since the rare Greek word *authentein* can no longer be understood as equivalent to the common word for exercising authority.

Returning now to 1 Corinthians 11, the essay fails to note that Paul praises the Corinthians for following his traditions. This is in contrast to verse 17, which introduces his teaching on the Lord's Supper. Here, even though the Corinthians were observing the Supper, Paul specifically says he does not "praise" them. Clearly they followed the tradition but not in the right spirit. This contrast points up the fact that what the Corinthians were doing about the ministry of men and women was praiseworthy, only the matter of head covering needed to be dealt with. This is quite different from the common idea that Paul thought women's participation in ministry was wrong, but postponed criticism of it until chapter 14.

Culver is right in saying that Paul wants to keep distinctions between men and women. In fact, some suggest that he is concerned with homosexuality or with the ritual sex change done in some pagan rituals. He states that "men and women did not sit together in Jewish synagogues" and may be unaware that recent archaeological research has failed to show any common practice of placing women in a separate part of the synagogue. He makes no reference to the fact that both Jewish and pagan moralists had strong conventions about the public function and appearance of women. Plutarch's comment that it is equally shameful for a woman to have a bare arm or for her to speak in public is relevant here. Since Paul has been talking about ways to be "all things to all men" (9:22), it would appear that he wants to avoid any action or appearance on the part of women that would, in that society, bring dishonor on their husbands. He makes it clear in his instructions to women and slaves in Titus 2:3-5 and 9-10 that their behavior must not bring the gospel into disrepute. A woman's public attitude toward her husband is very much a part of that testimony.

Culver's concept of ministry in the church at Corinth is quite different from what is actually described in 1 Corinthians. He seems to assume a scene with people sitting listening to a pastor preach, with the "sermon . . . open to discussion and questioning." "Women are not to interrupt or question the teacher (preacher)." It is hard to square this with the statement in chapter 14 that *everyone* comes with "a hymn, or a word of instruction" and so on. Reading a structured contemporary church service back into the New Testament church naturally makes it difficult to understand the freedom women had to minister. This same idea of women functioning in a structured system of pastoral authority is seen in Culver's allowance that if "a pastor in charge" invites her to speak or pray, a woman may do so if she does so in accordance with the conditions of this passage.

There is also an assumption that women participated only in group worship ("recitation of prayers, amens and the like"). Why he cites an Old Testament passage in which singing is called prophecy, instead of looking to 1 Corinthians 14 for a description of Christian prophecy, is hard to understand.

The efforts to discount 1 Corinthians 11:10 as supportive of women having authority overlook Ramsey's strong statement that to understand the Greek here as passive (that is, being *under*, rather than *having*, authority) is "a preposterous idea which a Greek scholar would laugh at anywhere except in the New Testament, where (as they seem to think) Greek words may mean anything that commentators choose."

Culver thinks that the silence of women in 1 Corinthians 14 refers to a *"public act of teaching"* (emphasis his), but he does not give evidence for that conclusion. One misses the submission of evidence for some of Culver's other statements also, but it must be kept in mind that his purpose is to cite tradition rather than to do exegesis.

There is a refreshing consistency in Culver's treatment of 1 Timothy 2. Many lift the sayings about women out of the context and ignore the other statements about jewelry. But is Paul saying that there is "something about woman's nature"? Is she really "more susceptible to temptation through deceit" than man is? Is it true that today "we could hardly find a more vivid illustration of the essential difference between masculine and feminine nature"? Of course Eve was deceived, and of course the common understanding of the significance of this event was that it rendered woman inappropriate to be a "teacher," that is, a transmitter of and witness to the apostolic tradition of Jesus' teaching and ministry. But the passage does not say that she was more easily deceived, nor does a teacher have the same authority in the church today as in the first century before the Scriptures were fully available.

Culver is right in saying that the words about man and woman in Genesis 3:16 are not called a "curse," as were the words about Satan and the ground. They described the way things would be after the Fall. But should we be any less concerned about ameliorating the undue domination of man over woman described in that verse than about ameliorating the sweaty agricultural labor of man by using farm machinery on the cursed ground?

As for the concluding quotations from the fathers, it is true that they restricted women. They also said some horrendous things about women (as well as other matters) with which most Christians today, certainly evangelicals, would disagree. I have recently coauthored a book with historian Ruth Tucker in which we trace women—and perceptions about them—down through the history of the church. I would not think of using the opinions of even the most well-known church spokesmen—ancient or modern—as guidelines on the subject.

In summary, Culver's essay contains straightforward opinions, including some almost incidental corrections of popular misapprehensions, but in my judgment it fails to pick up signals from the texts themselves that counter the traditions about restricting women.

AN EGALITARIAN RESPONSE
Alvera Mickelsen

Culver's traditional view assumes that traditions, both of biblical times and of today, are automatically good. He also assumes that the traditional view of limited roles for women has been quite universally accepted by all good people from the creation of the world until the present—that is, until the arrival of the modern feminist movement. Both assumptions are negated by the acts and teachings of our Lord Jesus Christ and of the apostle Paul, and by history itself.

Both Jesus and Paul clearly understood that tradition can be either good or bad. The right or wrong of tradition did not depend on how many hundreds of years it had been followed or how many respected teachers of the law promoted it. Rather it depended on what effect that tradition had on human beings who had been created in the image of God and for whom Christ gave his life.

The opposition of religious leaders to Jesus arose largely because he did *not* follow the accepted Jewish traditions. He healed the bent-over woman on the Sabbath day. He treated women as human beings instead of as the property of men—as was the tradition of the Judaism of Jesus' day. He permitted his disciples to pluck grain on the Sabbath.

In Mark 7:1-13 Jesus encounters the Jewish leaders on this exact matter of tradition. Jesus told them, "You have a fine way of rejecting the commandment of God, in order to keep your tradition!" (Mk 7:9 Amplified), and went on to say they were "making void . . . the Word of God through your tradition which you hand on" (7:13). And what did Jesus say were the commandments of God? "Love the Lord your God with all your heart, and with all your soul, and with all your mind. . . . And a second is like it, You shall love your neighbor as yourself" (Mt 22:37, 39 Amplified). Jesus gave his own version of this commandment when he said that his followers must treat others the way they want to be treated (Mt 7:12). Do Culver and others want the same gender restrictions on their ministry for God that they place on women?

Paul, too, battled traditions that he recognized as limiting the work of the Holy Spirit, the grace of God and the spread of the gospel. In fact, Paul wrote in Galatians 1:14 that he had *persecuted* the Christians precisely *because* he was so zealous for the traditions of his fathers. In Colossians 2:8 Paul warns Christians to beware of becoming prey to human tradition "and not according to Christ."

Paul's ability to turn away from the traditions of his own background when he saw them hindering the gospel and limiting the grace of God are indications of how fully he understood the message of Jesus. Paul, who had been reared as a "Pharisee of the Pharisees," who had been taught that circumcision was the sign of belonging to the covenant of God, was able to write in Galatians 6:15, "For neither circumcision counts for anything, nor uncircumcision, but a new creation" (RSV). He repeats the same idea in Galatians 5:6 and 1 Corinthians 7:19.

Paul was the one who confronted Peter and other disciples who were not able to accept the full implications of Pentecost and its demonstration of freedom in Christ. Paul went to the Jerusalem council to plead that Gentile Christians should not be brought under the legalism of Jewish tradition. Yet Paul adapted to some of the customs of his day when he saw that failure to do so would be misunderstood and bring disgrace on the message of Christ. Today we are bringing disgrace upon the message of freedom in Christ because we are unwilling to give up some of our traditions regarding women.

Other disciples had more trouble ridding themselves of hindering tradition. Peter, who had preached an all-encompassing message at

Pentecost, (that is, the Holy Spirit empowers both Jews and Gentiles, men and women, young and old, slave and free) failed to apply it when he was told to go to the Gentile Cornelius with the gospel. God had to send him a special vision to encourage his liberation. He finally had to say, "Can any one forbid water for baptizing these people who have received the Holy Spirit just as we have?"

The church today may be facing a similar problem regarding the gifts of women. "Can anyone deny pastoral or teaching ministries to these women who have been called by the Holy Spirit just as we have?"

More often than not it has been tradition, rather than biblical principles, that has limited the ministry of women. Culver argues that women can do everything *except* serve in positions of teaching and authority over men. What "authority" does a teacher have over a Sunday-school class of adults? Can the teacher forbid them to leave in the middle of the lesson? Can he or she insist they believe or act on what the teacher says? Can the teacher forbid some to take part in the discussion? Can the teacher insist that his or her teaching is "authoritative" over that of others who also believe and teach the Bible? A teacher who did any of these things would soon be without a class.

To some extent this limitation also applies to pastors and elders or other church officers. What actual "teaching authority" do they have over members? In cases of church discipline (very rare in our day) church leaders usually recommend action which must be carried out by the church body. The work of pastors, elders and other church leaders is largely in the formulation of policies which must ultimately be accepted by the congregation.

Actually, to be sure that no woman would hold authority over a man in the church, women would have to be denied the right to vote in churches. The denomination to which both Culver and I belong (Baptist) has a congregational form of government where ultimate authority rests with the congregation—and most churches have more women members than men! Only the *congregation* has the final authority to hire or fire pastors, authorize building projects, support missionaries, and decide on denominational affiliation.

A close look at traditional restrictions on women shows great inconsistency. In even the most traditional churches, women often function in "authority" over men and in "official or liturgical teaching and leading." For example, women are usually in charge of church kitchens, where they tell men how and where to set up tables and chairs for church functions. They recommend equipment that is needed and decide how it should be arranged. Women are usually in charge of church nurseries. They usually have primary authority over policies regarding the nursery—policies that affect fathers as much as mothers. Women are usually in charge of vacation Bible schools, where they plan and oversee any men who help (and how much those men are needed!). When women sing solos or duets in worship services, they surely are "leading" the congregation in worship. And the messages of their songs teach—we hope!

On the other hand, many activities that involve no authority are limited to men. The most classic example is serving Communion. What "authority" or "teaching" is involved in passing the elements to members? Yet women are usually restricted to preparing the elements in the back room, while men serve them. In traditional churches, we rarely see women ushers. Do ushers have some significant authority over those who come? In traditional churches we rarely hear a woman read the Scriptures or lead in prayer in a worship service. What authority is involved there?

A close look at our actual practices indicates that traditionally women can plan and greatly influence almost any church activity so long as they remain largely *invisible* or the activity is related to the usual domestic roles for women. The *invisibility* and the domestic roles are the practical determinants—not authority or the Bible.

Culver uses the usual "selective literalism" of those who through the centuries have tried to restrict women's service and calling in the church and society. When Paul's words do not suit, they are toned down. Culver says that Paul "does not forbid all ornament, but only the excess which is a mark of frivolity and love of display." The text does not say that. Paul simply forbids women to have braided hair or to wear gold, or pearls, or expensive clothing. Yet women in traditional churches do not wear cheap clothing, and they often wear gold or pearls. These commands of Paul appear in the same paragraph as the statement that women are not to "teach or have authority over men"—a statement that Culver believes must be rigidly applied. Apparently, Culver has no method of determining what are "highest norms and standards" and what are "regulations for people where they were."

The common reluctance to interpret the Bible with the literary, historical and cultural context in mind has led to the alignment of the church with dreadful causes. There was no "tradition" for democracy. Those who first suggested democratic concepts where told of the "divine right of kings" and that absolute power for kings was as old as history. The same arguments appeared for slavery. Since slavery had existed since the earliest recorded times, it had to be a part of the divine plan. These same arguments appear over and over regarding women in church and society.

Culver says that until recently, no one suggested that Genesis be interpreted any way except the traditional way of seeing male dominance as part of the divine plan. Researchers are finding writings all through church history that refute these traditional interpretations. In the 1920s, numerous books appeared carrying the same refutations. Katherine Bushnell's *God's Word to Women,* Jessie Penn-Lewis's *The Magna Charta of Woman* (1919) and many others appeared. They were largely ignored by men in control of ecclesiastical institutions.

One of the sad parts of our present situation is that arguments such as Culver's tend to drive intelligent women out of the church. Culver quotes with approval Ellicott's *Biblical Commentary for English Readers* (which he describes as "one of the most orthodox, dependable . . . commentaries of a few generations back") where H. D. M. Spence writes, "The deception [of Eve in the Garden of Eden] indicates a lesser ability in comprehension, and so this limitation is why it is not allowable for a woman to teach." Anyone who consults the academic records of women in seminaries today can only smile at such comments. Women are winning awards in all fields from preaching to theology out of proportion to their numbers. The one thing women are not winning is opportunities to serve in the traditional churches where they were nurtured in the faith and perhaps where they sensed God's call of service. Bad tradition is the real problem facing them today—not lack of ability or lack of the call of God.

1 Corinthians 12 clearly says that *God* is the one who gifts people

for service. Those gifts are to be used "for the common good" (1 Cor 12:7). Paul also states that when God's gifts are not used for the good of the body (the church), the whole body suffers. The body is suffering today.

God calls women to every area of service. He called in Old Testament times, in New Testament times, in all times up to and including the present. I agree with Culver that the *majority* of women will continue (as in days past) to find their primary service in the home and family, just as the majority of men find their primary service in secular work. But God can and does call some men and some women to serve his people in their vocations. Pastors encourage young men to listen for and hear the call of God in their lives for such vocations. They rarely encourage young women in similar ways, but God is still making his voice heard to responsive ears.

When we as individuals or as churches or as denominations set up barriers to keep women gifted by God from using their gifts, we do so at our own peril. Paul wrote in 1 Thessalonians 5:19-20, "Do not quench the Spirit, do not despise prophesying [according to 1 Cor. 14, prophesying includes preaching, teaching, evangelizing]."

We are forced to say that many parts of the Bible apply only to men if we are to maintain our traditions. In Colossians 3:16, Paul writes "Let the message of Christ dwell richly in you [plural—all Christian men and women], in all wisdom teach and admonish one another with psalms, hymns, spiritual songs, singing with grace in your hearts to God." How can we say that this is for men only?

May the church be unleashed from its traditions that have denied more than half its members the full use of the gifts that God himself may have poured out by his Spirit.

In the days of the apostle Paul, he sometimes had to adapt what he knew to be the highest ideals of our Lord to the social situation of his day so as not to bring disgrace on the gospel. In our day, we are bringing disgrace in the opposite way. We are unwilling to let go of our sexist traditions that are hindering the spread of the gospel. Many women honestly (and erroneously, I think) believe that the Bible makes women second-class citizens. They believe this because of the way they have heard the Bible interpreted. What would Paul say to our churches if he could visit us now? Would he say it doesn't matter that many of our best and brightest women see in the church a means of oppression rather than seeing the redemption and freedom that Christ came to provide?

James 2:1-7 condemns those in the church who show partiality. James illustrates his teaching by an example of giving a good seat and prominence in the church to rich people and keeping poor people in the shadows. James heaps condemnation on his readers because they failed to keep Jesus' highest standards of "you shall love your neighbor as yourself." He then adds the somber note: "But if you show partiality, you commit sin, and are convicted by the law as transgressors" (v. 9 RSV).

Is not our treatment of women in the church a similar example of partiality? And will we not receive the same condemnation?

2/A MALE LEADERSHIP VIEW:
THE HEAD OF THE WOMAN IS THE MAN

A MALE LEADERSHIP VIEW: The Head of the Woman Is the Man

Susan T. Foh

The organ prelude fills the sanctuary. From a side door, the minister, identified by his robe, a male song leader, and a woman enter the apse. What is a woman doing there, some wonder; women are not to lead in church but to be silent and submissive. Others, more in tune with the times, are not phased by her presence. During the service, the woman reads the Scripture and leads in prayer. Her participation is too much for some and too little for others. How should we react to her actions? How are we to evaluate them?

The Starting Point
The question of what women can do in the church, in terms of office-holding and participating in the worship service, has been answered several different ways. These various answers result from different views of the Bible or different methods of biblical interpretation.

The Bible may be approached as: (1) God's word without human error or opinion[1] or (2) God's word mixed with human opinion. Those who hold the latter view attribute Paul's commands concerning women to the human element in Scripture and thus believe these commands are no longer applicable today. The Bible, then, is not the final authority for faith and life since it is subject to the judgment of human reason.

One hermeneutical principle, the consideration of the cultural, historical and geographical context, has been used to relativize the biblical commands to women. For instance, some commentators argue that the command for wives to submit to their husbands occurred in a patriarchal society and thus is not binding today. To note the culture, however, should not relativize the command. God chose the time and place for his revelation to be recorded, and he is not bound by either. Only indications in the text can suggest its temporal or limited character.[2]

If the biblical material is in the form of a command to the church as a whole (as in 1 Cor 14:34 and 1 Tim 2:11-12), it ought to be seen as valid for all time. If there is nothing in the text to indicate that a command is limited to a special case or circumstance, we cannot presume to limit the text or to read Paul's mind. For example, some suggest that Paul, as a concerned pastor, deliberately limited the women in order to avoid upsetting the system too much all at once;[3] his commands were intended to be transitional and temporary (they self-destruct once society has progressed). Yet there is nothing in any of the passages about women to support this view.

Another cultural setting must be noted in the interpretation of Scripture: that of the interpreter. One must be aware of the trends and controlling ideas in one's own culture in order to refrain from reading them into the biblical text. Equality is a current banner held high (it is un-American to speak against equality), and it is assumed to be an indisputable theme in Scripture. But is it? Check a concordance. Only two references to equality refer to persons. Consider also the biblical emphasis on selflessness (Mt 5:39-41; 16:24-28; Rom 14:20; 15:2; 1 Pet 5:5), on responsibilities and duties (Eph 5:21-6:9; Col 3:18—4:1), and on submission (Rom 13:1; 1 Pet 2:13-22; 5:5; Heb 13:17; Jas 4:7).[4]

Because the Bible is God's word, several unique principles of interpretation are required. (1) The Bible must be interpreted under the guidance of the Holy Spirit (1 Cor 2:14). (2) The Bible is a unity, ultimately authored by the Holy Spirit; the unifying principle is Jesus Christ (Lk 24:27; 1 Cor 1:20; 1 Pet 1:10-12). The third is a corollary of the second. (3) Scripture does not contradict Scripture; Scripture interprets Scripture. The third principle is crucial in understanding what the Bible says about women because the Bible has been accused of contradicting itself on the position of women. In particular, the Old Testament is pitted against the New, Paul against Jesus, and the rabbi Saul against the Christian Paul. If the author of Scripture is the Holy Spirit, contradictions cannot exist; any appearance of contradiction results from the reader's lack of understanding. (4) The clearer passages interpret the less clear. Some of the differences concerning women's roles are derived from differences in how this principle is applied, differences relating to which passages are considered clearer.

Two seemingly opposite pictures of women emerge from the Scriptures. On the one hand, women are told to submit themselves to their husbands and to male leadership in the church. On the other hand, women played an active part in the church. Women are in the image of God, joint heirs of the kingdom, and there is no male and female in Christ. On the basis of this last assertion, some conclude that there should be complete role interchangeability between men and women. This latter view is currently in ascendancy.

Apparently, human nature tends to make things uniform, to smooth out the wrinkles in the biblical material to make it fit neatly in the boxes of the human mind. To create a logical, uniform system, both sides—the subordinationist and the egalitarian—must ignore or explain away the other. In addition, both sides make an illogical and unbiblical assumption: that subordination (which merely means ordering under) necessarily implies inferiority. The classic example that disproves this notion is that of God the Father and God the Son. God the Father and God the Son are both God (Jn 1:1; 14:9; Col 1:15-28; Heb 1:3). Nonetheless, Jesus says, "The Father is greater than I" (Jn 14:28), and he submits himself to his Father (Jn 5:30; see also 1 Cor. 11:3), even in the eternal state (1 Cor 15:27-28).

The Basics

The foundational principles for understanding women's roles are found in the first three chapters of Genesis. In Genesis 1 and 2, there are two accounts of the creation of man and woman. Chapter 1 ("So God created man in his own image, in the image of God he created him; male and female he created them," v. 27 NIV) is acclaimed by those who favor the absolute equality of the sexes, whereas the teaching of the woman's inferiority is often attributed to chapter 2. Neither extreme is true; the two creation narratives complement each other to give the complete picture.

On the sixth day, God created humanity in two sexes in his image. There is nothing in the text to suggest any difference between them. Both man and woman are equally in the image of God. Both are blessed by God, told to multiply and subdue the earth, and given stewardship over creation. This joint custody over the rest of creation has implications for women's roles in society or culture; their place in the work arena is no different from men's. Men and women have the same relationship to God (in his image) and to nature (to fill and exercise dominion over). This principle can be termed *ontological equality* or *equality in being.*

In Genesis 2, we learn more about the relationship between man and woman. Because it was not good for the man to be alone (an indication of man's dependence on or need for woman, 1 Cor 11:11-12), God created a helper fit for the man, the woman. The words *helper fit for* or *corresponding to* underline the likeness of the woman to man.[5]

Rather than a separate creation from the dust, the woman was created from the rib of the man. Why is the woman created in this surprising way? (1) It signifies her correspondence to the man. She is bone of his bone and flesh of his flesh; there is no superiority or inferiority in substance. (2) God's creation of humanity is one act that begins with the man and ends with the woman. (3) All of humanity comes from one source, Adam. As the source of humanity, Adam is the head and consequently the representative of all. As 1 Corinthians 15:22 says, "in Adam all die." (4) The woman's creation from the man establishes the basis for the one-flesh principle in marriage. It is the real, biological and historical foundation for the oneness that should exist between husband and wife (Gen 2:24). Reasons (3) and (4) pave the way for the principle of inequality between the man and woman. (5) Though the way the woman was created does not indicate inferiority, it does indicate a difference in function. The woman was created to help her husband; her function is dependent on him. As she followed him in creation, she is to follow his lead as her husband.[6]

How do we know that the man's temporal priority signifies the husband's headship? Though the answer has obviously failed to convince many, it is: "For man was not made from woman, but woman from man. Neither was man created for woman, but woman for man" (1 Cor 11:8-9; see also 1 Tim 2:13). God, through Paul, explains what we otherwise might have missed. It is likely that the Hebrew mind would have understood the connection between Adam's being the source of the woman and his position as head.[7]

But there is another clue that Adam is to be regarded as having authority over the woman. Adam named her. When Adam named the animals, it is clear that he was exercising his God-given rule over them. To name someone is associated with authority over that person. Even the name that Adam gives the woman indicates their relationship: *'ishshah* (woman) because she was taken out of *'ish* (man). The name stresses their similarity and their difference in function. James Hurley paraphrases Genesis 2:23, "She is indeed my own kind, from my own body. She is, however, derivative and it is my privilege to assign her a name. Let her be called by the name I give, 'woman,' because she was taken out of me."[8]

Is God's arrangement fair? Our objections, whether philosophical or emotional, to this hierarchical system arise because we do not know what a sinless hierarchy is like. We know only the tyranny, willfulness and condescension that even the best boss-underling relationship has. In Eden, none of these perversions existed. The man and woman knew each other as equals, each in God's image and each with a personal relationship with God. Neither doubted the value of the other or of himself or herself. Each was to do the same work, with husband as head and wife as helper. They functioned as one flesh, one body without discord. Does the rib rebel against the head or the head mistreat the rib?

There are three principles in operation before the Fall. (1) Man and woman are equal in being (Gen 1:27). (2) The woman is functionally subordinate to her husband. He was created first to set up his headship; the woman was created after, from and for the sake of the man to help him (Gen 2:21-23; 1 Cor 11:8-9). (3) Husband and wife are one flesh (Gen 2:24). Because of the third principle, the other two can operate harmoniously. The inter-relatedness of man and woman should prevent both from abusing their positions.

In the Fall, these three principles are also involved. Much speculation, usually with a chauvinistic slant, has revolved around the woman's sin. The serpent picked the weaker person; the woman usurped
her husband's place by leading him into sin; the woman enticed or
seduced Adam into sin. However, the text does not support any of
these notions. The serpent's subtlety consists in his method of argumentation, his persuasive half-truths. The woman's sin is directed
primarily against God.

She knew God's command; yet she dared discuss whether or not to
obey it with a fellow creature. In the end, she believed the serpent
rather than God. The woman sinned against her husband by helping
him (what she was supposed to do) in the wrong way, into sin ("She
also gave some to her husband, and he ate"—Gen 3:6). Adam is
judged not because he heeded his wife's advice per se, but because
he followed her bad advice to disobey God (Gen 3:17).

Their oneness and parity are shown in the results of sin: "Then the
eyes of both were opened, and they knew that they were naked" (Gen
3:7 RSV). It is as if they sinned simultaneously, as if Adam's sin were
a reflex action of the woman's (they were perfectly one flesh). Both
made aprons for themselves and hid from God in the garden. They
were one in their sin, reactions and guilt.

In Genesis 3:9 God addresses the man first because he is the appointed head. Nevertheless, the woman is also questioned; she is
responsible for her own actions. God insists on an explanation from
her as well as the man. On the other hand, the smooth-tongued
serpent is not allowed to speak. The man and the woman are alike
in their explanations; both shift the blame rather than admit their
guilt.

After the Fall the harmonious working of these three principles is
destroyed. In God's judgment against the woman, he tells how the
corruptions of these principles will develop, though the usual translation obscures this point. The RSV translation, "yet your desire shall
be for your husband, and he shall rule over you," suggests that somehow, through the woman's desire for her husband, he will be able to
rule her. However, the rule of the husband is in fact not made easier
after the Fall. Common experience suggests few husbands rule their
homes. In addition, many wives have no desire—sexual, psychological

or otherwise—for their husbands.

For a better understanding of Genesis 3:16, compare it to Genesis 4:7. The Hebrew of these two verses is the same, except for changes in pronouns, nouns and gender. The RSV translates the last part of Genesis 4:7 in an entirely different way: "its [sin's] desire is for you [Cain], but you must master it." Sin's desire[9] for Cain was to control or possess. Cain had to struggle; either sin or Cain would be the conqueror. God's words "you must master it" tell Cain what he should do, but they do not determine the victor.

In addition to identical construction, the proximity of the two passages indicates that they would have the same meaning. As in Genesis 4:7, the latter part of Genesis 3:16 describes a struggle between the one with the desire (the woman) and the one who must rule or master (the husband). The battle of the sexes is the result of sin and the judgment on it for the woman. The woman's willing submission is replaced by a desire to control her husband. Consequently, to maintain his headship the husband must fight for it. Sin has ruined the marital dance, the easy, loving lead of the husband and the natural following of the wife. In its place are struggle, tyranny, domination, manipulation and subterfuge.

This understanding of Genesis 3:16 is corroborated by experience. If it is translated "and he shall rule over you" (RSV), the words are not true; not every husband rules his wife. Instead, marriages are filled with strife and discontent. The loss of the wife's willing submission and the husband's loving "rule" each have two opposite aberrations. Wives manipulate and sometimes dominate their husbands; and some wives, losing all sense of their own worth, live only through their husbands or children. Some husbands, abdicating their position, absent themselves from the home through work, sports or alcohol; and some husbands physically or emotionally abuse their wives.

With this understanding of Genesis 3:16 in view, Paul, in Ephesians 5:22-33, focuses on the areas where wives and husbands tend to sin. As a result of sin, wives no longer naturally submit themselves to their husbands, so Paul says, "Wives, submit yourselves to your husbands, as to the Lord" (Eph 5:22 NIV). In their struggle to rule, husbands tend to resort to any means at their disposal, so Paul forestalls these "blows" with "Husbands, love your wives, as Christ loved the church and gave himself up for her" (Eph 5:25 RSV).

These three principles—ontological equality, functional subordination of the woman to her husband, and oneness—account for the seemingly contradictory strands of material in the Bible.

Illustrations from the Old and New Testaments

Recognition of the progressive nature of God's revelation adds to our understanding of the position of women in the Bible. The Old Testament breaks with the surrounding cultures, in which women were considered property, and treats women as persons of worth. According to the Old Testament, the woman was co-ruler with the man over creation. In marriage, the man was to leave his home and to cleave to his wife; hers was a position of importance.

God made his covenant with women as well as men (Deut 29:1-11); women were required to hear God's Word read aloud (Deut 31:12, Neh 8:2). Women "ministered" at the tabernacle door (Ex 38:8; 1 Sam 2:22). They offered their own sacrifices (Lev 1; 15; 1 Sam 2:19) and prayed directly to God (Gen 16:7-13; 1 Sam 1:9-18), and God spoke directly to them (Gen 25:22-23; Judg 13:3-5). Women could become Nazarites devoted to God (Num 6), prophetesses (Miriam, Ex 15:20-21; Huldah, 2 Kings 22:14), wise women (1 Sam 25:3; 2 Sam 14:2; 20:16-22) and judges (Deborah, also a prophetess and wife, Judg 4:4). Wives could not be sold, even if captured in war (Deut 21:14). The fact that such a prohibition existed points to the degradation of women in the surrounding cultures.

As a parent, the woman was on equal ground with the man. Honor is commanded for both parents (Ex 20:12; Lev 19:3). In Proverbs, the references to fathers and mothers are parallel (6:20; 10:1; 15:20; 17:25; 19:26; 20:20; 23:22, 25). The mother's instruction is as important as the father's (Prov 1:8). Proverbs 31:10-31 emphasizes the value of the woman; she is more precious than jewels. The wide variety of this capable woman's activities proves that the Hebrew woman was not just a housekeeper or childbearer.

Even though the woman, in the image of God, occupied a place of esteem, her position was not equal in every respect to the man's. Some legislation was designed to demonstrate the husband's headship concretely or visibly. For instance, the husband could annul his wife's vow (and the father his daughter's). But there were limits: he had to do so within the day that he heard about it (Num 30). This law had a practical reason—the wife's vow could affect her husband if she promised money or goods or abstinence from conjugal rights. On the other hand, widows were free to make their own vows; the principle of submission involves only wives to husbands and daughters to fathers.

In another significant area, the woman occupied a subordinate position: the woman could not be a priest, in contrast to the surrounding cultures. Part of the reason for this restriction is that the priest typified Christ, our eternal high priest. The New Testament provides the principle behind the Old Testament practice—the woman is to be subordinate in the church.

The Old Testament ideal for male-female relationships deteriorated during intertestamental times. Women were considered in the same category as slaves and Gentiles. A rabbi would not speak with a woman in public, and it was thought better to burn the Torah than to give it to a woman. In such a world, Jesus' treatment of women was shocking. In his encounter with the Samaritan woman (Jn 4), both she and his disciples were amazed that he would talk with a woman (vv. 9, 27). Yet Jesus taught women important spiritual truths (Jn 4:7-26; 11:25; 20:17), and he healed them (Mt 15:21-28; Mk 5:25-34).

Jesus challenged the first-century and twentieth-century stereotype that a woman belongs in the kitchen rather than the classroom (Mary and Martha, Lk 10:38-42). He calls attention to women's faith (Lk 7:36-40; Mk 12:41-44). In Luke 13:10-17 Jesus addresses a woman as a daughter of Abraham, a title of great honor. His rabbinic contemporaries would have seen it as almost a contradiction in terms. For the rabbis, the woman was a source of (sexual) temptation and was incapable of learning. In his public teaching, Jesus used illustrations involving both sexes (Mt 13:33; Lk 15:8-10; Mt 25:1-13; Lk 18:1-8); he (in contrast to the other rabbis) was concerned that men and women be taught God's Word. Women were a part of Jesus' entourage from beginning to end (Lk 8:1-4; Mt 27:55-56; Mk 15:40-41). This happened in a time when women appeared in public only when necessary. Undoubtedly, Jesus treated women as they should be treated—as persons of worth, made in the image of God.

In Acts, Luke carefully records the participation of women in the spread of the gospel. In contrast, in first-century Judaism, women were confined to a separate court in the temple and did not count as a part of the quorum needed for a synagogue. Women were among the disciples in the upper room (Acts 1:14) and spoke in tongues at Pentecost (Acts 2:17-18). Both men and women believed in Jesus, were baptized and were persecuted for their faith (5:14; 8:12; 9:2; 17:4, 12). Tabitha was "full of good works and acts of charity" (9:36), and she was raised from the dead. As soon as she was converted, Lydia invited Paul and company to stay with her (16:14-15). Both Priscilla and Aquila instructed Apollos (18:26), and Philip's four daughters were prophetesses (21:8).

In Romans 16, Paul greets and praises several women. Phoebe requires special attention; she is called a deacon or servant (v. 1) and patroness (v. 2). Was Phoebe a deacon? The Greek word can be translated servant or minister (in the broad sense, not as pastor, as we commonly use it). It could indicate that Phoebe was an exceptional servant in the church. On the other hand, the phrase in verse 1 reads like an official title: "Phoebe, being a *diakonon* of the church in Cenchreae." The instructions to women in the middle of the requirements for deacons in 1 Timothy 3:11 add weight to the idea that women could be deacons in the early church.

Patroness is perhaps more difficult to define. The noun occurs only here in the New Testament. The root verb[10] occurs in the following places. In 1 Timothy 5:17 this verb clearly describes the work of elders. In 1 Thessalonians 5:12 it refers to church leaders. In Romans 12:8, where it has been translated in various ways ("give aid" or "leadership" or "govern"), it describes a gift which may or may not correspond to a church office. In 1 Timothy 3:4-5 and 12 it is translated "manage" with reference to the elder's or deacon's household. In verse 4 it is parallel with "to care for," which occurs only here and in the parable of the Good Samaritan (Lk 10:34-35). In Titus 3:8 and 14 the verb has a different meaning: "to execute" or "apply oneself."

Even if the noun has the same meaning as the verb, the meaning in Romans 16:2 is not sure. Some commentators advocate translating the word as "leader" in an effort to demonstrate that women were as active in the early church as men. Even if "leader" is the correct translation (certainly Phoebe's being a deacon would make her a leader in the church), it does not mean that women were doing everything men were (such as being elders, pastor-teachers, or acting contrary to 1 Tim 2:12).

In Romans 16:2 the syntax (which suggests an official title in v. 1) argues against translating the noun as "leader." The verb for "help" and the noun "patroness" have the same root. The verb means "to stand beside or by" in the sense of help or support; the verb related to "patroness" means to stand before, which can have the sense of protect or care for. It is likely the two words are related, with perhaps different shades of the same basic meaning. Paul writes, "Help Phoebe as she has become a helper of many, even me." Another factor that militates against translating this noun as "leader" is that Phoebe is referred to as the "patroness" of Paul; it seems unlikely that Paul would refer to Phoebe as his leader. However, it is quite possible that Phoebe acted as a patroness or a protectress of Paul as well as others.

Paul continues in Romans 16:3 by hailing Priscilla and Aquila as "fellow workers" who risked their lives for Paul, and by acknowledging Mary who worked hard among the Roman congregation (v. 6). Several other women are also mentioned by name. In Philippians 4:2-3, Paul is concerned about two female workers who have labored by his side in the gospel—Euodia and Syntyche. Obviously, women had an active role in the spread of the gospel, and it included verbal help (Priscilla taught, Philip's daughters prophesied).

Yet, the New Testament gives no examples of female apostles,[11] evangelists or elders. There are no examples of women teaching in public. The primary figures in the advance of the gospel were men. What conclusions can be drawn from these historical examples?

The key to unlocking the significance of biblical examples is found in the specific commands and their theological base. In these, the three principles found in Genesis 1—3 reappear. But this key does not solve all problems. Almost every passage dealing with women has difficulties in the text, such as the cryptic reference "because of the angels" in 1 Corinthians 11:10 or the debated referent of women in 1 Timothy 3:11. There are four passages that are particularly relevant to the question of women in the ministry.

1 Timothy 2:8-15

In 1 Timothy, Paul is instructing the man he left in charge of the church at Ephesus on how one should behave in the household of God (1 Tim 3:14-15). After urging prayer for all men, especially government leaders, Paul says, "I want" the men to pray in a certain way and the women to dress in a certain way. "I want" on the pen of one who was appointed preacher, apostle and teacher (2:7; see also Tit 3:8) has the force of a command, not merely a wish or desire.

Paul's concern for both men and women does not focus on the external aspects but the condition of the heart that causes the outward signs. For men the primary duty is not to raise their hands when praying but to pray with a pure heart and without anger or quarreling. Raising hands is an appropriate posture expressing this attitude and should not be dismissed as inconsequential or purely cultural.

Likewise, for the women, the point is that Christian women should adorn themselves with the fruit of the Spirit, the virtues of reverence and sound judgment, and also good deeds. Paul does not forbid the use of jewelry or expensive clothing; however, women are not to spend the bulk of their time and energy on them. "Strength and dignity are her clothing" (Prov 31:25 NASB). Peter makes the same point: "Let not yours be the outward adorning with braiding of hair, decoration of gold, and wearing of robes, but let it be the hidden person of the heart with the imperishable jewel of a gentle and quiet spirit, which in God's sight is very precious" (1 Pet 3:3-4 RSV).

When Paul writes, "Let a woman learn in silence [or quietness][12] with all submission," he commands something the rabbis forbade: teaching women God's Word. Thus he makes an advance in women's education for his day. Quietness and submission are not negative qualities with reference to learning; they are the way to learn (see Eccles 9:17).

Though the woman should learn, she is prohibited from teaching and exercising authority over men. Learning in quietness is the inverse of teaching (v.11), and submission is the inverse of exercising authority. Paul's restriction[13] (v. 12) is based on his divine appointment as apostle, as noted above.

What is forbidden to the woman in verse 12? One answer is all forms of teaching and exercising authority over men, including any job with authority over men and teaching in a co-ed college. However, the context suggests that Paul is dealing with a church worship situation. It is likely that the public prayer of verse 8 would occur in a worship service. The commands regarding women's clothing surely are not limited to church, but church would be of special concern. Consider how the congregation would be and is affected when women try to outdo one another in jewels and high fashion on Sunday morning. In 1 Timothy 3:14-15, Paul explicitly states that his instructions are for behavior in the church.[14]

If worship is the context for these verses, there are still two alternatives: (1) all forms of teaching and authority, and (2) a specific type of activity defined by teaching and exercising authority (that is, the office of elder, including pastor-teacher or minister of the Word). In any case, the teaching forbidden to women does not include praying and prophesying (1 Cor 11:2-16), private instruction of men (Acts 18:26), teaching other women (Tit 2:3-4) and teaching children (2 Tim 1:5; 3:15; Prov 1:8).

The present tense of the infinitives "to teach" and "to exercise authority" suggests that the activities are habitual, something done regularly. Paul regularly uses the verb *teach* to mean authoritative teaching (Col 1:28; 1 Tim 4:11; 6:2; 2 Tim 2:2)—something he does as an apostle and Timothy does as the one in charge of the Ephesian church. Teaching and exercising authority are the two functions of the elder, whose qualifications follow immediately in chapter 3 (vv. 2, 5; compare 1 Tim 5:17). Possibly Paul aims to disqualify women from the office of elder before he defines the requirements of that office.

The verb "to exercise authority over" appears only here in the New Testament. Connotations of dictatorship, arbitrariness and interference in an inappropriate area have been associated with it. The NEB translates it: "nor must woman domineer over man." Some have therefore concluded that what is forbidden is being bossy or publicly defying husbands. However, Paul does not say that bossy or domineering women should not teach and exercise authority over men but that a woman should not teach or exercise authority over men. George W. Knight III has researched the use of *authentein* in extrabiblical literature. His conclusion is that this verb's meaning is neutral, without negative connotations. Its most commonly suggested meaning by translators and lexicographers is "have authority over."[15] What is forbidden to women in 1 Timothy 2:12 is the exercise of authority.

Paul gives two reasons for his prohibition: (1) Adam was created first, and (2) the woman was deceived, not the man. These two historical events cannot be altered or ignored. 1 Corinthians 11:8 also marks the significance of Adam's earlier creation; consequently, he is head of his wife (11:3), and she is to submit herself to him (Eph 5:22-23). The woman's relationship to the man founded at creation and Eve's deception make it inappropriate for women to teach and exercise authority over men in the church.

The woman's role in the Fall has sparked much unprofitable speculation. Some assume some deficiency in the woman—the woman is more easily deceived, or she is inferior in teaching gifts (if so, how could she be allowed to teach children?). Paul is not speaking of women in general or the nature of woman but of Eve. Verse 14 simply states a fact of the past; the tense is aorist, which means a completed act. Paul contrasts the way in which Adam and Eve sinned: Adam was not deceived (he knew what he was doing), but the woman was completely deceived.

This passage does not exalt all men above all women by giving men authority in the church. Authority is not given to all men, but only to the few who meet the qualifications of 1 Timothy 3:1-7.

Verse 15 is difficult to understand. It does not teach salvation by works (childbearing), and it is not a mandate to confine women to home and children. It is probably more closely related to verses 13-14 than to verses 11-12. The purpose of the passage is not to tell women that their role is childbearing (rather than teaching) but to encourage them in light of their position resulting from the Fall. Verse 15 relates to Genesis 3:16 as a relief of that judgment; and undoubtedly, Paul considers motherhood an honorable profession if the woman continues in faith, love, holiness and sound judgment. Paul did desire that younger widows marry and bear children (1 Tim 5:14).[16]

False teaching was a problem at Ephesus, which was Timothy's location when Paul wrote to him. One theory,[17] which intends to take into account the cultural situation, is that women were among these false teachers and that only false teaching is prohibited. The absence of any reference to false teaching in 1 Timothy 2:9-15 is explained by identifying the cause of Adam's Fall as false teaching. This theory is untenable for the following reasons:

1. The reason given in verse 14 for prohibiting women from teaching and exercising authority over men is not what Eve did to Adam (whether false teaching, persuasion or seduction), but rather the fact that Eve was deceived. The fact that Adam was not deceived implies that false teaching did not precipitate his fall.

2. This theory does not account for the first reason given for the prohibition, the prior creation of the man (v. 13).

3. The women in 1 Timothy 2:9-15 are approached differently from the false teachers. The false teachers know nothing, crave controversy, love money and live in immorality; some have wandered away from the faith (1 Tim 6:3, 10; 2 Tim 3:1-9; 4:3-4). Timothy is exhorted to correct them with the idea that "God may perhaps grant that they will repent and come to know the truth" (2 Tim. 2:25 RSV); in other words, at least some of these heterodox teachers are unbelievers who have attached themselves to the church (see 1 Jn 2:18-19). If the correction does no good, Timothy is to avoid such people (2 Tim 3:5; see also Tit 3:9-11). In 1 Timothy 1:3-7, in which the false teachers could be believers, perhaps Judaizers, Paul urges Timothy to command them not to teach different doctrines, nor occupy themselves with myths and genealogies.

In contrast, no mention of false teaching or correction of heterodoxy is made in 1 Timothy 2:9-15. This passage is in the middle of a section intended for believers (2:1—3:16); false teachers are not mentioned in this section. Teaching and exercising authority in verse 12 have no negative connotations in and of themselves. Unlike the false teachers and the women of 2 Timothy 3:5, who "can never arrive at a knowledge of the truth," the women of 1 Timothy 2:9-15 are believers who live in faith, love, holiness and sobriety, and who are exhorted to continue in those virtues.

4. If false or incorrect teaching were the object of Paul's prohibition, it seems unfair to apply it to all women (and only women), instead of specifying the incompetent, ignorant or heterodox ones. Priscilla was in Ephesus (Acts 18:24-28). Certainly, she was a capable and orthodox woman; yet, the prohibition does not exempt her. Paul attaches no

conditions or exceptions to his commands to women in verses 11-12.

1 Corinthians 14:34-35

On first reading, 1 Corinthians 14:34-35 seems more repressive to women than 1 Timothy 2:11-14. The verb used for "silence" in this passage connotes absence of speech. Is the silence demanded of women then absolute? If so, women should not sing, read responsive readings or pray aloud, even the Lord's Prayer. If so, all that comes before involving speaking in tongues, prophesying and sharing verbally in the church is of no concern to the women and should be marked "For Men Only." The "all" in 14:5 would then exclude women.

However, that the silence is not absolute should be evident from a comparison with 1 Corinthians 11:2-16, which regulates how women and men are to worship, specifically to pray and prophesy, so that God will be glorified. In addition, Paul's use of "to keep silent" in 1 Corinthians 14 suggests that absolute silence is not commanded and that the context defines what type of silence is in view. "But if there is no one to interpret, let each of them keep silence in church and speak to himself and to God" (1 Cor 14:28 RSV), and "If a revelation is made to another sitting by, let the first be silent" (1 Cor 14:30). In neither case is the silence presumed to be absolute; the one with the gift of speaking in tongues may certainly participate in singing, praying and so on, even if he or she may not speak in tongues without an interpreter.[18]

What does the silence of verse 34 include? An examination of "speak" does not solve the problem because the Greek word has as wide a variety of meanings as the English "speak" or "talk," from just talking to making a talk (see 1 Pet 4:11).

The context qualifies the meaning of silence first of all by reference to the law (v. 34). What law does Paul have in mind? Some suppose it is a rabbinic law that requires silence as a mark of the woman's subjection.[19] Although Paul uses *law* in different senses, here he cites the law in order to end any objections. It is *the* law. Such an authoritative usage indicates that the Old Testament is intended (compare the usage in 1 Cor 14:21). The reference is not to Genesis 3:16, which is a judgment, not a prescription; it refers to those parts of the Old

Testament which teach the woman's subordination to her husband. Paul's reference to the unchanging law of God marks this command as one for all times and places.

Paul's appeal to the law is usually felt as an overwhelming blow to keep women in check, but there is another way to see it. The law can be viewed as a limit. The woman is not required to submit herself in ways the law does not demand; the woman is only to submit herself in ways the law requires. The Old Testament allowed women to prophesy; therefore, 1 Corinthians 14:34 does not prohibit women from prophesying.

Submission, not silence, is what the law commands. The command in verse 34 would be better translated, "but should submit themselves." "Be subordinate" and "be subject" are passive and have a beaten-down ring to them. The Greek verb is reflexive. It is an act one performs on or to oneself. The woman, man's ontological equal, voluntarily submits herself in recognition of her position as a woman (1 Cor 11:3).

Verse 35 may also define the sense of silence or not speaking that Paul has in mind. Speaking would then be understood as asking questions. Dialog, with questions and answers, was a common form of education in the first century.[20] The women would not be permitted to ask questions in dialog because it was a form of teaching. (In the synagogue it was the rabbi or official teacher who asked the questions, not the students.) When Paul directs the women to ask at home, he is providing a way for them to learn; Paul does not neglect women's education. It is important that women learn, though they are not to take part in the official teaching of the church.

1 Corinthians 11:2-16

This passage concerns women's participation in the church in a positive way. Paul's main thrust is that men and women (when they pray and prophesy) worship God in a way that glorifies him. The glory of God is foremost in Paul's mind. He has just written, "So whether you eat or drink, or whatever you do, do all to the glory of God" (1 Cor 10:13). "Glory" (who gets it?) is the crucial factor in the issue of covering or not covering heads in verse 7. The subordination of the woman is not the primary thrust of the passage. The male-female relationship is discussed only because it is relevant to how men and women pray and prophesy during worship.

Do Paul's instructions still apply today? Frequently, the command for a covering is assumed to be a cultural requirement. This assumption is doubtful for several reasons.

1. It is often argued that Paul is righting a Corinthian wrong: the women of Corinth were acting up and ignoring social propriety, so Paul wrote to tell them to behave as proper women by covering their heads. However, Paul begins this section by commending the Corinthians (v. 2); it is not until verse 17 that he criticizes them. Possibly Paul is providing a theological basis for what the Corinthians were already doing. The inclusion of this section in Scripture cannot be rationalized as an exhortation to cultural conformity; it is included for a more profound reason, one going all the way back to creation.

2. The reason for covering heads is directly connected with the headship of the husband; the head is significant here. To suggest some other cultural expression, such as wedding bands to signify the wife's submission to her husband, ignores this integral connection.

3. Exactly what the customs in Corinth were is unclear.[21] Some scholars claim Paul rejected the customs of his day,[22] and some claim he upheld them to avoid unnecessary offense or because he could not see beyond them.

4. The discontinuance of coverings for women, by most denominations only in this century, was not done for theological reasons but for cultural reasons (hats went out of style and became too expensive).

Headship is the determining element in 1 Corinthians 11:2-16. What does it mean? In the Old Testament, *head* meant "the highest" or "front" in addition to "first thing" or "beginning." Because it included the ideas of height, elevation and precedence, *head* was associated with leadership (Ex 18:25; Num 1:16; 25:15). *Head* was used to denote the president of the synagogue. Paul relates authority and headship. In Ephesians 5:21-33 the woman submits herself to her husband precisely because he is her head, as Christ is the head of the church.[23] The idea of "source" is included. The church has its origin in Christ as the woman has hers in the man (1 Cor 11:8). Being "the source of" is the basis for headship, but the connotation of origin does not eliminate the idea of authority from headship. Being the head involves having authority (see also Col 2:10; Eph 1:21-23).

Nonetheless, headship does not automatically imply superiority. In the examples of headship (v.3), the head of Christ is God. God and Christ are both equally God. Therefore, the man is not head of his wife because he is intrinsically better. Rather, God established and appointed the man head.

That the husband's headship is not a passing fancy is indicated by verse 3. The man-woman hierarchy is placed between two unquestionable hierarchies: Christ is the head of every man, and God is the head of Christ.

A proper understanding of 1 Corinthians 11:2-16 is essential for the participation of both men and women in worship. The situation Paul regulated is that of 1 Corinthians 14, an informal service in which many made contributions. If the man prays or prophesies, he must be uncovered. If the woman prays or prophesies, she must be covered. This passage does not require women to wear coverings in church per se; they are necessary only when and if they participate verbally. The converse is true for men.

1 Corinthians 11:2-16 teaches that women can and should actively participate in worship by praying and prophesying. The only requirement is that they be covered so that the glory goes to God, rather than to their husbands; this requirement is necessary because of the husband's headship. In this passage, there are reflections of the three principles previously mentioned: (1) the subordination of the woman is implied in the acknowledgment of her husband as head, the necessity of the covering, and her being the glory of man; (2) the woman's equality is shown by her "authority" to take part in worship and the tacit agreement that she is in God's image; and (3) the interdependence of man and woman is related to the oneness of believers in the body of Christ. This third principle should check the possibilities for the abuse of the other two.

Galatians 3:28
According to the advocates of complete sexual equality, Galatians 3:28 was a time bomb dropped by Paul in one of his finer moments into the chauvinistic world of his day. The verse would gradually unfold its meaning until the church realized that there should be no distinc-

tions between women and men—that Ephesians 5:22-33; Colossians 3:18; 1 Corinthians 11:2-16; 14:34-35; and 1 Timothy 2:11-15 were just temporary measures or just Paul's inability to give up his patriarchal heritage without a struggle. One problem with this understanding of Galatians 3:28 is its approach to Scripture. It sets Scripture against Scripture; one verse is said (by some) to contradict another.

Another objection to the egalitarian interpretation of Galatians 3:28 is that it misunderstands the text itself. The point of Galatians 3:23-29 is that faith rather than the law is the way of salvation. Paul's message is that regardless of nationality, social status or gender, all are justified by faith (v. 24), all are children of God (v. 26), all have put on Christ (v. 27), all are heirs according to the promise (v. 29). Clearly the emphasis here is spiritual standing.

This assertion is no small thing, and it was especially good news in the first century. All classes and types of people have the same relationship to God through Christ. There are consequences for human relations, but not necessarily those egalitarians seek. Galatians 3:28 teaches oneness in Christ, not equality; the two words do not coincide in meaning.

In 1 Corinthians 12, Paul explains the practical applications of oneness. Jealousies, resentments and hostilities among believers are to end. This does not mean that the immediate causes—such as the headship of the husband or the variety of gifts—are bad and must be removed. Believers are to work together. Oneness means that what benefits one benefits all and what hurts one hurts all. There should be mutual care and help.

1 Corinthians 12 includes both oneness (v. 13) and hierarchy (v. 28). Therefore, oneness and hierarchy do not contradict each other in the body of Christ. Oneness, being part of one another, enables hierarchy to exist without worry about inferiority or superiority (1 Cor 12:15-26). Likewise, the oneness of husband and wife should eliminate questions of superiority and inferiority. Harmony should be further ensured by the knowledge that every believer has equal standing in Christ, that the hierarchy is appointed by God, and that all positions are necessary for the proper function of the body.

Paul does not say that all *will be* one in Christ; rather, he boldly proclaims that all *are* one. Galatians 3:28 was true when Paul wrote it, even though Jews scorned Gentiles, slavery existed, and women, by civil law and custom, may have been at their husband's mercy. The fulfillment of Galatians 3:28 does not depend on the existence or obliteration of any social institution or custom.

The three categories in Galatians 3:28 differ in nature. Because slavery is a social institution created by sinful humans who failed to see the image of God in all persons, it can be eradicated. Since this relationship can be erased, the biblical commands regulating slavery could be considered conditional or temporary. However, insofar as the categories still exist, as in the case of employer and employee, the commands still apply. The Jew-Gentile distinction has not been removed, and the Bible does not mandate its obliteration. Instead, Paul exhorts the two groups to be reconciled (Eph 2:14-16); this command is still valid. The male-female distinction is more fundamental; God established it at creation, and it cannot be removed. Since the categories of husband and wife and male and female remain, the relevant commands apply. Each of the pairs must be understood in its own terms as the Scriptures present them.

Galatians 3:28 does not annul the passages that teach the submission of women in the church or in marriage. The concepts of equality in being and subordination in function coexist in the Bible (1 Cor 11:2-16; 1 Pet 3:1-7; 1 Cor 12:13, 28). Oneness between husband and wife and among believers in Christ binds the other two principles together.

In summary, both Old and New Testaments teach the same three principles: (1) Men and women are equally in the image of God and have the same relationship to God through Christ (Gen 1:26-27; Gal 3:26-29; 1 Pet 3:7). (2) Women have a subordinate role in the church and in marriage (1 Cor 11:3; 14:34; 1 Tim 2:11; Eph 5:22-24). (3) In church and marriage, God has established a unity which harmonizes and balances the first two principles. The oneness of believers in Christ and of husband and wife are based on love (1 Cor 12—14; Eph 5:25-31).

The Next Step

How do these principles and passages relate to what women can do in the church? Unfortunately, exegesis of the relevant passages does not answer all the questions.

The most pressing question is: Can a woman occupy the position of pastor or minister (elder or pastor-teacher, to use biblical terms)? If the answer is yes, then no further questions need be asked, because if she can hold the "top" job, all others would be open to her.

The significant aspect of ordination for this discussion is that it recognizes the specific gifts God has given a person. Ordination confers nothing; it is merely the church's acknowledgment of what God has given. Thus, ordination to the ministry (or to the office of elder or pastor-teacher) is not a right to be fought for; it is a matter of God's grace.

Some denominations, like the early church, ordain deacons. Acts 6:1-6 is commonly understood as the ordination of the first deacons. If women can be deacons, it is proper to ordain them. Ordination to the diaconate is irrelevant to ordination to the ministry.

There have been invalid arguments on both the pro and con sides of the question of women ministers. The following are some improper arguments against women ministers.

1. The argument from nature: women are inferior and therefore cannot become ministers. This argument assumes that the subordination of women taught in the Bible necessarily implies inferiority (a false assumption). As stated before, the Bible teaches the subordination of women in the church, based on two objective facts: creation and Fall. It never suggests that women are inferior or incapable in any way.

2. The argument from the nature of God: God is Father; Jesus was incarnate as a man. Since the minister represents Christ, he must be male also. Though the use of masculine terminology with reference to God is significant and Jesus' incarnation as a man was theologically necessary, Scripture never proposes this argument. In fact, there is no evidence to indicate that the minister represents Christ to the congregation. In addition, the argument based on God's nature against women's ordination to the ministry can be balanced by one for it: both men and women are in God's image. But the Bible suggests neither argument in relation to the ministry, nor should the church.

3. The argument from biblical example: when Jesus chose only men as apostles, he set the standard for the church. The apostles were

also all Jews. Should all ministers be Jews? Which actions and choices of Jesus are normative and which are not? Another objection to this argument is that the office of apostle is discontinued and that it is not the same as that of elder or pastor-teacher. The two offices existed contemporaneously in the first century.

4. The argument from tradition: throughout its history, the church has not ordained women as ministers. In the past, women have become ministers only in sects or heretical groups, such as the Montanists. Although the practice of the church deserves careful attention, it is not infallible; it does not have authority over us. Only Scripture has.

There is only one valid argument against women's ordination to the ministry: scriptural prohibition. This prohibition is found in 1 Tim 2:12. It is debatable whether this passage specifically excludes women from the office of elder or not. But even if it has a more general application, it still prohibits women from becoming ministers (elders or pastor-teachers) because the particular duties of the elder are teaching (1 Tim 3:2) and ruling (1 Tim 5:17). The reason women are not permitted to teach or rule men is not found in any of the above invalid arguments. To use them weakens the case against women's ordination. The reasons are (1) the man was created first and (2) the man was not deceived but the woman was. Whether or not these reasons make sense to us or meet our standards of justice is immaterial. They are God's reasons, and we either submit ourselves to him or not.

Are God's reasons arbitrary? To ask that question seems to head in a wrong direction. Perhaps the answer is no, of course not, but finite human reason may not be able to comprehend them. The Bible is clear that we are not let in on everything and that our reasoning powers are not to be totally trusted (Prov 3:5-7; 14:12; Is 55:8-9; Rom 9:20). But there are hints as to why God chose to create humanity in two sexes with one as head.

In the Old Testament, God compares his people to a wife and himself to a husband. With this tangible illustration, God teaches his people how they are to submit themselves to him and how he loves them. In the New Testament, after Christ's perfect example and the internal dwelling of the Spirit in believers, the comparison is reversed.

Paul tells the wife to model her submission on the church's submission to Christ and the husband to model his love on Christ's self-sacrificing love for the church. The husband-wife authority structure functions as a picture of the relationship of the church to Christ her Lord. Our submission in authority structures reminds us (even those in the position of leader) of our need to submit to God.[24]

God created humanity from one person; Adam's being created first enables him to represent the whole of humanity. He is its head (Rom 5:12-21; 1 Cor 15:45-49). The woman is included in the man in a way that the reverse is not true. This aspect of the male-female relationship may indicate why elders must be male—so that they can represent the whole congregation, men and women. This line of reasoning is not an argument for male elders but rather an attempt to understand why only men may be elders.

The choice of an all-male apostolate results from the principle expressed in 1 Timothy 2:12-14, the subordination ("ordering under") of women in the church. Though biblical examples on their own are not conclusive, they can be mentioned as support, to show that 1 Timothy 2:12-14 is not an isolated prooftext. Biblical history from beginning to end illustrates this principle. In the Old Testament, only men could be priests and elders; men are conspicuous as patriarchs, kings, prophets, judges and authors of Scripture (all known authors were men). Only men were apostles (see footnote 9); every evangelist and missionary mentioned in Acts was a man. The commands to women in 1 Corinthians 11:3-16 and 14:34-35 confirm the prohibition in 1 Timothy 2:12-14. Even the commands to wives (Num 30:1-15; Eph 5:22-25; Col 3:18-19; 1 Pet 3:1-6) add support because they agree that the creation order has consequences and that hierarchy is not contrary to God's will.

The Objections

Proponents of the ordination of women to the ministry are well aware of the scriptural commands to women. Why do they regard them as void? The following are some of the arguments for the ordination of women to the ministry.

1. Biblical example. Scanzoni and Hardesty say, for example, "From the beginning women participated fully and equally with men."[25]

Women did play an active part, but the omissions are also notable. There are no examples of women teaching the assembly or even a miscellaneous group of people. There is no recorded incidence of disobedience to 1 Timothy 2:12-14.

2. Tradition. Like biblical example, tradition witnesses to women's invaluable activity in the church but not to their ordination to the ministry.

3. Experience. The preaching of women has been blessed by God. Times have changed, and women are well educated and would be accepted as ministers now. These points ignore God's Word. We know that God can bring good from wrongdoing (Phil 1:15-18), but that does not justify, much less encourage, disobedience. The Holy Spirit who gives gifts is the same one who authored the Scriptures, including 1 Timothy 2:12-14. He does not contradict himself by endowing women with a position he has denied them in the Word. Women's gifts need to be used, but they can be used in other ways.

Another experiential argument is that some women "feel" called to the ministry. To decide whether or not one has a "call" to the ministry is difficult. The starting point is the Bible. If a woman examines herself in its light, she should conclude that her feelings have misled her because 1 Timothy 2:12-14 forbids women to become elders.

The Holy Spirit does give women gifts such as the ability to teach or counsel, and some women are adept at exegesis and public speaking. These gifts and talents must not be wasted by the church. But the church, in search of creative ways to employ the gifts of its women, must not make void God's Word.

4. The universal priesthood of believers. This concept is unrelated to women in the ministry. There is no continuity between the office of priest, which ceased when Christ sacrificed himself once for all (Heb 7:11—10:25), and the office of elder or pastor-teacher. The duties of the two are very different. The priest's primary duty was to offer sacrifices for sin. The minister teaches God's Word, administers the sacraments, cares for the congregation and governs the church (including church discipline).

The universal priesthood of believers involves our offering ourselves as spiritual sacrifices to God (Rom 12:1; 1 Pet 2:5) and our access to God through Christ's blood (Heb 10:19-22). Women are priests in these senses just as men, but this status does not qualify anyone for any church office.

5. *Preaching is equivalent to prophecy, and women are allowed to prophesy (1 Cor 11:3-16).* Preaching and prophecy, however, are not the same. The sermon is a form of teaching and so is forbidden to women. With prophecy, God puts the very words into the mouth of the prophet (Deut 18:18-19); they are not the result of the prophet's reasoning. Preaching is the result of the speaker's preparation and study. Its source is Scripture, not the mouth of God. In addition, a prophet is distinguished from a pastor-teacher and evangelist (those who preach) in Ephesians 4:11.

6. *Galatians 3:28.* Does this text really teach sexual equality across the board? As previously indicated, Galatians 3:28 does not teach equality but oneness in Christ. This "spiritual equality" without "practical equality" has been greatly criticized with a cry of "not fair." But this "not fair" call demonstrates a shift in priorities. The most important thing is our spiritual standing (Mk 9:43-48). The as-yet-unseen spiritual world is the reality. The oneness of the body of Christ does not imply uniformity or removal of all distinctions, as Paul's comparison to the human body shows. Galatians 3:28 abolishes hostilities between the three pairs and affirms their equal status—children of God and heirs of the promise, regardless of nationality, social status or gender. All believers are equally important in the kingdom of God, but that does not give everyone the right to become heads or eyes or ears (1 Cor 12:14-30).

What May Women Do in the Church?
The church is confused about what the scriptural prohibitions for women mean. As a result, there has been waste of spiritual gifts and frustration and disappointment for many women. Letha Scanzoni and Nancy Hardesty write: "The church does actively discourage women. If they report that the Holy Spirit has given them gifts for changing diapers, corralling seven-year-olds, baking cakes, or rolling bandages, the church has a place for them. But if their gifts are administration, accounting, theological investigation, or public speaking, forget it."[26]

Some churches, partly in response to the secularly stimulated cries for women's liberation and partly out of confusion about interpreting the difficult passages related to women, "fence" the law. They take the prohibitions at their most comprehensive application; to make sure that no command is disobeyed, they forbid more than Scripture does. Some denominations have no female choir directors, directors of Christian education or Sunday-school superintendents. Some individuals think women may not teach in co-ed colleges or hold any position, ecclesiastical or secular, that puts men under their authority.

Other churches have succumbed to the call for sexual equality and have removed all distinctions. Without serious attention to the Scriptures, some churches randomly allow women to do some things and not to do others; tradition may account for this situation.

The first step in answering the question of what women may do in the church is a proper understanding of 1 Corinthians 11:2-16; 14:34-35; and 1 Timothy 2:11-14. We have concluded that women are to pray and prophesy[27] in the congregation as long as they are covered, that the silence of 1 Corinthians 14:34-35 refers to not asking questions during the period of instruction, and that the intent of 1 Timothy 2:12 is to eliminate women from consideration for the office of elder, the teaching-ruling position of the church. Unfortunately, these exegetical conclusions do not answer all the questions. The New Testament worship service and church structure were quite different from today's. There are positions in today's church that did not exist in the early church—boards of directors, treasurers, Sunday-school superintendents and teachers, denominational officers and committee chairpersons. How do we know which of these positions women may occupy?

My understanding of 1 Timothy 2:12 is that it refers specifically to the duties of the elder. Therefore other offices are open to women. For the elder, teaching and exercising authority are inseparable; he has the right to teach and to enforce his teaching by church discipline. The elder's authority is over human souls (1 Tim 4:16; Heb 13:17); he is to teach others God's truth and correct them so that they may grow in God's grace. It is his responsibility to ensure that the faith, as it was originally taught, is kept and passed on (2 Tim 1:13-14). Other types of authority, however, can be delegated to women. Women may have input on the use of funds, choice of programs, church property and the like, just as any layman. This sort of authority is not in the same category as the authority over individuals' doctrine and life that the elder has.

Some of the positions potentially available to women are church librarian, treasurer, Sunday-school director, trustee, editor of the church paper, choir director, committee chairperson and writer.

One caution must be sounded regarding opening all non-elder church offices to women. In some instances, other officers, such as a trustee or deacon, may have assumed some of the functions of the elder. Clarification is needed. It may be better to return those duties to the elders rather than refuse these positions to women. This situation raises the question of church government. Is there one form that is biblical and normative for the church? There is no easy solution, but I think that the more the church conforms to the biblical picture, the easier it will be to apply Scripture and to see what women can do in the church.

The position of Sunday-school teacher requires special attention. Traditionally, women have taught children and other women in Sunday school, but the above understanding of 1 Timothy 2:12 opens the door to all levels of Sunday school, including the mixed adult class. Is this proper? This question is more complex than that of administrative positions because the Sunday-school teacher often appears to be doing exactly what the minister does in his sermon. Often the Sunday school more closely resembles the instruction period of the early church (1 Cor 14:34-35), in which women were told not to ask questions.

What is the nature of the Sunday school? Commonly, it is not considered part of the regular worship service. It is optional; church members are not required to attend. For this reason, if no other, Sunday school should be distinguished from the gathered church, which all of God's people are to attend.

The Sunday school was begun in 1781 by Robert Raikes in England to teach poor children to read and write and to reform their rough behavior, as well as to give them religious instruction. Because of its success, it spread rapidly. That its origin was outside of the church (through an individual) contributes to its nonofficial status.

The Sunday-school teacher does not enforce his or her teaching with church discipline. It has a more informal, nonofficial, open-to-discussion character (that resembles the mutual teaching among all believers, Col 3:16) than the official teaching of the minister during the worship service. Even if the minister teaches the Sunday school, his style usually reflects this difference. The work of the Sunday-school teacher and that of the minister are not the same.

What the Sunday-school teacher does differs from what the minister does in his sermon in the authority behind it. The fact that Sunday school takes place on Sunday should not cloud the difference. To do full justice to biblical authority, this distinction should be clarified for the church members so that they would know 1 Timothy 2:12 is being obeyed. If a denomination or church wishes to extend the time and place for official teaching into the Sunday school, the teaching should be done by an elder and women should not participate, even in asking questions. In either case, the type of teaching should be defined for the participants so that the biblical commands can be obeyed. The same approach applies to Bible studies. The nature of the teaching should be defined so that women will know their limits, if any.

To what extent may women take part in the worship service? Asking this question raises another: Is there a biblical format for worship? The "woman" question challenges the traditional order of worship, partly because 1 Corinthians 11:2-16 and 14:34-35 are part of a larger section dealing with the whole church meeting (1 Cor 11—14), and partly because women with their recently raised consciousness want to use their gifts in worship.

In the traditional service, there is little if any opportunity for lay people to participate, except as a group. Women's participation in these group activities, praying the Lord's Prayer, singing hymns and anthems, and reading responsive readings are sanctioned by 1 Corinthians 11:2-16 (women should pray and prophesy, including reading God's inspired Word) and Col 3:16. The silence commanded for women in the church in 1 Corinthians 14:34-35 concerns the instruction period, that is, the sermon in today's service.

In a more informal service, resembling those in the early church, there are problems to be solved. First, the covering of 1 Corinthians 11:5 must be determined. This issue is crucial because men, including the minister, need to know what it means to be uncovered also. Rather than postponing permission for women to participate because of the difficulty in identifying the covering, however, it may be better for a denomination or a church to make a provisional decision, such as a standard for hair length or style. Possibly women should be covered during corporate prayer and Scripture reading, but without doubt, women should be covered when they pray and read Scripture individually. In 1 Corinthians 11:2-16, Paul seems to have only individual prayer and prophecy in view because he says each (or every) man (v. 4) and each (or every) woman (v. 5), and prophets were to speak one at a time (1 Cor 14:29-32).

Other questions arise too. May a woman share her testimony, prayer requests and praises? May a female missionary give her report in the assembly? If a woman can pray, it would seem that she could also share her requests and praise. It is during the instruction period, the sermon and its discussion, that women are to be silent. Since personal testimonies and missionary reports, though instructive, are not authoritative, official teaching, they would be appropriate for women, if they were not substituted for the sermon.

May a laywoman do everything a lay man can do? It is tempting to say yes based on 1 Timothy 2:11-14. After all, not all men are authorized to teach and exercise authority; being male is not the sole qualification for being an elder. However, 1 Corinthians 14:34-35 seems to imply that any man could ask questions and that only women are excluded from the discussion. Therefore, the answer to the question is a qualified yes, with the exception of any participation in the instruction period, including asking questions.

What if there are no men qualified to be elders and there are trained women, such as on a mission field? May the women then assume leadership? God's laws do not change even to fit the exceptional case. Nonetheless, it is presumptuous (and untrue in experience) to assert that God will always provide able men for the eldership.

Elisabeth Elliot was faced with such a situation after her husband and several other missionaries were massacred by the Auca Indians. She was the only theologically trained person left who could speak the language of the Aucas. Her response was to hold Bible studies and to "teach" a sermon to one of the Auca men who appeared able before the worship service. She refused to preach in the official service. Is she being a legalist, obeying the letter of the law but ignoring the point? Or does her solution resemble that of Priscilla and Aquila? When they heard the defective preaching of Apollos, they did not usurp his place as teacher; instead they taught him privately, and he continued his ministry. Elisabeth Elliot privately trained Auca men so that they could become elders in their church. This type of solution to the exceptional case honors God's Word.

In 1 Corinthians 12:28, Paul lists several gifts given to Christians in hierarchical order: apostles, prophets, teachers, workers of miracles, healers, helpers, administrators, speakers in tongues. Because the Corinthians, like modern Christians, resisted the idea of hierarchy, Paul wrote to them about the body of Christ. Like the human body, the church is composed of different functioning units, persons with different gifts. Some gifts or functions seem more important than others, but that is a deception, worked by the self-seeking pride and discontent of the old nature. Every part is essential to the proper working of the body, and so each is equally important. Love, the application of oneness, is more important than any gift or position, and it transforms the hierarchy of Christ's body.

Of the gifts mentioned in 1 Corinthians 12:28, only two are not given to women. Historically, there were no female apostles. And since in this context *teacher* refers to the official teachers of the church, women were excluded from this position. All other offices are open to women. Ephesians 4:11 has a slightly different listing: apostles, prophets, evangelists and pastor-teachers. Based on the previous discussion, it is evident that women should not be pastor-teachers, the biblical designation closest to the modern concept of minister. The pastor-teacher is an elder (Acts 20:17, 28; 1 Tim 5:17; Tit 1:5-9; 1 Pet 5:1-3).

But what is an evangelist? May women be evangelists? Are evangelists elders? The noun *evangelist* occurs only three times in the New Testament (Eph 4:11; Acts 21:8; 2 Tim 4:5). In Ephesians 4:11, it is one of the gift-offices of the church and is distinguished from apostle, prophet and pastor-teacher. Timothy, an evangelist (2 Tim 4:5), is a man who teaches authoritatively and who is responsible for the elders and people of the church. Paul told him, "Preach the word, be urgent in season and out of season, convince, rebuke and exhort, be unfailing in patience and in teaching" (2 Tim 4:2 RSV). If such are the duties of the evangelist, the office is closed to women. However, Timothy wore several different hats, and it is not unequivocally clear which one gave him the authority to teach and to discipline. Philip the evangelist (Acts 21:8) fits the modern notion of an evangelist, a preacher who travels from town to town and who is not tied to a local church, an itinerant pastor-teacher. Philip was empowered to baptize (Acts 8:38), an act conveying the church's authority.

The verb *preach* or *preach the gospel* occurs frequently. Who preaches? Angels, Jesus, John the Baptist, the twelve apostles, Paul, Philip, Barnabas and those who were scattered as a result of persecution (an indeterminate reference). Nowhere in the New Testament is a woman specifically depicted as evangelizing or preaching.

Thus the biblical data relevant to the question of women evangelists is inconclusive and scarce. There are two basic ways to consider the office: as an elder not attached to a local church or as a "glorified" witness. If we consider who evangelized, the former understanding is closer to the scriptural picture. The primary function of the evangelist would be authoritative teaching or preaching. He differs from the pastor-teacher in that he is not connected with a specific church and probably in that he addresses mostly non-Christians. To start new churches, the evangelist must be able to administer the sacraments (baptism and the Lord's Supper) and to teach new converts with authority.

To deny this office (as a type of elder) is not to reject women missionaries. As in the case of Elisabeth Elliot, women missionaries should not act as elders to the mission church by preaching, exercising discipline or administering the sacraments. For this reason, a missionary team should include an ordained elder. Nonetheless, there are many contributions a woman missionary can make—Bible studies, teaching individuals, translation, counseling. One does not have to be an ordained evangelist to tell the good news of Jesus Christ to others. Women can witness to their Lord freely.

May women be deacons? Once more, the biblical evidence is inconclusive, but it is better understood if women are admitted to the office of deacon. In Romans 16:1, Phoebe is called *diakonon,* and the evidence supports its being translated "deacon."

In the middle of the instructions to deacons in 1 Timothy 3:8-13, Paul addresses women (v. 11). It is possible to interpret this as reference to deacons' wives; however, no such requirement is made of elders' wives. In addition, deacons' wives could be considered already covered in verse 12, in which deacons are told to have one wife and to manage their households well. Verse 11 begins with "likewise" as does the section addressed to deacons (v. 8). The repetition of this conjunction suggests that another similar group is involved—a group of female deacons. The feminine noun "deaconess" does not occur in the New Testament. In order for Paul to address the issue of women deacons, he would have to refer to them by sex. That is why Paul inserts a command for women in the middle of his instructions to deacons. The requirements for the women in verse 11 are comparable to those for the deacons in verses 8-9. In a culture in which the sexes were separated, the church would have needed women to visit sick women and perform other tasks of service among women.

The duties of a deacon, though not clearly described in Scripture, are not inappropriate to women. They do not include authoritative teaching forbidden to women in 1 Timothy 2:11-14. The deacon is primarily a servant with a focus on material or physical service. The qualifications (serious, not double-tongued, sober, not greedy, not slanderers) are suited for one dealing with financial, administrative and social service. The office probably arose out of the need for fair distribution of food to widows (Acts 6:1-6).

The witness of the early church (the Greek Fathers and Theodore of Mopsuestia) confirms the reference of 1 Timothy 3:11 as to female deacons. In A.D. 111, Pliny, governor of Bithynia, questioned two maidservants who were called deaconesses *(ministrae)*. This reference may be to a church office.[28] There are clearer examples of deaconesses in the third and fourth centuries.

In the Didascalia (early third century) and the Apostolic Constitutions (late second century), a deaconess's duties are delineated. The deaconess was to help the clergy in the baptism of women and in the instruction of female catechumens; to minister to the poor and sick, particularly to women; and to visit women in pagan households. She was to act as an intermediary between the clergy and the women in the congregation. The office of deaconess disappeared in the West in the fourth century and in the East in the twelfth century.

Women deacons today could (and should) be performing the same functions, including the financial and administrative aspects of those services. In churches where deacons have taken on some of the elders' duties, the work should be redistributed along biblical lines; that is, women should not be denied the office of deacon because in a particular church deacons are teaching with authority or exercising church discipline. In addition, the work of female deacons should not be confined to preparing communion and cleaning up afterwards, though that work is also appropriate for them.

In summary what may women do in the church? In the worship service, they may participate in all but the instruction period and the discussion. Women who are covered may lead in prayer and prophesy (including Scripture reading). In regard to church office, women may not be elders (neither pastor-teachers, nor evangelists, nor ministers, as commonly termed), because these offices involve teaching and ruling. They may be deacons or administrators. In general, the church wastes the gifts of its women and its laity as a whole. A greater effort must be made to help members of the body identify their gifts and use them for the growth of the body and the glory of God.

Notes

[1]God witnesses to his Word in the Bible (2 Tim 3:16-17; 2 Pet 1:20-21) and by his Holy Spirit (1 Cor 2:14). Paul affirms that all Scripture is God-breathed; it is the result of God's creative breath and therefore profitable to us. Without denying human agency in the writing of the Bible, Peter, in 2 Pet 1:20-21, eliminates all possibility of human contamination. No prophecy of Scripture results from human initiative, will, determination, study or imagination. The individuals who wrote the Bible were moved by the Holy Spirit who spoke God's words. The proof of the inspiration and authority of the Bible does not depend on 2 Tim 3:16-17 and 2 Pet 1:20-21 alone. For a detailed discussion, see John Murray, "The Attestation of Scripture," in *The Infallible Word: A Symposium* by the members of the faculty of Westminster Seminary (Philadelphia: Presbyterian and Reformed, 1946); Benjamin Breckinridge Warfield, *The Inspiration and Authority of the Bible* (Philadelphia: Presbyterian and Reformed, 1948); Edward J. Young, *Thy Word Is Truth: Some Thoughts on the Biblical Doctrine of Inspiration* (Grand Rapids: Eerdmans, 1957); and Susan T. Foh, *Women and the Word of God: A Response to Biblical Feminism* (Phillipsburg, N.J.: Presbyterian and Reformed, 1980), pp. 8-21.

[2]In the case of the Old Testament, the New Testament indicates the temporality of some of its laws, but there is no Newer Testament. Biblical revelation is progressive to its end point. The nature of the Old Testament is preparatory, with typologies and symbols. It led up to the coming of Jesus Christ, the culmination and fulfillment of

God's promises. The New Testament explains the significance of Christ's coming; it is the final revelation of God.

[5]Richard and Joyce Boldrey, *Chauvinist or Feminist? Paul's View of Women* (Grand Rapids: Baker, 1976), pp. 50, 55-58. See also Harvie M. Conn, "Evangelical Feminism: Some Bibliographical Reflections on the Contemporary State of the 'Union,'" *Westminster Theological Journal* (Spring 1984), p. 120.

[4]Foh, *Women and the Word*, pp. 37-43.

[5]"Fit for" means "in front of" (as looking into a mirror).

[6]Foh, *Women and the Word*, pp. 60-61.

[7]James B. Hurley, *Man and Woman in Biblical Perspective* (Grand Rapids: Zondervan, 1981), p. 210.

[8]Ibid., p. 212.

[9]The etymology of the word *desire* supports this interpretation. The root is the Arabic *saqa*, which means "to urge," "drive on" or "impel."

[10]Bo Reicke defines the verb as (a) "preside," "lead," "conduct," "govern," "direct"; (b) "stand" or "go before" in the sense of "protect," "assist," "represent" or "care for"; or (c) "arrange," "handle," "execute" ("προΐστημι," in Gerhard Kittel and Gerhard Friedrich, eds., *Theological Dictionary of the New Testament*, 10 vols. [Grand Rapids: Eerdmans, 1964-76], 6:700-701).

[11]There is some dispute over whether Junia (Rom 16:7) was an apostle and whether Junia was a man or a woman. The name *Junia* was a common Roman name for a woman; however, all the nouns and pronouns in Rom 16:7 are masculine, and some scholars have suggested that Junia is a contraction of a man's name. In any case, it is unlikely that Andronicus and Junia were apostles in the official sense. "They are noted by the apostles" is a possible translation. The only apostles mentioned in the New Testament are the Twelve, James (the brother of Christ and the head of the church at Jerusalem, Gal 1:19), Barnabas (Acts 14:14) and Paul. In Acts 1:21-26, the eleven chose one man to replace Judas as an apostle (v. 25). This action implies that those who met the qualifications in vv. 21-22 were not necessarily considered apostles; only the chosen Twelve were apostles. Because of this exclusiveness, Paul had great difficulty being recognized as an apostle. Repeatedly, he was forced to give proof of his apostleship (1 Cor 15:9-11; 2 Cor 12:11-13; Gal 1:1, 11—2:10; Eph 3:1-13). Paul's call to the apostleship was a special case. If Junia and Andronicus were apostles, it would seem that more than an occasional reference would have been made to them in the New Testament (Foh, *Women and the Word*, p. 97). Hurley suggests that Junia and Andronicus may have been apostles in a nontechnical sense; perhaps they were "sent out" (*apostle* means "one who is sent out") by the church for a specific task (as in 2 Cor 8:23; Phil 2:25—Hurley, *Man and Woman*, pp. 121-22). Hermeneutically, it would be improper to interpret a brief, unclear reference as an example of a female apostle in disagreement with a relatively clear command supported by theological arguments (1 Tim 2:12-14).

[12]The Greek word connotes quietness or rest, rather than absence of speech.

[13]"I permit" connotes command; it is stronger in meaning than "urge" or "advise". It is in the present tense, which indicates continuing action.

[14]"Dei is an impersonal verb meaning 'one must' or 'one ought.' In Pauline and in general New Testament usage it points to a strong degree of necessity, generally involving divinely based moral obligation" (Hurley, *Man and Woman*, p. 196).

[15]George W. Knight III, "*ΑΥΘΕΝΤΕΩ* in Reference to Women in 1 Timothy 2.12," *New*

Testament Studies 30 (1984): 154.

[16]1 Cor 11:12 may add some light: the woman's dependence on man, based on her creation after and for him is balanced by his dependence on her now through childbearing. The woman is "saved" from total dependence on the man (and possible domination by him) by performing part of the cultural mandate, the part which balances her derivation from the man and stresses the interdependence of the man and woman. Another explanation of v. 15, which is usually rejected because of its obscurity, is that childbearing refers to the birth of the Child, Jesus Christ. Several factors commend this interpretation: (1) the verb "save" is taken in its usual New Testament sense, to save from sin and death; (2) the definite article with childbearing is accounted for; (3) the noun refers to the birth of children (or a child), not raising them, as some have suggested; a different noun means to raise children; and (4) the immediate context alludes to Gen 2—3, which closely associates the promise of the seed (the savior) and the judgment on the woman (Gen 3:15-16). Obscurity is not alien to Paul's style, and his choice of *childbearing* could be intended to recall Gen 3:16. Childbearing is not only the arena of judgment for the woman; it is also the avenue of salvation for her: through *the* childbearing, Jesus. The force of the conditional clause would then be the same as in Mt 24:13, "But he who endures to the end will be saved."

[17]Aida Besançon Spencer, "Eve at Ephesus (Should Women Be Ordained as Pastors according to the First Letter to Timothy 2:11-15?)," *Journal of the Evangelical Theological Society* 17, no. 4 (Fall 1974):215-22.

[18]Hurley, *Man and Woman*, pp. 190-91.

[19]Paul K. Jewett, *Man as Male and Female* (Grand Rapids: Eerdmans, 1975), p. 114.

[20]The rabbis, posing questions which other rabbis or their students would answer, used dialog to teach. The Greeks (Socrates, for example) also used dialog to instruct. Since the early church modeled its worship on that of the synagogue, it may have also used it. In Acts 20:7-12, Paul, in the teaching part of the Sunday gathering, dialogs. His talking is also called "the speech" and "to confess" or "declare," the verb from which the word *homily* is derived.

[21]Conzelmann reports that the Jewesses and respectable Greek women of this time did not appear in public uncovered (Hans Conzelmann, *I Corinthians* [Philadelphia: Fortress Press, 1975], p. 185). The Woman's Bible includes this information: Corinth was destroyed in 146 B.C. by the Romans, who recognized it as a Roman colony in 46 B.C. The Roman women did not veil themselves and mingled freely with men. Elizabeth Cady Stanton, *The Original Feminist Attack on the Bible (The Woman's Bible)*, part 2 (New York: Arno Press, 1974), p. 151. Jewish and Roman men covered their heads for prayer and Greek men prayed with uncovered heads, R. C. H. Lenski, *The Interpretation of St. Paul's First and Second Epistles to the Corinthians* (Minneapolis: Augsburg, 1961), pp. 434-35. If the population were mixed, the customs may have been also.

[22]Peter Brunner, *The Ministry and the Ministry of Women* (St. Louis: Concordia, 1971), p. 23.

[23]Concerning the meaning of "head," Hurley writes, "Christ's rule is for the sake of his body, the church. Here [Eph 1:20-22; cf. Eph 5:22-23] the idea of love, unity and rule for the sake of another are introduced. Paul draws the rule of Christ and Christ's love for his church together by means of two meanings of the word 'head' *(kephalē)* Hurley, *Man and Woman*, p. 146.

[24]Susan T. Foh, "Women Preachers—Why Not?" *Fundamentalist Journal* 4, no.1 (January

1985):18.

[25]Letha Scanzoni and Nancy Hardesty, *All We're Meant to Be* (Waco, Tex.: Word Books, 1975) p. 60.

[26]Ibid., p. 178-79.

[27]Whether or not prophecy still exists is beyond the scope of this chapter. An equivalent act is the reading of Scripture, since the Scriptures are God's direct word to the church, as is prophecy.

[28]A. F. Walls, "Deaconess" in *New Bible Dictionary*, ed. J. D. Douglas (Grand Rapids: Eerdmans, 1962), p. 298.

A TRADITIONALIST RESPONSE
Robert D. Culver

I read some time ago Susan Foh's *Women and the Word of God*,[1] and now I have tried to digest her essay. I have been informed by her on several aspects of the general teachings of Scripture about women, and I am in general agreement with what she writes and the spirit and standpoint from which she writes. She calls a spade a spade and not an instrument of steel and wood for moving coal or sand. Her interpretation of Scripture and practical suggestions in the present essay are almost all in the book, but I found them somewhat less persuasive, even though again I agree in the main.

Mrs. Foh bluntly reminds us all that we must beware lest we read our culture into Scripture. She says, "Equality is a current banner held high (it is un-American to speak against equality), and it is assumed to be an indisputable theme in Scripture. But is it?" She shows how truly anti-biblical it is. Bravo! She and her sources have demonstrated that the various Bible versions which specify authority are correct. Again, Bravo!

She points out that there is a strong current in so-called biblical feminism—to set "Scripture against Scripture." So they set Galatians 3:28 against all else Paul said about male and female in Christ. This she not only rejects but shows to be absurd. I could not agree more.

I have quoted Karl Barth to the same effect.

She finds "three principles" announced in the early chapters of Genesis. While it is not the way I would choose to comment, I agree fully and find her summary paragraph worthy of repetition here: "In summary, both Old and New Testaments teach the same three principles: (1) Men and women are equally in the image of God and have the same relationship to God through Christ. . . . (2) Women have a subordinate role in the church and in marriage. . . . (3) In church and marriage, God has established a unity which harmonizes and balances the first two principles. The oneness of believers in Christ and of husband and wife are based on love."

I found much more than this to be not only sound but helpful. The bibliography of sources in her book is an excellent guide to literature on the subject, though I notice no literature on the theology of church and ministry in the early church fathers. Though I did not pursue the subject in my essay, I have read far enough to be convinced that there was unbroken concern, not only for the office of presbyter-overseer through the first centuries, but that it functioned both in oversight (rulership) and teaching. It seems never to have occurred to anyone that women could hold such office. Far from first appearing in Cyprian, it seems more likely that the office of the local bishop (pastor, presbyter) in charge of a flock has first-century origins. It was certainly prevalent when the *Didache*, the *Sources of the Apostolic Canons* and the *Letters of Ignatius* were composed—all very early.

It would seem like nit-picking to comment on every point in Susan Foh's manuscript where I placed a question mark or noted what I think may be a minor error. One or two points which seem important to me and wherein I hope she will consider a change of mind follow.

Mrs. Foh takes a very unusual view of Genesis 3:16, "Yet your desire shall be for your husband, and he shall rule over you." She asserts that the harmonious working of the "three principles" (ontological equality, functional subordination of the woman to her husband and oneness) was "destroyed" by the Fall. I'll have to ponder that; and it may or may not be true, as several commentators claim, that the translation "suggests that somehow through the woman's desire for her husband, he is able to rule her."

Most interpreters I have read think the "desire," while not precisely sexual, includes that, and covers the whole range of things a woman (Eve the archetypal woman) expects from the man who is her husband. But Foh is confident that the desire is not sexual at all and that it has nothing to do with "psychological dependence." Rather it is desire to dominate her husband. This verse, in her opinion, is the textual "beginning" of what she calls "the battle of the sexes."[2]

What is the exegetical basis of this view? The key is said to be correspondence between Genesis 3:16 and 4:7. In the latter, "its [sin's] desire is for you [Cain], but you must master it." The idea is that sin wants to control Cain. So, according to the analogy that Mrs. Foh sees, the woman, whose desire is for her husband, will want to control her husband. "As in Genesis 4:7, there is a struggle in Genesis 3:16 between the one who has the desire (wife) and the one who must/ should rule or be master (husband)."[3]

Against this interpretation I present the following:

1. Whether there be simple prediction or curses involved in Genesis 3:16, there is no reason in Hebrew grammar or syntax for introducing the mode of command, as Mrs. Foh would have it, "He must rule over you." Nor does the situation require it as in Genesis 4:7.

2. It is not true, as her essay states, that sexual desire or other features of the mating urges in young women are foreign to *teshuqah* ("desire") in 3:16. True, it seems to be absent in 4:7. Yet this word occurs only three times in the Bible, the third being in an exceedingly erotic love song, "I am my beloved's, and his desire is for me" (Song 7:10). The constructions except for the prepositions, *'al* in Song 4:7 and *'al* in Genesis 3:16, are virtually identical. Domination of a second party by a first party has nothing to do with the mating impulses of young female love in the Song, and there is no clear reason for it in Genesis 3:16.

3. Neither the book by Mrs. Foh nor her essay presents any supporting opinions of scholars ancient or modern. As far as I know the view is original with her. She has, however, made a good many converts, as I am learning.

4. What she calls "the judgment" and "the curse"[4] on the woman is not by any means *only* that. There may be punishment (the pain now accompanying parturition), but there is also God's plan for perpetuating the race and for the Redeemer to consider.

A more inclusive and accurate view seems to be that now that sin had come, God was adjusting physical and social affairs so that the human race could "be fruitful and multiply." Soon both Adam and Eve would die. Never would there likely be more than four or five generations living at the same time, at least after the time of Moses. If the race was to fulfill its creation mandate to "fill the earth" and to master it, then there would be a need for a great increase in conception, that is, many more babies. As a guard against overpopulation there is the caution that childbearing is accompanied by greatly increased pain. In such a situation women who do some thinking might calmly decide never to mate. But God did something to insure that such would rarely happen. He did also change her so that "thy desire shall be to thy husband," that is, desire for a mate will be stronger than aversion to the pains of multiple childbearing. Views similar to this are widely held by competent and reputable interpreters, among them Franz Delitzsch *(New Commentary on Genesis)*, G. Von Rad *(Genesis)*, H. C. Leupold *(Exposition of Genesis)*. Perhaps there are more facts, both agreeable and disagreeable, in the text and context of Genesis 3:16 than Susan Foh has yet seen, or if seen, acknowledged.

There are more than enough agreed consequences of the sin of our first parents—guilt, corruption of nature, punishment. We struggle with these grim theological and personal realities every day. We do not need another one—a putative inevitable husband-wife contest for power. Let us be spared this till-now-undiscovered consequence of the Fall. I hope Susan Foh will withdraw her insistent assertion that there is something like an automatic, built-in impulse in all brides to dominate the lives of their unsuspecting husbands. Is there some impulse, irresistible and immutable in every man, *not* to love his wife as we are commanded? Certainly not. Then please do not try to convince us of the existence of some universal desire of women to dominate their husbands. God forbid it!

Another matter on which I register disagreement is Mrs. Foh's insistence that there are no important psychical differences between men and women. Chapter six, "The Metaphysics of Sex," of her *Women and the Word of God,* is devoted to this proposition. She does not even think the Bible favors any division of labor between men and women.

I suggest Titus 2:5, which among other things directs the older women to teach young women to be *oikourgous*, "working at home." Can you imagine such instruction for young men by their fathers?

Susan Foh lists four "invalid" arguments, also labeling them "improper." One of these is said to be "the argument from nature." If she did not reject differences of a psychic, emotional and mental sort between men on the *average* and women on the *average*, she would not, as she does, insist that this argument is the same as "women are inferior and therefore cannot be ministers."

I have noted in my own essay how people through the ages have regarded men and women as "cut out" for different roles in society precisely because that was the way things move in harmony with the nature of things. Mixing of the roles, as pointed out convincingly by Weaver in *Ideas Have Consequences*, is largely due to a rejection of nature. Somehow the fitness of men for certain places and functions in society and of women for others has always been in relation to the unique natures of women and men. If this is not so, then man's prescribed leadership in home and church is rooted more in Islamiclike capriciousness in the Godhead and less in relationship to God, holy and wise, who knows more than we about the "fitness of things." I have argued against this outlook in my own essay.

Another of Mrs. Foh's "invalid" and "improper" arguments is "the argument from biblical example"—male-only apostles are mentioned. The observation that they "were all Jews" also is supposed to dispose of that. Hold on. How about kings, writing prophets and apostles? I doubt that Mrs. Foh will allow herself to assign that to paternalistic customs of antiquity. It seems more reasonable to assume that God who made a "help meet [that is, appropriate] for the man" and "woman for the man," and not the other way around, must have been operating on stated providential policy. Means in nature are fitted to ends (see Psalm 104). Precedents mean something. Even the "laws of nature" are frequently said to be nothing less than "the habits of God." Maybe male leadership is one of God's habits also. There is more than a little of a mild form of crypto-feminism in Mrs. Foh, I surmise.

She also insists that traditions mean nothing. It seems evident to me that the authoress has something to learn about the art of persuasion—not quite the same as laboratory proof and the rules of formal debate. What we know from observation about the behavior of men and women as well as from biblical and historical precedents is apt to have more force with many people than some of our sharpest exegesis. And does not tradition—through millennia of biblical and church history—say something about how preceding generations interpreted the Word of God? None of us should lightly reject it. I cannot help but wonder why Susan Foh wishes to get rid of it. Latent female prejudice? Hmmm. No, of course not. As a matter of fact, late in her essay she seems to acknowledge some of what I have been saying in these last three paragraphs.

Notes

[1]Susan T. Foh, *Women and the Word of God: A Response to Biblical Feminism* (Phillipsburg, N.J.: Presbyterian and Reformed, 1980).
[2]Ibid., p. 69.
[3]Ibid.
[4]Ibid., pp. 66-67.

A PLURAL MINISTRY RESPONSE
Walter L. Liefeld

Foh's essay contains much good exegesis and many thoughtful observations. It is unfortunate, therefore, that she works on the basis of two oversimplified and unfair assumptions. She begins her essay by stating that differing views on women stem from differing views on the Bible. One is that of inerrancy, and the other is that which allows human opinion. The implication is that all who agree with her are in the first category and all who do not are in the second. The other assumption is that the issue of what commands are applicable today is resolved by an appeal to the first assumption.

Her reasoning is, therefore: If the Bible is inerrant and without human opinion, every command applies today. She believes that to take into consideration the social context in and to which a command was applied is to relativize it. According to that reasoning we cannot place the names of any widows under sixty years of age on a deacons' list for assistance (1 Tim 5:9), even though the social situation is different. To suggest that the sense of a loving Christian sibling relationship can be expressed in a culturally different way than by the holy kiss would, following her logic, "relativize the biblical command."

Foh would immediately remonstrate that these are in themselves cultural expressions. But we need to realize that the public appearance and demeanor of women is also a cultural expression. Foh confuses the *principle* of a woman's relationship to her husband with the cultural *expression* of it, thereby missing a basic element in hermeneutics. I, like Foh, am a biblical inerrantist and strongly oppose rendering the Bible culturally relative. I am concerned, as she certainly is, about some feminist writers over the past several decades who in my judgment have defaulted on both of those matters. But Foh has overreacted and weakened her own case in the process.

Her hermeneutical problem is reflected in her use of 1 Corinthians 2:14 to support the statement that "the Bible must be interpreted under the guidance of the Holy Spirit." Of course we should do everything, and this certainly includes reading the Bible, under the guidance of the Holy Spirit. Romans 8:14 tells us that being led by the Spirit characterizes the "sons of God." But the attempt to apply the concept that we call the "illumination" of the Holy Spirit to the interpretation of Scripture is wrongly based on 1 Corinthians 2:14.

That Scripture speaks of accepting and understanding the things that come from the Spirit of God, but does not teach that in some way God shows us what the right interpretation is. If this were the case, and if it were pressed to its logical conclusion, then when two Christians differ over the interpretation of a verse, say, on the issue of predestination, the problem would be that one of them was not led by the Spirit. It would become a spiritual matter rather than one of careful exegesis. Does Foh mean to imply that those who disagree with her are not interpreting the Bible "under the guidance of the Holy Spirit"? It is strange that some Christians seem to be able to acknowledge graciously that there are legitimate differences of opinion among spiritual believers over, say, the issue of predestination and yet are unable to acknowledge legitimate differences among Spirit-led people on the subject of women.

Another problematic "principle of interpretation" is that the clearer passage interprets the less clear. That sounds self-evident. We must sometimes ask, however, whether one passage may *seem less* clear only because we need more information from context or background circumstances and whether another passage may seem *more* clear only because it contains apparently transparent words or phrases that in actuality do not mean what they seem to on the surface. 1 Corinthians

11:1 and 1 Timothy 2:12 are in the latter category.

Another "principle" Foh cites is that "Scripture does not contradict Scripture." It is important to apply this in both directions. Can one or two verses that restrict women's ministry contradict biblical examples elsewhere of women in positions of ministry and leadership?

Considerable space has been devoted to these preliminary assumptions because they can so easily be used to validate one position or to undercut another. There are a number of other statements in the essay that I will address only briefly. First, while it is true that the creation of humanity ends with woman, does that imply inferiority? What about the fact that both man and woman came after the animals? Next, how does the creation of Eve through Adam "pave the way for the principle of inequality"? Attention should be centered on the Fall and on the reversal of the effects of the Fall in the church, where "there is neither male nor female" (Gal 3:28). Even if there were subordination in creation, could we not expect a higher level of relationship in the *new* creation in Christ? Further, Foh stresses the fact that woman came from man, but does not mention the reversal in 1 Corinthians 11:11-12: "In the Lord, however, woman is not independent of man, nor is man independent of woman. For as woman came from man, so also man is born of woman" (NIV).

Foh says that to "name someone is associated with control over that person." She fails to observe that while Adam did speak of his wife as being a "woman" (*'ishshah*) in Genesis 2:23, he did not *name* her "Eve" until *after the Fall.* If there is any control it follows the terrible effect of man assuming dominion over the woman (Gen 3:16).

Foh's interpretation of the woman's "desire" for her husband as being "a desire to control" him depends on a verbal parallel within a different topic in Genesis 4:7. It overlooks a passage on the same topic, the intimate relationship of man and woman in Song of Solomon 7:10: "I belong to my lover, and his *desire* is for me." It is striking that here the word is applied to the man, not the woman—a difficult fact for Foh's theory.

Neither the discussion of Phoebe as "patroness" (Rom 16:1-2) nor the accompanying note mentions classical sources (or recently cited information from the papyri that I also failed to cite in my essay). But she is right in not reading too broad a leadership role into that single word. Her comments on Junia, including the relevant note, are cautious. She is willing to acknowledge the viewpoint that Junia may have been a woman apostle in a "nontechnical sense." She thinks, however, that 1 Timothy 2:12 should restrict one's interpretation because it is more clear, rather than allowing this example to bring her interpretation of the Timothy passage into question.

Current discussions over the meaning of the rare verb *authentein* in 1 Timothy 2:12, including Foh's, are heavily dependent on an article by George W. Knight III, cited in one of Foh's footnotes. Knight assigns a "neutral" rather than "negative" meaning, claiming that it refers simply to the exercise of authority. Another study has confirmed that the word group to which this verb belonged was used around the New Testament period with more than one level of meaning.[1] Some used it in the sense of exercising authority while at the same time others used it with a more intense meaning. Since its use over that general time period in various contexts includes meanings of initiating action, originating something, taking authority into one's own hands or domineering, exegetes must be very slow to conclude that in 1 Timothy 2:12 it means simply to exercise authority. Paul had the normal and customary word *exousiazō* at hand, were that what he meant. All this bears heavily on Foh's interpretation.

The discussion of 1 Corinthians is thoughtful, and the conclusion about the avoidance of shaming the husband aims in the right direction. Attention to the vocabulary of shame and honor in that part of 1 Corinthians and in the literature of contemporary moral convention would have led Foh to a more accurate understanding of the passage. If she would acknowledge the relevance of the circumstances of 1 Corinthians 11 (that is, in the church) and of culture (that is, in society) she would be better able to see that (1) the command about headcovering or style of hair was significant then but not now, and (2) that other commands of Paul about the appearance and demeanor of women in public may be connected to the proper impression Paul wanted to make on nonbelievers.

In summary, much in this essay depends on the author's interpretation of 1 Timothy 2:12, an interpretation I consider defective. But in other cases there is a welcome careful moderation of more traditional views. If the implication that only one interpretation fits an inerrant view of Scripture and that consideration of cultural factors is a threat could be set aside, perhaps further moderation of those traditional views would be forthcoming.

Notes

[1]L. E. Wilshire, "The TLG Computer and Further Reference to [Authenteō] in 1 Timothy 2:12," *New Testament Studies* 34 (1988): 120-34.

AN EGALITARIAN RESPONSE
Alvera Mickelsen

Susan Foh's essay illustrates the perils of inadequate hermeneutical principles for interpreting the Bible. She lays down four principles:

1. The Bible must be interpreted under the guidance of the Holy Spirit. (I agree.)

2. The Bible is a unity, ultimately authored by the Holy Spirit, with Jesus Christ as the unifying principle. (I agree, except that the authorship of the Holy Spirit was *through* human beings.)

3. Scripture does not contradict Scripture; Scripture interprets Scripture. "Contradictions cannot exist," says Foh. According to her, what are apparent contradictions are a matter of the reader's lack of understanding. Whether we choose to call certain passages "contradictions" or "diversity," the result is the same, and Foh as well as the rest of us must deal with them honestly.

4. Clearer passages interpret the less clear. This is a slippery slope where the preconceptions of the interpreter may very well determine which passage is "clearer." Is Galatians 3:28 ("There is neither Jew nor Greek, there is neither slave nor free, there is neither male nor female; for you are all one in Christ Jesus" RSV) more or less clear than 1 Timothy 2:12 ("I permit no woman to teach or to have authority over men" RSV)? This ultimately leads back to the sad situation of

one group claiming one verse, the other another because "this one is clearer to me."

Rather than such subjective criteria, we must have a sound *basis* for determining which passages are highest ideals and which are "regulations for people where they were." Foh does not give us such a basis.

Foh also attacks consideration of cultural, historical and geographical contexts because such consideration "relativizes the biblical commands to women." She explains, "If the biblical material is in the form of a command to the church as a whole, . . . it ought to be seen as valid for all time. If there is nothing in the text to indicate that a command is limited to a special case or circumstance, we cannot presume to limit the text or to read Paul's mind."

Unfortunately, those who espouse this view are unable to carry it out. For example, five times Christians are commanded in the New Testament to "greet one another with a holy kiss." There is nothing in any of the contexts to indicate that this command is limited to special cases or circumstances. Yet traditional churches in the Western world rarely carry out this command.

The general command to all gentile churches in Acts 15 is another command that has been ignored. Gentile Christians *in all the churches* were commanded to "abstain from what has been sacrificed to idols, and from blood, and from what is strangled, and from unchastity." The only part we still try to maintain is the command about unchastity for that was clearly stated by Christ himself. True, most of us do not have to worry about food being offered to idols. But I have yet to hear of a Christian who felt he could not eat a rare steak (blood!) because of this command. As a child growing up in the country years ago, I often saw poultry killed by a quick snap of the neck. We don't usually ask at the meat counter or at a friend's house how the chicken was killed. These commands do not appear in church covenants. Why not? On what grounds do those like Foh neglect this clear command of the New Testament that was never revoked?

The list of similar situations could go on and on. Many churches use twelve words of 1 Timothy 2:12 as absolute grounds for denying women's participation in many areas of service, but these same churches totally ignore not only 1 Timothy 2:8-10, but also the fourteen verses in 1 Timothy 5:3-16 that give detailed instructions to the church on supporting widows. Nothing *in the text* indicates that these verses were only for the church at Ephesus at that time.

Actually, Foh's application of 1 Timothy 2:12 to *all* situations and all times relativizes Pentecost—Peter's proclamation that men and women alike would prophesy, that is, carry God's message.

Foh says that the presence of false teaching at Ephesus cannot be considered a reason for the prohibition of 1 Timothy 2:12 because nothing about false teaching appears in verses 9-15. Paul's concern with false teaching permeates the entire book! The first and fourth chapters are devoted almost exclusively to the perils of false teaching, and chapter six ends with a warning against it in language that clearly suggests Gnosticism ("what is falsely called knowledge"). The double mention of chastity or modesty (vv. 9, 15) suggests that "false teaching" included lifestyle as well as ideas. We dare not look at verse 12 apart from Paul's deep concern about false teaching.

Obviously we need sound principles to sort out the "highest ideals and norms of Scripture" from the dozens of "regulations for people where they were." In practice, all Christians do this, whether they admit it or not. Unfortunately, most simply follow the tradition of their own church rather than examine for themselves the basis for the choices that are made.

Since, as Foh says, the unifying principle of the Bible is Jesus Christ, we must be sure that our Savior's words are not nullified by the way we interpret other parts of the Bible. How do we reconcile his command to "treat others the way we want to be treated because *this is the law and the prophets"* with practices that are directly contrary to it? If men would not want to be restricted in the use of their God-given gifts on the basis of their gender, then they dare not similarly restrict women if they profess to be followers of Jesus Christ.

Foh's restrictions nullify the Great Commission of Jesus so far as women are concerned. Christ said, "Go therefore and make disciples of all nations, *baptizing* them in the name of the Father and of the Son and of the Holy Spirit, *teaching* them to observe all that I have commanded you" (Mt 28:19 RSV). Her response that women can teach male converts privately so that they in turn can teach and preach is irrelevant to the discussion. Any good missionary, male or female, will work through national Christians as much as possible. But before there *are* converts, how are people to hear?

Neither Foh nor Culver mentions one of the most important teachings of Christ—his condemnation of power structures and hierarchy. This teaching was *at the very heart* of his ministry, for it is repeated in each of the four Gospels, and in some it is mentioned more than once: "You know that the rulers of the Gentiles lord it over them, and their great men exercise authority over them. *It shall not be so among you;* but whoever would be great among you must be your servant, and whoever would be first among you must be your slave; even as the Son of man came not to be served but to serve, and to give his life as a ransom for many" (Mt 20:25-28 RSV [emphasis mine]).

This prominent teaching of Christ is rarely mentioned in discussions regarding women in the church and home by those who believe in female subordination. Such people nearly always lean strongly on hierarchy, finding it in strange places and never dealing with Jesus' strong words of condemnation of hierarchy. Foh finds hierarchy in Paul's simple listing of God's appointments to the church. The list: apostles, prophets, teachers, workers of miracles, healers, helpers, administrators, speakers in tongues.

If this *is* a hierarchy (not so indicated in the text), then where are the pastors? They are not even on the list. Pastors do appear in the Ephesians 4:11 list *after* apostles, prophets and evangelists. Prophets appear second in both lists. We clearly have women prophets in the New Testament—Philip's daughters and Anna in the Temple when Jesus was presented. On Foh's grounds, women prophets are higher in the hierarchy ladder than pastors and teachers. I doubt that Paul had hierarchy in mind at all—he was too familiar with the teachings of Jesus. The whole purpose of 1 Corinthians 12 was rather to emphasize the oneness and interdependence of members of the body of Christ—the opposite of hierarchy.

Foh insists that prophecy is different from preaching or teaching because prophecy is not the result of the speaker's preparation or reasoning. Therefore the women prophets in the Old and New Testaments were not in violation of her interpretation of 1 Timothy 2:12 that women are never to teach men. But did not Moses, Isaiah, Micah, Deborah, Huldah and other prophets use their reasoning when they prophesied? A common-sense reading of their prophecies certainly seems to indicate so. Micah writes in 3:8, "But in very deed I am filled with power, with the Spirit of the Lord, and with justice and with might *for the purpose* that I make known to Jacob his transgression and to Israel his sin." He knew why he was prophesying and in whose power he spoke. This does not sound like God "dictating" the words to his mouth without Micah's thought processes being involved. Rather it shows that God's Spirit energized him to proclaim God's message.

Foh says there are no biblical examples of women teaching the assembly or even a miscellaneous group of people. In the Old Testament, Huldah the prophet delivered God's message to the *the High Priest and several men who were with him.* The women at the tomb "taught" the message of the resurrection *to the assembled body of disciples,* who did not believe them because women were not considered credible witnesses in the Jewish culture of that day. Foh says that no women evangelists appear in the New Testament. But the Samaritan woman appears to be the very first evangelist. "Many Samaritans from that city believed in him because of the woman's testimony" (Jn 4:39). Her testimony was clearly to a group of people (Jn 4:28). Acts 9:2 indicates that Saul intended to arrest both men and women believers. Why would he bother with women believers if they were not evangelizing and spreading the gospel?

1 Corinthians 14 seems to indicate the same for New Testament prophets. Verse 3 says, "He who prophesies speaks to men for their upbuilding and encouragement and consolation." Verses 24-25 seem to show the evangelizing effect of true prophecy, for when an unbeliever enters the assembly and hears someone prophesying, "the secrets of his heart are disclosed; and so, falling on his face, he will worship God and declare that God is really among you." Foh's diminution of prophecy hardly does credit to either Old Testament or New Testament prophets, but it indicates the lengths to which some go to support a particular interpretation of 1 Timothy 2:12.

When Foh attempts to apply her own principles, more problems appear. Her definitions of "authoritative" and "official" teaching on the part of elders or pastors are hard to understand in the context of today's evangelical churches. Liefeld has well said that the *authority* of biblical teaching does not rest in the person teaching, but rather in the *Word of God* that he or she proclaims. Foh, on the other hand, says the *elder* has "the right to teach and enforce his teaching by church discipline; it is his responsibility to ensure that the faith, as it was originally taught, is kept and passed on." He has "authority over individuals' doctrine and life."

This sounds more like the older Roman Catholic position than that of Protestant churches that teach that every individual Christian is responsible to God and capable of reading and understanding the Scriptures. The Scriptures emphasize that pastors and other church leaders are to serve the believers, to encourage them in their Christian walk with God, to help them understand the Scriptures, to pray for and with them, to lead *by example*, to help the community of believers reach out to others. The "authority" approach that Foh promotes seems far out of keeping with the spirit and ministry of Christ himself. Desire for power over others was the original sin in the Garden of Eden and is at the root of many sins in our churches and society.

Other problems inherent in the principles that Foh espouses become clear as she tries to apply them to the church situation today. She says that women may teach Sunday school because it is different from the regular worship service in that church members are not required to attend. In what churches are members *required* to attend worship services? She says the Sunday-school teacher does not *enforce* his or her teaching with church discipline. Does the pastor or elder? There is probably more discipline among children taught by women than among adult classes taught by elders.

The work open for women includes, according to Foh, writing. Actually, written commentaries or lesson materials about the Bible often have far more authoritative influence on both men and women than sermons do. Sunday-school curriculum material is probably as close to "official teaching" as most churches ever get. Yet, according to Foh, it is permissible for women to teach men by writing such material.

Application of other teachings becomes even more difficult. In regard to 1 Corinthians 11, Foh suggests that a denomination or church should set a standard for hair length or style for women who will participate in the service. (Obviously the same should then be done for men, for the passage also discusses their hair length.) The idea of churches or denominations embarking on a new legalism in such matters as hair length would be appalling to most Christians and rightly so. The apostle Paul took pains to teach Christians that such kinds of legalism hinder rather than help the gospel. The Bible stresses that God is more concerned with a willing and a contrite heart, love for neighbor, and love for God than with such things as the hair length of those who sing or pray.

The concept of keeping women in a restricted place runs counter to the "freedom in Christ" that Jesus demonstrated and that Paul preached. It invalidates the Pentecost event that was to empower the "new life" that Christ came to provide—one in which classism, racism, sexism, ageism were to have no place. The Christian church was *not* intended to be a revised version of Judaism. It was to be "new wine" in new wineskins. Unfortunately, some churches resemble the exclusively male-dominated Jewish synagogues more than they resemble the Spirit-filled church of Jesus Christ that honored and used all the gifts of all believers.

In Galatians, Paul strongly proclaimed freedom in Christ for all men and women. He warns his readers to beware of those who would put a yoke of Jewish legalism around their necks. He illustrated his meaning with a reference to Sarah (the mother of the free) and Hagar (the mother of the bound). He writes, "So, brothers, we are not children of the slave [Hagar], but children of the free woman [Sarah]. For *freedom* Christ *freed us*. Stand therefore, and stop being loaded down with a yoke of slavery" (4:31; 5:1).

Legalistic restrictions such as Foh and Culver propose are a yoke of bondage for Christian women and for the church of Christ. Christ came to deliver us from a bondage that has handicapped the church through the centuries.

3/A PLURAL MINISTRY VIEW: YOUR SONS AND YOUR DAUGHTERS SHALL PROPHESY

A PLURAL MINISTRY VIEW:
Your Sons and Your Daughters Shall Prophesy
Walter L. Liefeld

The conclusions we reach with regard to women and ministry are inevitably affected by the way the questions are posed. It could be said, for example, that there is only one question: Should Christian ministry, which by all testimony of Scripture is *spiritual* in nature, be limited by the gender of the minister, which is by nature a *human* distinction? That is a basic and straightforward way of putting it. It cuts through to the heart of the issue and sets the agenda without ambiguity. It puts the burden of proof on the disputant who would say that there is some distinction—physical, mental, social or spiritual—that makes a woman unfit for certain aspects of ministry. It confronts the opposition with one apparently unambiguous text: "There is neither . . . male nor female, for you are all one in Christ Jesus" (Gal 3:28).

The opposite approach is to cite the two passages that impose restrictions: "Women should remain silent in the churches" (1 Cor 14:34) and "I do not permit a woman to teach or to have authority over a man" (1 Tim 2:12). The question then becomes, Can a person hold to the apparent restrictions Paul introduced and at the same time deny that one's gender has some relation to ministry? Theological scaffolding, such as the "headship" of the husband, is then put in place and the structure goes on to completion.

Responses to the two positions just outlined tend to attribute more to the opposing position than their opponents intend to affirm. Few positions are defended at the extreme pole. Instead they are nuanced, either to make them more acceptable or for the sake of precision. Perhaps one of the most common examples of this scenario of attack and nuance occurs when Christian feminists accuse traditionalists of considering women to be subordinate and therefore inferior. The nuanced response is that they do indeed hold to subordination, but that this is a matter of function, not essence, and does not imply inferiority. Discussion then proceeds on whether there really can (in human society, that is, apart from the theological example of the Son's subordination to the Father) be any subordination without some sense of inferiority.

Not only are the positions modified in such ways, but the reasons for the positions vary. Thus Christian feminists may explain (or explain away, depending on one's viewpoint) the restrictive verses by assigning them to a bygone culture or to specific and limited circumstances; by attributing them to Paul's opponents or, in a few instances, to the unreformed Jewish patriarchal mind of Paul himself; or by interpreting them in a way that seems to accord better with the whole testimony of Scripture as they understand it on women's dignity, gifts and suitability for ministry.

Traditionalists may base their conclusions on a particular understanding of headship, the assumption that women are easily deceived, an interpretation of 1 Corinthians 14:34 that women are to be silent at all times, not just under certain circumstances, or an identification of preaching with the kind of authority Paul wanted withheld from women in 1 Timothy 2:12. These points are, of course, not exhaustive, but they illustrate the complex variety of approaches.

The Importance of Perspective and Perception

It can be a great help, when discussing a matter that deeply affects the church and, in this case, at least fifty per cent of church members, to back off, gain some perspective and even recognize some inconsistencies (perhaps humorous ones) in our own position. To see ourselves as others do is always healthy.

What does a visitor to church think, for example, when a woman can "share" from the platform, but not "preach"? Why, in some groups, can men listen to a woman if they are in an adjoining room, but not in the same room? Why is it all right for a woman to teach in the basement but not on the first floor? What inner transformation suddenly prohibits a teen-ager who is used to praying in the young people's meeting from praying among adults? Is there something to learn from the comment by a student from another continent who felt it was a matter of racism and an insult to him that women missionaries could teach him there but not teach men in America?

Is it consistent to hold, as some do, that the speaking in tongues described in 1 Corinthians 14 is no longer in effect, but that the silence of women described in the same chapter still holds? Is it consistent to forbid women to teach because of 1 Timothy 2, while allowing braided hair with gold and other jewelry, which is clearly forbidden in the same chapter—as though one is related to culture and the other not? Why do some Christians insist on head coverings but forbid women to speak, although the head coverings in 1 Corinthians 11 were specifically connected with women speaking?

Why allow women to sing in church, when churchmen of an earlier generation insisted on using boy sopranos so a woman's voice would not be heard on the high, and therefore leading, part? Why allow a woman choir director to select hymns with doctrinal content, written by women and to be sung by women, but not allow a woman to teach the same doctrine without music? Why can a woman speak of the love of God in John 3:16 but not of the other attributes of God in didactic passages? Why alleviate the pain of childbirth and provide labor-saving machinery for farmers to overcome the effects of the Fall and the curse, while still insisting on maintaining man's inordinate rule over woman, also a result of the Fall? Why listen to a woman teaching on tape or in a film, but forbid her from speaking in church in person?

The above illustrations are one-sided, and some have received answers, but they illustrate the sort of question that is being raised by observers of the current scene. This is largely a matter of social perceptions, but we shall observe that such perceptions play a large role in the reasons behind certain New Testament instructions concerning women and their roles in church and society.

The Importance of Framing the Right Questions

We can easily see that the issue of women and ministry is not mono-lithic; it is composed of several strata of subissues. The solution of the major issue must come from the solution of the others. But we also find different opinions as to what these other issues are. It is also helpful to identify practical questions, such as those mentioned above, that arise day by day in a variety of situations. To gain a clear picture of such questions, along with a realization of some of our inconsistencies in attempting to answer them, may help keep our feet on the ground while discussing the exegetical issues.

If this were a full-length study, two comprehensive questions would present themselves for exhaustive research. Based on the phrase "women and ministry," they are: (1) How does gender affect ministry? and (2) How does the nature of ministry affect women's roles?

Further questions attend the first. Among them are: Is there anything inherently different between men and women that renders one capable of ministry and the other not? What significance is there to the order of creation: man first, then woman? How does the Fall affect woman's suitability for ministry? How does the redemption of Christ affect the consequences of the Fall? What can one conclude from the actual instances of women's ministry in biblical history? What did Jesus intend us to conclude from his attitude toward and teaching about women? Why did Paul write as he did about women?

It is the second question, How does the nature of ministry affect women's roles? that will receive more attention here, because I consider it relatively neglected and misunderstood. The ultimate question in this connection is: May women be ordained? This has been the subject of various articles and books,[1] and of much discussion within several denominations. But clouds of uncertainties and unresolved questions prevent clear vision of this ultimate issue. One major problem is the divergence of views among Christians as to what ordination means and implies.

Is it a recognition of spiritual gifts? Is it permission to preach? Is it permission to teach? Is it permission to administer the sacraments? Does it grant authority over the church? Does it bestow rank above other believers? What is the "laying on of hands"? What did it signify at the time of the New Testament? Did it, as often maintained, convey teaching authority to rabbis and therefore, by analogy, to Christian ministers? Why did Jesus not lay hands on any apostles? Should elders be ordained? Can a woman be an elder? Is there any correlation between commissioning a missionary and ordaining a pastor? Can the former, if a woman, sustain an instructional relationship with Christian disciples that a woman could not have as a pastor at home? What does teaching mean in the New Testament? Does it imply authority? Does preaching imply authority? Where does authority ultimately lie in a New Testament church? What is the role of servanthood in connection with ministry?

No single sweep of the pen can underline the right answer to the question of women in ministry. Few denominations will answer all the above questions in the same way. How then can all Christians agree on the basic issue of women's ordination and ministry? The agonizing discussions among Roman Catholics are well known, as are the struggles among Episcopalians. There are some independent fundamentalists who grant a great deal of freedom to women in various ministries, including teaching in Bible schools, yet others who claim that one cannot hold to inerrancy and be a feminist.

It is not unusual to find among fundamentalists and evangelicals a concept of the ministry that vests as much de facto authority in the pastor as do some highly structured denominations. In some cases the pastor has so much power that it is psychologically difficult for members to conceive of a woman in that role. This fact, combined with a particular understanding of 1 Timothy 2:12, makes it impossible for them to be open to a woman in the pulpit.

Given the above circumstances, I want to give special attention toward the end of this essay to questions about the nature of ordination and of ministry in the biblical sense. This should help us to achieve some clarity on what we are all talking about and to see the ministry of women in what may be for some a different perspective.

What Assumptions Need Re-evaluation?
The discussion of women in ministry has been clouded by a variety of assumptions. One is that it is impossible to be a feminist and still

hold to the inerrancy or even the infallibility of Scripture. Is it fair or accurate to say, as Susan Foh has said, that biblical feminists "have taken one step further away [that is, even beyond rejecting biblical infallibility in matters of science, geography and history] from the biblical concept of the trustworthy Scriptures"? That statement is followed by the claim, "*The* [emphasis mine] biblical feminists have abandoned the biblical and historic position of the God-breathed inerrant Scriptures."[2]

Certainly *some* feminists have done that. But does it help the discussion to imply that only one's own interpretation is consistent with biblical trustworthiness? If biblical feminists honestly think that Ephesians 5:23 and 1 Timothy 2:12 (her examples) have meanings other than what she assigns to them, does that necessarily mean that they therefore "maintain that the Bible is defective," as she asserts? It strikes me as strange that although Christians have taken opposite sides on many issues (ranging from Calvinism and Arminianism to the nature of millennium to modes of baptism) without needing to insinuate that those who disagree with their interpretation are thereby rejecting the doctrine of inerrancy, this charge enters the discussion on women.

Another cloudy area is the role of culture. The assumptions take two forms. One is that the ideas of Christian feminists come from secular sources. Is this fair? Is it not better to acknowledge that (1) some Christian feminists have indeed been affected by secular movements, but that (2) this does not mean they have not also openly searched the Scriptures? The other assumption regarding culture is that Christian feminists relativize the Scriptures, making them subservient to culture. Thus Foh also says, "If Paul's teaching about women in the church is cultural, maybe his teaching on justification or his faith in God is too. Once we start amputating parts of the New Testament, how do we know when to stop?"[3] There is a fallacy here: a failure to see that the *roles* of men and women in a social context (which the church is)—where public speakers will be viewed from the standpoint of contemporary social norms regarding sex roles—are quite different from a *doctrine* such as justification and from one's personal *faith.*

Furthermore, there is confusion among some evangelicals between

Scripture being *subject* to culture and Scripture *speaking* to culture. It is significant that Paul discusses orderliness in 1 Corinthians 11 and 14 in terms of social perceptions, such as shame, honor and other terms having to do with propriety. And it is also significant that this follows a section in which he shows how to be "all things to all [Jews and Gentiles]" in order to win some to Christ (1 Cor 8:19-23). How can we avoid connecting this with the fact that Paul gives social perception as a reason for the submission of both slaves and women in Titus 2:5, 10? The situation is not that Paul's teaching is culturally determined, but that his evangelism is culturally directed.

Another false assumption that needs to be dispelled is that traditionalists believe women to be inferior. Probably few would want to say that, though admittedly one's understanding of certain biblical passages may sometimes seem, rightly or wrongly, to indicate such thinking subconsciously. It would help the discussion considerably if we men would acknowledge how easily we can subconsciously assume that our work or ministry is more important than that of women. It would also help if feminists would acknowledge that traditionalist interpretations of specific passages may have intrinsic validity even if the feminists think they are wrongly motivated.

There is another double-sided assumption. Side one is that if women are given leadership in the church, they will "take over"; side two is that if a woman is in the pulpit, men will not come to church. The best way to deal with this at present is to say that such fears should be subordinated to the question of what the biblical text actually says, not vice versa.

One final cloudy issue regards the meaning of *head* (Greek, *kephalē*). Traditionalists tend to assume that it always means "rule" or "authority" and interpret Ephesians 5:22-33 on wives and husbands and 1 Corinthians 11:2-16 on women's head covering accordingly. Other scholars have shown that it sometimes was used in the sense of "source." Although scholars are dealing with the same evidence, differences in selecting and weighing the evidence have led to sharply opposing conclusions. A study that selected a number of figurative uses out of a bank of some 2,000 occurrences[4] seemed at first to support the meanings of "rule" and "headship," but the methodology used has been heavily criticized by other scholars. If one depends largely on the biblical context of each occurrence, the picture changes with the topic. In Ephesians 5:22, for example, the headship of the husband is linked both with the wife's submission and with the husband's loving nurturing of his wife. There is not a word about the husband "ruling." In the larger context of Ephesians *kephalē* means both "rule" (1:22) and "source" (4:15-16). Along with confusion on such issues, the popular linking of feminist ideas with such matters as illicit sex, abuse and the breakdown of the family has contributed to muddled thinking and strong emotion.

What Can We Learn from Biblical History?

If the proper questions are to be asked, they must be set against the teachings and examples in all of Scripture. The biblical examples of women who were involved in various ministries show that ministry as such was not forbidden to women. There can surely be little question now remaining that women have had significant ministries in biblical times and throughout church history. However, because attention is often centered so heavily on the restrictive passages, it is easy to undervalue this and lose a proper balance. The instances of women prophetesses are now well known, though the fact that the Bible calls Miriam a leader (Mic 6:3-4) and that Deborah was a leader ("judge") *prior* to Barak's reluctance to lead in battle is not always noted (Judges 4:4-6).

Even if, as some claim, God raised up women like Deborah (or Huldah—2 Kings 22:14-20, 2 Chron 34:22-28—whose decision regarding the rediscovered Law affected the entire nation) only because of the defection of men, a twofold question remains: (1) Did God do right or wrong in allowing women such leadership ministries? (2) Assuming God can only do right, can we ask whether this indicates that it is not intrinsically sinful for women to have ministries of leadership and that God would commit ministries to women today, even if it were only because of need? The fact that ancient Jewish society was patriarchal makes it even more striking that he chose women.

The extrabiblical Jewish literature that began to appear in the period between the Old and New Testaments and continued into the New Testament period contained many references to women, some positive, many negative. There were several outstanding examples, including the saintly and stately figure of Judith. But for many the value of a woman lay mainly in her role as wife and mother. The prominence of women in the life and ministry of Jesus stands in contrast to his background. Rabbis did not have women disciples, but Mary sat at the feet of Jesus, which was a position not of worship, as is so often thought, but of discipleship. Luke even tells us that Mary was "listening to what he said" (10:39). The biblical text makes it clear that there were other women who ministered to and with Jesus (Mt 27:55; Lk 8:1-3).

Acts 2:17-18 contains a statement of crucial importance. During his explanation of Pentecost, Peter quotes the promise in Joel 2:28-32, "Your sons and daughters will prophesy. . . . Even on my servants, both men and women, I will pour out my Spirit in those days." In Old Testament times, God's chosen prophets were few; now this ministry would be distributed widely, among women as well as men. Given the importance of this event for the church in the present age, it is surprising that the significance of the quotation is so easily lost.

Some would say, because of 1 Corinthians 13:8-12, that prophecy ceased at the completion of the New Testament canon. This is incorrect, as can be seen by the fact that this passage refers to a yet future time, when we shall see "face to face" and shall "know fully," just as we are fully known. God did not bestow the gift of prophecy on men and women as a major feature of the new church age only to withdraw it almost immediately. This gift of prophecy was—as we see in 1 Corinthians 14:5, 26, 31—for the encouragement and instruction of the church.

Feminists claim this proves women were teaching; traditionalists claim that the instruction and edification were only incidental results of the prophesying. Of course, it was not the same as the inspired authoritative prophecies of the Old Testament. This is seen in the fact that the church was to evaluate the prophecies (14:29). But anyone who thinks that men should not learn from women should note that this was happening in 1 Corinthians 11:5 and that Paul praised them for it (in striking contrast to the following passage, where he did *not* praise them in connection with the way they approached the Lord's Supper, vv. 17-34).

The presence of women among the fellow workers of Paul receives ample attestation in Romans 16. Phoebe was a *diakonos.* The way this is interpreted provides an example of the effect of the differing assumptions mentioned above. Feminists claim her as a "deacon"; traditionalists say that the word does not have to be a technical one, but could simply mean "servant." It has often been remarked that had Phoebe and the other women who are mentioned in this chapter been males, no one would have hesitated to translate the descriptive words with such terms as "deacon," "leader," "minister." The other word used to describe Phoebe comes from a word group that has connotations of strong leadership. Space does not permit detailed support here, but the feminine form can, at the least, be taken to mean one who was a benefactress, perhaps recommending who would be welcomed by a community as worthy of financial support.[5]

The difference in approach can be seen again with respect to the name of Junia[s], whom Paul describes as "outstanding among the apostles" (Rom 16:7). As of this writing, I am not aware of any instance in which that appears as a masculine name in ancient literature.[6] As expected, traditionalists and feminists have differing appraisals of this, and also of whether "among the apostles" is the proper translation or whether it means "by the apostles." In my judgment the Greek preposition *en* favors the former.

The ministry of Priscilla and Aquila, also mentioned in this chapter (v. 3), will come under discussion later, but here we may note the placement, as elsewhere, of Priscilla's name first.

In summary, any discussion of Pauline restrictions on the ministry of women must be seen against the impressive background of women who did minister in both Old and New Testament history. This ministry is all the more significant against a social background of negative or, at best, mixed opinions concerning the status of women.

How Do We Handle Apparent Differences in Scripture?

The two passages in the New Testament that appear to restrict the ministry of women are 1 Corinthians 14:34 and 1 Timothy 2:12. If a reader came across 1 Timothy 2:12 with no knowledge of the instances of women prophesying in the Old and New Testaments or of the description of Priscilla teaching Apollos or of the foundational verse Galatians 3:28 that "in Christ there is neither male or female," he or she would probably conclude that the Bible takes a dim view of the ability of women to teach. Given that knowledge of other Scriptures, however, the reader is more likely to conclude that there is something about the circumstances of 1 Timothy 2:12 that, if known, would help in the understanding of Paul's perspective. Since Priscilla did indeed teach doctrine and since the women who prophesied at Corinth (and presumably elsewhere) were providing instruction and were edifying the church as they did this, it is reasonable to ask whether the teaching in 1 Timothy was of a different sort.

It is generally agreed (in practice, if not expressly affirmed) that this passage does not prohibit women from teaching other women or children or "natives." But if the following verses about the deception of Eve mean, as many take it, that the teaching of women may not be reliable, one would think that it would be precisely the other women and children and "natives" (who presumably would have no way of determining the correctness of what they have been taught) who should not be subjected to the teaching of unreliable women. Or to put it another way, if women are easily deceived why should we let them teach at all or even be witnesses?

There are strong reasons for suspecting that either the teaching referred to in 1 Timothy 2:12 was some specialized kind of instruction or that there was some particular reason why the women in the congregation served by Timothy were not suitable as teachers. Neither of these proposals minimizes the force of Paul's reference back to Genesis 3 and the deception of Eve. Paul does not explain why he makes that allusion. Many assume that he intends to prove by it that women are *incapable* of teaching. It could be equally taken to show why women are *suspect* as teachers.

1 Timothy 2:12, and 1 Corinthians 14:34 as well, must not be isolated from the rest of Scripture. We have already seen that they must be understood against the background of the Old Testament, the Gospels and Acts. In addition they must be viewed honestly in comparison with other specific Scriptures that seem, at least, to lead to a different conclusion.

One of these passages is Galatians 3:28, which states that in the Lord there is "neither male nor female." This is a crucial passage that tends either to be cited as governing the interpretation of all other relevant texts or, on the other hand, to be minimized as to its implications. It is important to understand this verse in its context lest we go to a wrong extreme. In Galatians, Paul is dealing with such matters as the law, justification and the liberty of the Spirit. The immediate context is a contrast between law and promise. Verses 23-25 describe the chronological sequence in which law is followed by faith, by which we are justified. "Now that faith has come, we are no longer under law" (v. 25). Instead (v. 26), "You are all sons of God through faith in Jesus Christ." This is a new relationship to God, which is accompanied, as verse 28 will state, by a new relationship to one another.

The idea of newness, seen thus far in terms of chronological succession and then in terms of relationship, is also indicated by the terminology of baptism and then of being "clothed with Christ." We know from Ephesians 4:20-24 and Colossians 3:9-11 that this is the language of conversion and new life. In the latter passage Paul continues, "Here there is no Greek or Jew, circumcised or uncircumcised, barbarian, Scythian, slave or free" (Col 3:11). The implication of this is seen in the immediately following exhortations relating to mutual forbearance and love (vv. 12-14). Obviously in the Colossians passage, when one has put on the new clothing of Christ, the obliteration of differences in Christ affects not only *position* but *practice*.[7] It is no less so in the Galatians context. That is to say, there are implications for social relationships, not only for spiritual standing.

The fact that in the Greek Paul moves from "neither Jew *nor* Greek . . . neither slave *nor* free" to "neither male *and* female" may indicate that he has equality in the original creation as well as in the new creation in Christ in mind. Genesis 1:27 says, "So God created man in his own image, in the image of God he created him, male *and* female he created *them*" (emphasis mine).

It is argued by some that this verse is basic to all others, and that no matter what functional differentiation other verses may seem to teach, the social equality of Galatians 3:28 renders any distinction between men and women in the church inadmissible. Others, in contrast, take their stand on verses about women's silence or exclusion from teaching, and restrict the meaning of Galatians 3:28 to soteriology. I cannot accept either approach as satisfactory.

The latter approach distorts the context and blunts the force of the verse, while the former approach ignores that Paul did specify different customs for men and women in the church (for reasons we shall discuss below). It should also be observed that the equality of the sexes in Christ does not abrogate the differences in marital relationships (see Eph 5:22-33; Col 3:18-19).

Further, although we belong to the new age and to the heavenlies, we still live in God's present created order and function in earthly families. Therefore, in the church, Paul did require women to wear veils (or long hair bound up) to avoid hindering the people of his day from accepting the gospel of Christ. He also restricted their public participation. It is therefore impossible to say that there is no difference between Christian men and women in the church, but neither can we say that Paul is not addressing social relationships when he says there is "neither male nor female."

Galatians 3:28 must be seen as a contrast to the inferior status usually given women in Paul's day. It is a dramatic affirmation that must not be ignored or watered down in order to maintain a restrictive position. Galatians 3:28 does apply to social relationships within the church and not merely to the spiritual realm of soteriology. At the same time, it does not mean that all distinctions are obliterated. Neither a positive statement, like Galatians 3:28, nor a restrictive one, like 1 Timothy 2:12, should be considered apart from the totality of biblical revelation on the subject.

Another passage that needs to be studied in connection with 1 Timothy 2:12 is Acts 18:24-26. Here is a case where a *narrative*, concerning Priscilla and Aquila teaching Apollos, seems to be in conflict with a *command*, that women are not to teach. Are we to say that the principle that women can teach is established in Acts and that our interpretation of the Timothy passage must be molded by this, or do we take the latter passage as normative and seek to explain Priscilla's activity in a way consistent with our interpretation of that?

We may make several observations regarding the incident of Priscilla and Aquila. One is that the wording of the text indicates that both he and she taught Apollos. Priscilla did not teach him alone, but neither was she excluded from that ministry. A second observation is that her name occurs first. Interestingly, at one stage of the manuscript tradition someone changed the order of the names to the more common one of the male first. In that same manuscript tradition the copyist minimized the reference in Acts 17:12 to prominent Greek women by a deft realigning of the words.[8] It is clear that it offended the prejudices of some in that patriarchal society that the woman's name appeared first. A third observation is that the man she instructed was an educated, intelligent and able teacher in his own right (Acts 18:24-26). Priscilla was not teaching a child or some ignorant native from the frontier of the Roman Empire.

Priscilla's instruction was apparently given privately. What are we to conclude from this? Are we to assume that private teaching (but not public) was all right for a woman in the New Testament period? If so, does this mean that the crucial question is whether the teaching is done publicly or privately? This hardly seems compatible with the emphasis in Scripture on that which is inner, essential, spiritual, rather than what is external or circumstantial.

Is the crucial question then whether the teaching is done in an "official" capacity or not? The New Testament does not teach the existence of "office" itself in the church, in spite of the fact that there were elders and other leaders. The concept of "office" is a development in the early church that is not explicit until the writings of Cyprian.

Further, we may ask whether the New Testament would attach more significance to the public teaching of what we might call "lay" people in the church than to the private teaching of a man who went on to become an influential teacher of many others. Obviously the text in Acts gives no hint that Priscilla was wrong in the teaching of such a potentially influential person. Can we not by analogy conclude that it is therefore biblically acceptable for a woman to teach potential teachers and leaders in a seminary or other Christian training institution?

Is there a third possibility? Is the issue whether a teacher ministers authoritatively? Does the New Testament teach that some people are authorized in a way others are not to teach the word of God? Is there some kind of commissioning ritual that confers authority or power or legal jurisdiction over others? Where does the Bible itself place the locus of authority in the church? That is a major question to be addressed shortly.

Another possible conclusion with respect to the permissibility of Priscilla's teaching is that the crucial question regarding whether or not it is appropriate for a woman to teach is whether her spiritual life is pleasing to God and whether she has a sufficient grasp of Scripture and of doctrine to teach. One of the explanations of 1 Timothy 2:12 is that the women in Paul's day (and perhaps especially at Ephesus, where Timothy was) were unsuited for teaching. If so, that passage would not be a general prohibition against women teaching, but rather a restriction in a specific and therefore limited situation. In the case of Priscilla, there is clearly no such problem.

It is sometimes claimed that when Paul supports his argument with a reference or allusion to the Old Testament, this means that the application of his teaching is to be made in the same way universally and for all time. This is a subtle shift from the more accurate statement that what such a quotation establishes is a *principle* that needs to be applied appropriately in each comparable situation. For example, in 1 Corinthians 11, where there is a reference back to the order of creation, the *principle* is that a woman should not dishonor her husband, who is her "head," but most Christians would agree that the *application* of this principle today is *not* the wearing of a veil (or long hair bound up) as it was in the first century when loose hair signified a prostitute.

What we may not realize is that not only women's appearance, but even the very act of their speaking publicly had serious implications in first-century society (and not merely at Corinth or Ephesus). Plutarch, who lived in apostolic times, said that it was equally shameful for a woman to speak in public and to have a bare arm.[9] We need to realize that in Paul's day a woman's speaking and teaching in the church could constitute a moral problem and bring shame on the church and on the Lord, thus keeping people from Christ. That is simply not true in most societies today, at least in the Western world.

In fact, the situation is reversed: to prohibit a woman from having the same dignity and opportunity in church as she does in society is a stumbling block to many people. Therefore, by earnestly trying to make the same application (the silence of women) rather than following the same principle (avoiding shame and dishonor to the husband), we can actually commit the very error Paul sought to avoid—that is, offending people's moral sensibilities and hindering them from accepting the gospel.

In summary, the principles of the Old Testament and the teachings of Paul in such matters are indeed universally true for all time, but where this has to do with public perception and the consequent acceptance of the Christian gospels, the particular application may differ. We acknowledge this principle when we substitute a handshake for the holy kiss (commanded *five times* in the New Testament), when we do not insist on raising hands in prayer (which is commanded in 1 Timothy 2, the same passage that prohibits women from teaching), when we permit support to widows who are under sixty years of age (which is forbidden a few chapters later in the same book of 1 Timothy), and when we substitute other acts of humble service for foot-washing (which was a demonstration of the *principle* of Jesus' teaching authority and lordship in John 13:13-14).

It is also worth noting that when Paul refers to a woman's equal standing with men (Gal 3:28) or to the relationship between husbands and wives (Eph 5:22-33; 1 Cor 11:11-12) he refers to Christ and being in Christ. But when he places *restrictions* on women, he refers to the Old Testament (1 Tim 2:12-15 and also 1 Cor 14:34, if, as many think, the word *law* is Old Testament law). It would seem that Christian women should follow pre-Christian norms in order not to offend Jews ("as under the law to win those who are under the law," 1 Cor 9:20), just as they follow conventional ethics not to offend pagans (1 Cor 9:21). But on the grounds of redemption and new creation, which supersede both the curse and the Fall, it is still true that there is "neither male nor female in Christ."

Paul's principle, then, is not the wearing of veils or the silence of women, but rather conforming to Jewish and moralistic pagan norms for the sake of the gospel. As we have seen, in biblical times even for a woman to speak publicly was considered a symbol of impropriety. To substitute the *rule* (a woman's veil or her silence) for the *principle* ("all things to all men, that I might by all means save some"—1 Cor 9:22 KJV) is not only to substitute the letter for the spirit, it may actually reverse the principle.

If a woman speaking in the first century was an offense to the people Paul sought to reach, today it is just the reverse. A society that accepts women as corporation executives and university presidents will find it difficult to listen to a church that silences them. And if the above reasoning sounds like conformity to the world (as is sometimes charged) perhaps the problem is a misunderstanding both of the principle I have argued for here and of the principle argued for by Paul, of being "all things" to win people to Christ.

How Do Paul's Missionary Principles Relate to All This?

The following observations are brief but important. Paul had a basic principle that required the temporary subordination of other principles. To understand this may help us to understand his instructions concerning women. It will be useful to note some differences between Galatians and 1 Corinthians.

In Galatians Paul established the principle that the believer is "dead to" the law. Salvation is not earned by doing the works of the Old Testament law. Along the way, Paul insists on his authority as an apostle. As we have seen, he also established a principle regarding male and female in Christ. But in 1 Corinthians Paul says that he, the apostle of freedom from the law, is willing to become "as under the law" to win those who are under the law. The fact that he takes this remarkable position so as to remove barriers to the gospel, without changing his position on salvation apart from the works of the law, should alert us to the fact that he can also accommodate the social norms of Jews and others regarding the public activities of women, without changing his position on women's equality with men.

If some in Paul's day considered it shameful for women to speak publicly, or to appear without a facial veil, or to have their hair flowing down, what are the implications of the fact that it is shameful in our society today to restrict women from full equality and opportunity? If Paul could accommodate principle without abandoning it, can we say something to those we seek to reach by the equality and opportunities given women in the church, without abandoning whatever convictions we may have (thinking of Eph 5) about the relation of husband to wife in the home? If not, we may be perpetuating form (the silence of women) while actually abandoning Paul's principle of accommodation.

But suppose not all of the above is accepted? Suppose Paul's restriction is against not only the usurpation or assumption of authority but against any exercise of authority. Does that mean that women cannot be ordained? The next topics in this presentation will therefore be the nature of ordination (and the laying on of hands) and the "ultimate" question, Should a woman be ordained? Following that we shall probe the nature of New Testament ministry. Finally, we shall consider some of the relevant biblical texts.

The Question of Ordination

The preceding sections have dealt with biblical background and with various questions pertaining to the relation of gender to ministry. The next sections will deal with the nature of ministry and its implications regarding women. The main insight to be gained is that the New Testament church did not ordain people to positions of *authority,* but designated people to ministries of *service.*

By the time the church at Antioch laid hands on Paul and Barnabas (Acts 13:1-3), they had already been in the Lord's work for some time. This was a commission to a new task, not the conferral of rights, rank or authority. Paul and Barnabas appointed elders (Acts 14:23). The verb originally meant to point out with the hand and later became associated with ordination, but it did not mean to lay hands on someone.

The laying of hands on Timothy (1 Tim 4:14; 2 Tim 1:6) was done in connection with the bestowal of a spiritual gift; it was not the conferral of authority or rank. It is often claimed that this laying on of hands is to be understood along the lines of the laying of hands on rabbis to authorize them to teach. Recent research, however, has proved that there is no evidence for this in the first century.[10] There are a number of references in rabbinic literature to ordination. Not only is the practice later than the New Testament period, but the significance of the rite was different from that in 1 and 2 Timothy. It involved bestowal of judicial authority. Further reference to the laying on of hands in connection with rabbinic ordination is lacking. Hands were laid on the Sanhedrin, but that was not to confer teaching authority.

In the Old Testament hands the laying on of hands was a means of recognition or identification; for example, people singled out for blessing, animals offered in sacrifice, people being designated for particular service, such as Joshua and the Levites.[11] Joshua was commissioned as Moses' successor and the Levites to minister to the Lord. There is no use of the laying on of hands to commission someone to a teaching office.

In summary, there is no uniform use of the laying on of hands in Scripture. In the New Testament, Jesus did not lay hands on the apostles or any other group of disciples, which is strange if this was a standard way of ordaining people. In Acts, the only possibly relevant passages are 6:1-6 (where hands are laid on the seven who were designated, not for a teaching ministry, but to serve the needs of the Greek-speaking widows), 9:17 (where Ananias lays hands on Paul so that he might see again and be filled with the Holy Spirit; see also 8:17; 19:6) and 13:1-3, cited above. Thus there are many instances in Scripture of the laying on of hands, but not in the sense of an ordination to teaching. Scholars are now recognizing that what was formerly thought to have been common rabbinical practice simply was not.

There was thus no standard act in Scripture of ordination that elevated people to a position of superior rank and authority. The laying on of hands signified the conferral of the Holy Spirit and the commissioning of people for service. Only in the case of Joshua was it connected with authority, and there it was to a ministry of leadership under the guidance of Eleazar the priest, not to a ministry of teaching or preaching as we know it.

In many evangelical churches today ordination is simply a way of designating those whom God has called to the ministry. Such "privilege" as ordination may confer is *not* the same as an exclusive right to preside over certain sacramental rites or to exercise governing authority over the church, practices that have no precedent in Scripture. All believers share in a spiritual priesthood, sacramental functions not being assigned to any class (or gender). Scripture uses the word *priest* only of Christians in general, not of an individual to the exclusion of other believers.

If ordination is understood to be the conferral of priesthood or of a superior rank, it must be identified with a rite that developed in the early church, not with any practice in the New Testament. Without debating here the legitimacy of such a tradition, we may say that the role of women in churches of that heritage has to be determined within that understanding. But if we are dealing only with practices already established within the New Testament church, we may well ask whether women should be excluded from a designation or commissioning to spiritual service. Even if one is reluctant to confer superior rank or judicial authority to a woman, this understanding of ordination should present no barrier to a woman.[12]

The Locus of Authority

While it is true that some pastors arrogate to themselves a large measure of authority, such as the right to veto the church's selection of board members, this does not mean that the Bible intended such authority to rest in one person. There is one head of the church, our Lord Jesus Christ. The Holy Spirit exercises divine authority on earth ("The Lord is the Spirit"—2 Cor 3:17).

Evangelicals assert that the Bible is our authority, with some using the phrase "our only rule for faith and practice." In Scripture elders are told to guard the flock (Acts 20:25-31; Tit 1:9). They govern the church as its leaders, but are warned not to dominate (1 Pet 5:3). The concern of, say, Presbyterians over women elders is thus understandable if 1 Timothy 2:12 does indeed refer to a normal exercise of authority (though see below). It should be noted, however, that no Scripture pictures an elder holding personal authority as an individual.

In many evangelical churches the locus of authority is the congregation. In such cases, in any congregation where the women are in a majority, women already are in authority! It may be argued that the preacher in the pulpit has personal authority, but this is not taught in Scripture (apart from apostolic authority). The authority is in the Word itself, not in the individual teaching it. Spiritual gifts (which of course are given to women as well as to men) do not convey authority. This is seen in the fact that the congregation at Corinth was to evaluate what the prophets said (1 Cor 14:29).

What Is the Implication of Ministry as Servanthood?

Biblical ministry is servanthood, not the assumption of authority over others. In Mark 10:35-45 Jesus contrasted the tendency of Gentile rulers to seek lordship and authority with the way he, the Son of man, came not to be served but to serve. The Christian minister is to be like the Lord Jesus. In contrast, contemporary discussion over the ordination of women almost always includes, and may even center on, the issue of authority. The question should not be, "What *authority* does Scripture permit to women?" but "What *ministry* does Scripture permit to women?"

The next question should be, "How do we publicly recognize God's choice of this servant?" Is there any reason why the same mode of recognition for servanthood should not be employed for women as it is for men? Scripture knows nothing of rank among the servants of the Suffering Servant of God, nothing of domination among the undershepherds of the Chief Shepherd. The shepherds are told to be "eager to serve; not lording it over those entrusted to you, but being examples to the flock" (1 Pet 5:2-3). It is striking that when Paul lists the qualifications for elders, his reason for mentioning the importance of ruling one's family well is not so the elder can "rule" the church, but rather so he can "care" *(epimeleomai)* for it (1 Tim 3:4-5).

In conclusion, since ministry is servanthood rather than the personal exercise of authority, not only women, but men as well should not seek elevation to a position of power over others. Conversely, if ordination is understood as a simple recognition or commendation of those who are going out to serve, why should it be denied to women?

What Does Authority Imply?

There is reason to doubt that the kind of authority which Paul did not want women to have was what we think of as normal ecclesiastical authority. It may be that the kind of authority prohibited to women in 1 Timothy 2:12 was not a normal kind of authority.

The simple fact is that the normal Greek verb for exercising authority *(exousiazō)* is not the verb used here. An extremely rare verb, *authenteō*, is used instead, one that does not occur anywhere else in the New Testament. Unfortunately, some writers have taken extreme or poorly argued positions with regard to this verb.[13] In earlier centuries it had indicated violent action ("to murder," "to commit suicide," "to project oneself sexually"). In New Testament times it does not seem to have been generally used this way (contrary to the opinion of some), but neither (as others maintain) did it simply mean to "exercise authority." Rather it had come to be used for domination and the arrogating to oneself of the right to initiate or originate something.

The circumstances of the Pastoral Epistles may explain the use of this strange verb. It is increasingly recognized that the circumstances of 1 Timothy and the other Pastoral Epistles were radically different from those of today. The difficulty lies in knowing just how to assess the relationship of the circumstances of Paul's day to his teaching.

Some feminists propose constructions that are difficult to establish with certainty and almost seem to be efforts to circumvent the text. But there are other evangelical scholars who are convinced of the unity of biblical teaching on the ministry of women and desire honestly to reconcile what appear to be differences between passages on the subject. They therefore are willing to study the circumstances to see if there were particular reasons why Paul, on the basis of the Genesis narrative, forbade women to teach. I do not necessarily draw the same conclusions others do from the observations that follow, but I think their potential relevance to the issue ought to be acknowledged:

1. Women were the particular victims of false teachers who took sexual advantage of them (2 Tim 3:6-7). Some suggest that women may also have propounded false teaching.

2. Women were not educated and were not capable of teaching.

3. Women were considered unreliable as witnesses. (Even though they were the first at the empty tomb, Paul does not cite them as witnesses in 1 Cor 15.)

4. The church was about to be (if it was not already) faced with early gnosticizing tendencies. Among such tendencies were the idea of a female principle in God, and a stress on Eve over Adam (which, it is claimed, required Paul to issue a correction affirming that Adam was created first).[14]

5. It was long understood in the Greek world that women were acceptable as prophetesses, but not as teachers.[15] This would help explain why Paul permitted women to prophesy in 1 Corinthians 11, but forbade them to teach in 1 Timothy 2.

6. Among the Jews, teachers of Scripture were not only highly honored but actually revered. The Lord Jesus alluded to the fact that the judges of earlier times who applied the revealed Word of God in legal cases were even thought of as divine (see Jesus' quotation in Jn 10:34 of Ps 82:6, "You are gods"). Women would not be acceptable as teachers in that environment.

It is a principle of biblical interpretation to seek out the immediate circumstances to which Scripture is addressed. To be sure, sometimes the cultural background is obscure, and sometimes commands that are intended for all time are wrongly restricted by an appeal to culture. Yet if the role of women were even partially a matter of social perception (so that certain activities of women, such as public teaching, or speaking without a headcovering, would bring the gospel into disrepute), this certainly should have a bearing on our own application of the relevant texts.

More than one of the six circumstances I have outlined above may be relevant to our interpretation and application today, even though there is much need for further clarification. In addition, the remainder of the paragraph in 1 Timothy 2:12-15 provides a reference to the fact that Christian women can be "saved." Space does not permit a summary of all the views, but it is worth considering that Paul may be showing that God has provided for the reversal of the effects of the Fall (the "curse"). The undue subordination of women to fallen men was dealt with in the redemption of Christ. Some think "the childbirth" in this passage is a reference to the birth of Christ, the "seed of the woman" predicted in the same Genesis 3 passage that tells of the curse. It may be that Paul is implying that women who continue in faithful devotion (1 Tim 2:15) are thus qualified to minister when conditions permit.[16]

In summary, the kind of authority Paul forbade to women was something more than and different from what we normally conceive of as ecclesiastical authority. The preceding several sections have led to the following conclusions: Hindrances to recognizing women for ministry on the ground that they must not exercise authority over men may be considered removed for the following reasons: (1) Ordination does not biblically mean the conferral of authority over another. (2) In Scripture, ultimate authority under God does not rest with a minister or an elder as an individual. (3) The heart of biblical ministry is service, not the exercise of authority. (4) The reference to authority in 1 Timothy is a special case, difficult to understand, but not presenting a hindrance to the normal ministries of women. While these four points are related, they are not dependent on each other. Any one of them should call into question the restriction of women from recognized ministry.

What Is Teaching?

Contemporary restrictions of women from Bible teaching are based on a concept of teaching that differs from that in 1 Timothy 2:12.

The "teaching" prohibited to women in 1 Timothy was not the explanation of biblical texts, since the Bible was not yet complete or widely disseminated. At that time teaching meant the transmission of the apostolic tradition. The authoritative teachings of the Lord Jesus and of the apostles were transmitted at first in an oral form before these were universally available in written form in the New Testament.

But it must be recognized that the witness to such a tradition would not have been accepted from the mouths of women, who were considered unreliable as witnesses. Whatever the theological or circumstantial reasons Paul had for prohibiting women from teaching, the fact is that this teaching depended on the authority of the teacher in a way it does not today.

Some think the teaching authority Paul denied to women was the kind of authority possessed by the writers of Scripture. The closest parallel today would probably be carrying the gospel in oral form to unreached peoples, a ministry few people would deny to women. On the other hand, the greatest contrast would be the teaching of Scripture to an audience that has the Bible in its hands with biblically literate teachers available to correct any misinterpretation. Yet that is just the setting in which a teaching ministry is often denied to women.

The frequency of the word "teach" (*didaskō*) and its related forms diminished in Christian writings over the early decades of the church, while the use of the term from which we derive our word "catechism" seems to have taken its place.[17] That is, the early ministry of teaching, which was the transmission of the apostolic tradition, gave way to a more formal uniform repetition of Christian doctrine.

The entire New Testament eventually became recognized as canonical Scripture and became available widely throughout Christendom. Any hesitancy one might have had in listening to teaching about the sacred traditions by women would now be gone. Today we have the completed canon of Scripture as our authority. We stand, not under the authority of some teacher, but under the authority of the *written Word of God.*

What Can We Conclude?

The preceding questions and comments should (1) warn us against dogmatic and extreme positions, (2) indicate the importance of taking all of Scripture into consideration, (3) show us that apparently differing Bible passages can be resolved without loss of their distinctive emphases, and (4) caution us against forcing the biblical data into our contemporary ecclesiologies.

The main biblical characteristic of ministry was service rather than authority. Since the completion of the New Testament canon, authority has resided in the biblical message, not in the messenger. Difficulties over women teaching or having authority can be resolved by a better understanding of what teaching and authority meant in the time of the New Testament church and what they mean today.

While the Bible is not to be thought of as culturally rela*tive*, it is culturally rele*vant.* Some passages are intended to show us not just what Paul did, but why he did it and how we can follow his principles in our own day. It is possible both to believe the "letter of the law" and to follow its spirit. Some feminists have been in danger of forsaking the former because of where they have seen it lead some of their contemporary traditionalists. But there are traditionalists who have missed the spirit of the Scripture in their attempt to be faithful to the "letter." Neither extreme is necessary; neither is healthy. The answer is not compromise, but a better understanding of both *woman* and *ministry* in Scripture.[18]

Notes

[1]See the bibliography at the end of this volume for a wide variety of books pertaining to the ordination of women.

[2]Susan T. Foh, *Women and the Word of God* (Phillipsburg, N.J.: Presbyterian and Reformed, 1980), pp. 6-7, 14, 19-20.

³Ibid., p. 46.

⁴Wayne Grudem, "Does [Kephalē] ("Head") Mean 'Source' or 'Authority Over' in Greek Literature? A Survey of 2,336 Examples," published both as an appendix in George W. Knight III, *The Role Relationship of Men and Women* (Chicago: Moody, 1985) and in the *Trinity Journal* n.s. 6 (1985): 38-59. One of the sharpest criticisms of Grudem's article is by Gordon Fee in his 1 Corinthians commentary in the New International Commentary on the New Tetament series (Grand Rapids: Eerdmans, 1987), pp. 502-3, footnotes 42-46. A strong argument for the meaning of "source" has since been presented by Catherine Clark Kroeger in "The Classical Concept of *Head* as 'Source,' " in Gretchen Gaebelein Hull, *Equal to Serve* (Old Tappan, N.J.: Revell, 1987), Appendix III, pp. 267-83. See also Gilbert Belizikian, "A Critique of Wayne Grudem's Treatment of *Kephalē* in Ancient Greek Texts" (ETS 0025; Theological Research Exchange Network, 1987) 20.

⁵The most recent evidence from the papyri on the use of *prostatis* describes a widow who was given guardianship and full control over her son's inheritance.

⁶Aida Besançon Spencer has a good discussion on Junia in *Beyond the Curse: Women Called to Ministry* (Nashville: Thomas Nelson Publishers, 1985), pp. 101-2. Recent extensive research by a student of mine, Matthew Arnold, including both Latin and Greek sources, produced no evidence of a masculine form of the name.

⁷Both Ephesians 4:20-24 and Colossians 3:9-11 speak of "putting on" the new man like new clothing. This seems to be common language to describe the new life in Christ. The use of clothes as a figure of behavioral characteristics goes back to the Old Testament; see Job 29:14; Psalm 35:26; 109:29; 132:9; Isaiah 11:5; 59:17; Romans 13:12, 14; 1 Thessalonians 5:8. See F. F. Bruce, *Epistle to the Colossians*, The New International Commentary on the New Testament (Grand Rapids: Eerdmans, 1984), pp. 145-46, and note 72.

⁸Acts 17:12. The variant is listed in the Nestlé-Aland text (Stuttgart: Deutsche Bibelgesellschaft) but not in the current United Bible Societies text, ed. K. Aland et al. Both texts list another variant in the same manuscript tradition that subtly minimizes women (Acts 17:4) and one in which mention of the woman Damaris, who became a believer through Paul's Areopagus address at Athens, is completely omitted (Acts 17:34), All of this is discussed in Bruce M. Metzger, *A Textual Commentary on the Greek New Testament* (London: United Bible Societies, 1971), pp. 453-54, 459-60.

⁹Plutarch *Moralia*, "Advice to Bride and Groom," trans. Frank Cole Babbitt (Cambridge, Mass.: Harvard University Press, 1928), p. 31.

¹⁰Two such works are: Edward J Kilmartin, "Ministry and Ordination in Early Christianity against a Jewish Background," *Studia Liturgica* 13 (1979), and Lawrence A. Hoffman, "Jewish Ordination on the Eve of Christianity," *Studia Liturgica* 13 (1979).

¹¹See, for example, Genesis 48:14, 17, 18; Leviticus 1:4; Numbers 8:10,12; 27:18, 23; Deuteronomy 34:9.

¹²On the whole question of ordination, see Marjorie Warkentin, *Ordination: A Biblical-Historical View* (Grand Rapids: Eerdmans, 1982).

¹³Among the published literature are Catherine Kroeger, "A Strange Greek Verb," *Reformed Journal* 29 (1979): 12-15, and George W. Knight III, "AUTHENTEO in Reference to Women in 1 Timothy 2:12," *New Testament Studies* 30 (1984): 143-57, who take opposite sides. Kroeger has continued her research and includes a few comments on the verb in "1 Timothy 2:12—A Classicist's View," in Alvera Mickelsen, ed., *Women, Authority and the Bible* (Downers Grove, Ill.: InterVarsity Press, 1986), pp. 225-

43. See my response that follows her essay on pp. 244-47. See also L. E. Wilshire, "The TLG Computer and Further Reference to [Authenteō] in 1 Timothy 2:12," *New Testament Studies* 34 (1988): 120-34.

¹⁴For differing opinions on Gnosticism and women, see Elaine Pagels, *The Gnostic Gospels* (New York: Random House, 1979), pp. 48-69, and Louis A. Brighton, "The Ordination of Women: A Twentieth-Century Gnostic Heresy?" *Concordia Journal* 8 (1982). The Gnostic texts can be found in the *Nag Hammadi Library*, translated by the members of the Coptic Gnostic Library Project of the Institute for Antiquity and Christianity, James M. Robinson, Director (San Francisco: Harper & Row, 1977).

¹⁵James Sigountos and Myron Shank, "Public Roles for Women in the Pauline Church: A Reappraisal of the Evidence," *Journal of the Evangelical Theological Society* 26 (1983): 283-95.

¹⁶One recent study that takes this approach is Aida Besançon Spencer, *Beyond the Curse: Women Called to Ministry* (Nashville: Thomas Nelson Publishers, 1985), pp. 91-95. Extensive exegetical work has been done on this and other issues connected with the 1 Timothy passage. See especially Douglas J. Moo, "1 Timothy 2:11-15: Meaning and Significance,' " *Trinity Journal* n.s. 1 (1980): 62-83; Philip B. Payne, "Libertarian Women in Ephesus: A Response to Douglas J. Moo's Article, '1 Timothy 2:11-15: Meaning and Significance,' " *Trinity Journal* n.s. 2 (1981): 169-97; Douglas J. Moo, "The Interpretation of 1 Timothy 2:11-15: A Rejoinder," *Trinity Journal* n.s. 2 (1981): 198-222: Philip B. Payne, "The Interpretation of 1 Timothy 2:11-15: A Surrejoinder" (Available from the Evangelical Free Church of America); M. D. Roberts, "Women Shall Be Saved: A Closer Look at 1 Timothy 2:15," *TSF Bulletin* 5 (1981): 4-7; Aida Besançon Spencer, "Eve at Ephesus," *Journal of the Evangelical Theological Society* 17 (1974): 215-22; David M. Scholer, "1 Timothy 2:9-15 and the Place of Women in the Church's Ministry," in Mickelsen, *Women, Authority and the Bible*, pp. 193-223, followed by a response by Walter L. Liefeld, pp. 244-47.

¹⁷G. W. H. Lampe, *Patristic Greek Lexicon* (Oxford: Clarendon Press, 1961), pp. 364-65, 732-33.

¹⁸For further general reading, see the bibliography at the end of this volume.

A TRADITIONALIST RESPONSE
Robert D. Culver

Walter Liefeld's essay seems to say there is no such thing as "the ministry." Such issues as ordination, authoritative teachers and teaching, church overseers (rulers) and the like are therefore illegitimate issues. I will try to summarize his arguments in order to address them.

I sincerely regret that I must be mostly negative throughout, even though Liefeld plainly wishes to avoid offense. (1) In my opinion, he begins with essentially erroneous explanations both of the issues involved and the several views taken. No one in this discussion says a "spiritual" ministry is limited by the merely "human distinction of gender," though this may be imputed to some of us. The distinctions I make and the limitations are not human at all. Either they are apostolic in origin or they do not exist. (2) It does not seem quite cricket for him to ascribe my arguments to me before he has read them. I do not object to citing previous writings of mine or general knowledge of my views, but I must reject the procedure of claiming to say what traditionalist or feminist opponents are going to say. It would be far more constructive to pursue his own agenda.

Liefeld's first major heading is "The Importance of Perspective and Perception." It appears there is nothing in his pages on that subject, except allegations of inconsistency in current practice among churches which think Scripture restricts certain offices to adult men. I respond to one supposedly typical remark: "Is there something to learn from the comment by a student from another continent who felt it was a matter of racism and an insult to him that women missionaries could teach him there but not teach men in America?" On the contrary, Is there something to learn from the fact that the restriction of the office of elder and church pastor-teacher to men tends to be more rigid in black Africa than in America? Perhaps the student might reflect further on the stance of the female missionary who instructed him? Was she an obedient Christian witness or was she the appointed (ordained) "teacher of the church" in his locality? She almost certainly was not the latter.

Also, which part of 1 Timothy 2 *forbids* "braided hair with gold and other jewelry"? I do not know any important work of exegesis which agrees. Does Liefeld mean to tell us that Paul does not mean what he says about anything in that troublesome passage? I don't think he does. If Liefeld is only reporting the hazy ad hoc protests of others, would it not be well to say who these people are or possibly to furnish some answers or even to ignore them?

I will address some of what Liefeld asserts are "the right questions." It seems to me that there is only one basic question for most of us: Does the Word of God restrict something understood as "*the* ministry" to men? Liefeld, following a point of view held by early Quakers and later by the Plymouth Brethren, thinks there really is no such *office* as the pastorate, as most understand it. So he asserts, if I may simplify his argument, there is no such thing as *the* ministry. If he is correct, my essay as well as the other two in this book are unnecessary and irrelevant.

Liefeld argues that Susan Foh is unfair when she asserts that "biblical feminists have abandoned the biblical and historic position of the God-breathed inerrant Scriptures." But he himself could furnish the names of several who abuse biblical inspiration, I think. Not long ago some feminist writings by P. K. Jewett, in which he sought to correct Paul's views on this subject, were viewed with alarm and given serious rebuttal as abandoning a high view of Scripture and of apostolic authority. The matter ran on for a good while in several journals, including the *Journal of the Evangelical Theological Society*. So let us not be too severe on Susan Foh.

Further, it is Liefeld's "perception" that Paul discusses the issues of this debate "in 1 Corinthians 11 and 14 in terms of social perceptions," as well as the issues of "slaves and women in Titus 2:5, 10." Perhaps true in part, but I feel he should notice that Paul finds several aspects of the doctrine of creation in support of the correctness of Paul's own "social perception" in these cases. Paul nowhere says specifically that in the matters under discussion in these essays the tradition or order he insists upon is rooted only in current social perception or that they are only matters of prudence in evangelistic effort. It seems to me that in the main, though elements of custom and social perception are present, they are not the decisive matters of Paul's concern. They certainly are no primary basis for tradition and order. Yet the rules for women's hair and head covering at worship in 1 Corinthians 11 are said by Paul to be apostolic *tradition* and *order*. Liefeld denies this specifically. (See my essay and comments on 1 Cor 11:2 and 34.)

Under "What Can We Learn from Biblical History?" Liefeld calls attention to matters which none of the participants will find much to disagree with. But I think he omits some other important lessons from history, and I do not agree with some of his inferences. I restrict my response to the following.

The cases of the many women who ministered to and with Jesus (Mt 27:55; Lk 8:1-3) seem to prove only that Jesus depended upon their ministrations *to him and his party* and had nothing directly at all to do with Jesus' ministries of healing, preaching and teaching. There are no examples of women in *the* ministry—the ministry of Jesus and the apostles. They really did less than either Foh or I of this dialog would gladly allow. The same goes for Paul's female helpers.

In my judgment, this preliminary skirmishing, occupying more than a third of the essay, does not really lay the ground for what he wishes to establish in the main sections: "How Do We Handle Apparent Differences in Scripture?" and "The Locus of Authority." It appears that Liefeld thinks the trend of our times toward full female leadership in every department of life is also the wave of the future for Christian churches. He tries manfully (if I may use such a naughty word) to disclaim association with either feminism or traditionalism in preference to what he calls a balanced view. Nevertheless, the essay comes out in somewhat diffuse, but definite, endorsement of what Mickelsen hopes will come to pass. But he does so with a difference. He has two main claims to make: First, the New Testament church had no offices, only gifts and functions, which apparently operated without any authoritative oversight. There is nothing like *subordination*—of one person or function to another and no *superordination*— in other words, no hierarchy (to use an accepted if misleading word). Second, the many injunctions of Paul to Timothy and Titus to exercise "rule" or "authority," and for members to "submit" and "obey" do not apply to anyone today.

Rather, he says, (1) the concerns of Paul's day were to pass on the apostolic tradition *verbally*, in absence of a finished and collected New Testament, and (2) the need was therefore not exposition of biblical texts as in preaching today but "reliable" (authentic, certified) witnesses to what Jesus or Paul or another apostle had said. (3) This gave way later to "formal uniform repetition of Christian doctrine." The reason, then, why women were forbidden by Paul to speak formally in church (for Liefeld has them speaking quite a lot, to be sure) was the practical fact that the age did not regard women as reliable witnesses. Theology or divine revelation seem to have had nothing to do with Paul's restrictions.

In response to this argument I observe that no attention at all is given to several texts which I think effectively dispose of the theories shared by Liefeld and typical Plymouth Brethren, Quakers and many amorphous independent groups of today. These Christians hold that there was no ecclesiastical structure of authority (hierarchy) in the New Testament church at all. (Early Quaker "meetings" have been described as simple folk gatherings, and only gradually have the Brethren developed "principles of gathering" and any formal leadership.) I think Walter Liefeld's assertions of the absence of evidence for a structure of authority in New Testament churches flies directly in the face of all the truly relevant evidence. Consider:

1. "Paul and Timothy, servants of Christ Jesus, to all the saints in Christ Jesus who are at Philippi, with the bishops ["overseers" is a better translation] and deacons" (Phil 1:1 RSV). Does that sound like a church without any sort of structure or ecclesiastical authority? Lie-

feld does not treat this text. Neither does he refer to "overseers." I think it is plain why he prefers "elders."

2. "Let the elders who rule [Gr. *proïstēmi*] well be considered worthy of double honor, especially those who labor in preaching and teaching" (1 Tim 5:17 RSV). This verse is precious to all advocates of Presbyterian polity. The first meaning of *proïstēmi* is "be at the head of, rule, direct." So we can understand why among the qualifications for "bishop" or "overseer" the candidate for this office must "manage his own household well" ("ruleth well" 1 Tim 3:4 KJV). The same word is used again. Does this sound like a church in which there were overseers and elders [rulers] who neither took oversight with ecclesiastical authority nor exercised any sort of rule?

3. "But we beseech you, brethren, to respect those who labor among you and are over you in the Lord and admonish you" (1 Thess 5:12 RSV). Here, as in the above-cited passages, the word for what the elders or bishops do is *proïstēmi*, translated "are over you." Again does this sound like a place where there was no superordination, no offices or officers, no people whose office required respect and obedience— "for their works' sake"?

4. "Obey your leaders and submit to them; for they are keeping watch over your souls, as men who will have to give account" (Heb 13:17 RSV). Necessarily, the readers knew who their leaders were. Christian antiquity tells us that the acknowledgment of definite, known, universally recognized local leaders (bishops, elders) was a primary concern of the Christians of that day. "Obey" in the text is a passive form of *peithō*, which in passive voice means "to be persuaded," "obey," "take someone's advice" (Bauer, Arndt & Gingrich, *A Greek-English Lexicon of the New Testament*). Also, Liddell and Scott in *A Greek-English Lexicon* has "middle and passive . . . to obey." The *Theological Dictionary of the New Testament* is in agreement, except that it is more clear that "obey" is the *extended* meaning, not primary.

In the construction here authorities say the word means "obey, follow." "Submit to them" employs *hypakouō* for "submit." I see nothing ambiguous about this word. It is employed of the relations of servants to masters in the New Testament. And this striking use appears in 1 Peter 3:6, "As Sarah *obeyed* Abraham, calling him lord." Again, does Hebrews 13:17 fit a church such as Liefeld describes? It is noteworthy that the essay gives critical treatment to none of these texts. Several of them are not mentioned.

A few sentences from a book review by Walter Liefeld clarifies and enlarges somewhat what is left unsaid in his present essay. The quotation will tell us why he mentions few of the texts I have used in rebuttal. In his review of a book which argues against *officers* and *ordination,* he says: "There is no specific call to the ministry, such as was experienced by the OT prophets. We are all called at conversion and spiritually gifted. NT ministry is that of service, not of domination of others. Elders are set in the church (Acts 20:28), not 'over' it [yet see the passages which I have cited above]. The Greek terminology in Heb. 13:17; 1 Thess. 5:12 is not strong enough to support the language of rulership found in those passages."[1]

It seems to me that it is precisely the Greek terminology which makes certain that the New Testament describes an apostolic tradition (*paradosis*—1 Cor 11:2), or "order" (1 Cor 11:34), of an organized, structured, local church with functioning officers called elders (presbyters) and bishops (overseers). Obedience of some sort, sometimes called "submit yourselves," is due these leaders. For these reasons the apostolic tradition, excludes women from the highest office in the churches. Paul, who states the tradition, articulates the reasons. Some are based on natural feeling, some on the created order of things; some are related to the Fall of mankind, and some are for the sake of good "order." All were designed to promote good feeling within the community of Christians. It seems to me that insofar as feeling, as such, is contrary to the tradition and order, the feeling, not the traditions and order, should yield.

Note

[1]Walter L. Liefeld, "Review of *Ordination: A Biblical Historical View* by Marjorie Warkentin (Grand Rapids: Eerdmans, 1982)," in *Journal of the Evangelical Theological Society* 27, no. 3 (1984):366.

A MALE LEADERSHIP RESPONSE
Susan T. Foh

First of all, I appreciate very much Liefeld's reasonable tone and his fairness to the varied views of women and ministry. I also appreciate his willingness to face the difficulties in harmonizing the biblical materials concerning women. The right questions could perhaps lead to the right answers, but sometimes an excess of questions can create more confusion than clarity. Liefeld's questions are thought-provoking, but I felt somewhat confused after reading through them.

Liefeld's approach is to distinguish between a principle being taught in the prohibitive texts and the means by which that principle should be expressed (determined by culture, such as head coverings or silence). The principle he extracts is to conform to "Jewish and moralistic pagan norms for the sake of the gospel." This concept is taught in 1 Corinthians 9:19-23, as Liefeld notes, though being all things to all persons has never included disobedience to God's commands. But the question remains: Is this idea present in 1 Corinthians 11:2-16; 14:33-35; and 1 Timothy 2:9-15?

It is tempting to answer yes in the case of 1 Corinthians 11:2-16, mainly because the idea of requiring a covering for women in worship and forbidding one for men seems trivial to us. For me, there are several reasons for still answering no. (1) Paul begins this section with a commendation to the Corinthians for keeping the traditions he has delivered to them (v. 2). It seems that what follows would be among those traditions deserving praise. (2) Paul makes a play on words with "head." He could have used another word in verse 3 to express the relationship of man and Christ. "Head" is chosen because it is significant in its figurative and its literal senses. (3) Verse 16 indicates the universality of the custom. (4) When Paul considers eating food that has been offered in sacrifice (1 Cor 10:23-30), he makes it clear that eating is acceptable and that not eating is also acceptable for the sake of others' consciences. In contrast, there is no either/or attitude in 1 Corinthians 11:2-16.

In the cases of 1 Corinthians 14:33-35 and 1 Timothy 2:9-13, I see no separation of a form from a principle. There is a prohibition and then a reason for that prohibition. Paul did not relate his commands to women to his day's cultural requirements. Paul's appeal to the Old Testament law in 1 Corinthians 14:34 is not an escape clause. Rather, it provides unquestionable and, for Paul, unquestioned force to his argument. In 1 Timothy 2:13-14, Paul bases his prohibitions on two past, unchangeable events—creation and Fall. If Paul meant for his commands to be temporary, why did he support them in these ways? If Paul was unaware of their temporary status, why did God allow them to become part of the canon?

I am not sure how Liefeld distinguishes between the commands to wives and the commands to women in the church. Why does he consider the former still valid and the latter invalid for today?

Liefeld's concept of letter versus Spirit (2 Cor 3:6) is a misunderstanding. It is true that there are some commandments that are more important than others (justice, mercy and faith are more important than tithing mint, dill and cummin, Mt 23:23). Yet that is not the contrast of 2 Corinthians 3:6. The thing written, the letter, is the law of God (all of it, including the broad principles and the lesser commandments) that pronounces the sentence of death upon those who cannot keep it in every aspect. It is contrasted with the Spirit of God that gives life. The contrast is between a religion of merit that results in death and a religion of grace that results in life.

Concerning the locus of authority, a more detailed discussion would be helpful. Authority is an unavoidable point in the discussion of women and the kind of ministry permitted (or denied) to them. It is also unavoidable because there is authority involved in what the elders or pastors do (1 Thess 5:12; 1 Tim 5:17; Heb 13:17). They are responsible for the souls of their congregation. In Mark 10:35-45, Jesus tells his disciples to serve, but the context is how to lead. Service, caring and acting as an example are how Christian leaders are to rule and guide; these attitudes do not undercut their responsibility for those under them. The facts that ordination does not confer anything, that the authority of elders is derivative, and that their leadership is to be exercised in loving service do not change the reality that they do have authority.

Liefeld suggests that 2 Timothy 2:15 may be a reversal of the Fall—a distinct possibility. Yet, there is a jump in thought to say that Paul implies faithful women are then qualified to minister (if by that, Liefeld means teach and exercise authority) when conditions permit.

It seems unlikely that those who, like Liefeld, see an unexpressed principle of cultural concession (whether intentional or not) in these passages and those who, like me, see them as part of God's unchanging Word will ever agree. I am sure that to each side, one's own interpretation seems self-evident (somewhat like, "If you don't see it, then I can't explain it") and true to the will of God. From my point of view, the choice is between taking a position that seems right to me ("Why should women be discriminated against on the basis of sex? Is not God too big for such a thing?") and taking a position that accepts God's Word for what it says (of course, considering the literary and cultural contexts and the whole of Scripture).

It still seems farfetched to me to suggest that 1 Corinthians 14:33-35 and 1 Timothy 2:9-15 actually command (in principle) the opposite of what they say. There are difficulties in interpreting the passages directed to women, but it seems clear to me, as I have argued, and unavoidable that there are certain restrictions on what women can do in the church. The question is what the restrictions are, not if they exist.

It was not a mistake for the Pharisees to obey the Old Testament law in detail; their mistake, in part, was to focus on detailed obedience without love for God and others (and to put their trust in that obedience). If we make restricting women the major focus in our faith, we will miss the point of our faith, to love God and others (Mt 22:37-40; Rom. 13:10). But put in perspective, submission to the commands to women is one part of our obedience to the Lord.

AN EGALITARIAN RESPONSE
Alvera Mickelsen

Walter Liefeld is to be commended for his keen examination of the inconsistencies in the arguments put forth by those who say the Bible limits the role of women in ministry. He also gives excellent examples of the inconsistencies in the practices of those who hold this view.

His discussion about the meaning of ordination is particularly helpful. Different denominations have differing views about the meaning of ordination—and rarely are those views based on biblical teachings. Instead they are usually based on the traditions that have been handed down in particular groups. This does not mean that their practices of ordination are wrong, but it does indicate that we can hardly talk about a "biblical base" for male-only ordination—or for any ordination.

The "laying on of hands" (usually the only biblical concept put forth in support of ordination) was used in biblical times in many circumstances—for healing (Acts 9:12), to receive the Holy Spirit (Acts 8:17), to commission for special service (Acts 13:3), in connection with receiving a spiritual gift (1 Tim 4:14), and in a few other similar circumstances. Liefeld points out that there is no example in the New Testament of "laying on hands" to commission someone as a teacher or pastor. Nor did Jesus ever "lay hands" on any of the apostles.

Furthermore, however we may see ordination and its significance, there is no scriptural base for assuming that ordination gives exclusive rights to preside over the Lord's Supper or baptism—although that is the usual practice in most churches, including those that do not hold to apostolic succession. Nor is there a biblical base for the idea that ordination gives a person governing authority over the church. Actually, the New Testament clearly teaches that *all believers* constitute a *kingdom* (with allegiance to a common king—Jesus Christ) and *all believers* (males and females alike) are *priests* (Rev 5:9, 10; 1 Pet 2:4-9), with the responsibility of interceding with God on behalf of others, of representing God to others and of bringing sacrifices of praise to God. If there is any authority involved in these activities, it is an authority shared by every believer. Ordination does not confer authority—it only recognizes God's call to ministry, a ministry of servanthood. Ordination does not confer rights or rank. Actually, the whole idea of rank is alien to the New Testament.

Liefeld's discussion of authority as resting in the revealed Word of God is a refreshing change from the usual emphases in some churches. We rarely hear emphasis on the explicit, and oft-repeated teaching of Jesus on *servanthood* as the mark of ministry and leadership rather than authority. No man or woman can desire power over others and still be faithful to the teachings of Christ, for Jesus clearly condemns the gentile (pagan) chain of command (Mt 20:25-28). Yet much of the discussion regarding women in ministry rides on the concept of authoritative teaching and positions of authority as belonging to men only. They don't belong to anyone! The concept of rank among the servants of Christ is utterly foreign to everything the Suffering Savior did and taught.

Liefeld also points out (as do other writers in this book) that the traditional limitations on women are often espoused by churches that follow a congregational form of church government—where the ultimate earthly authority rests in the congregation rather than in pastors or elected officials. And in most churches, women form the majority of members. Thus the pastor and elders in these churches *are now* under the authority of women.

The teaching structures of New Testament times and the importance of oral teaching were clearly different from our situation, now that we have a completed canon that we recognize as the written Word of God. In that written Word of God lies the *spiritual* authority in the church of Jesus Christ—not in a person or that person's *interpretation* of Scripture. Truly spiritual pastors or leaders recognize that their only teaching authority is that inherent in the Word of God.

Liefeld makes passing comment to an appendix (to a book by George Knight III) contributed by Wayne Grudem, which asserts that he examined more than 2,000 instances of *kephalē* ("head") in classical Greek literature and found many instances of its meaning "authority over" but only a couple where it could mean "source."[1] It is not necessary to examine 2,000 instances to find several Greek references where the meaning is clearly "source" rather than "authority over."

Actually, the word *kephalē* ("head") basically means "extremity." All other meanings are derived from that basic concept. Richard Broxton Onians, professor of Latin at the University of London, has written a volume entitled *The Origins of European Thought.*[2] He gives many illustrations to show that approximately from the time of Homer to the classical Greek period (the time of Plato and others) the head was regarded as the *life* or the *seat of life,* and because of that was to be highly honored. "It was natural and logical to think that the 'life' issuing from a man must come from the 'life' in him, from his *head* therefore, and, helping that location, to see in the seed, which carries the new life and which must have seemed the very stuff of life, a portion of the cerebrospinal substance in which was the life of the parent."[3] This explains why, when the god Zeus wished to have a child and dispense with a mother, he "gave birth" to it (Athene) "from his head."[4] The author of the Homeric Hymn to Pythian Apollo says that he "engendered it . . . in his head." Later, it was generally believed by the Greeks that the seed (sperm) was stored in the head.[5]

This, of course, explains the Orphic line that appears in numerous places in Greek literature. In some instances *kephalē* appears and in other writings *archē* ("beginning") appears in the same place in the line describing Zeus. *Archē* ("beginning") could hardly be considered a synonym for "ruler," but it surely could for *kephalē* ("source"). Grudem attempts to draw a great difference between the meaning of "source" and "beginning," but such a distinction is in most instances largely artificial. The headwaters of a river can be considered either the "source" or the "beginning."

In the Orphic references to Zeus, the contexts sometimes also use the term *aitios*, which means "cause"—an idea closely related to "source." Some of the references to Zeus where he is called *kephalē* ("head") include the following (Fragment 21a [46]):

Concerning the world: And as the Totality spoke being heavenly and that which sprang from the earth, giving the Totality's name [Zeus] to all nature and providence in reference to which things he [Zeus] is *cause* of all things. Wherefore also in the Orphic sayings it does not say wrongfully:

Zeus became first; Zeus is last, ruling the thunder;
Zeus, Source *[kephalē]; Zeus, Middle, and from* Zeus all things are
    brought to completion. Zeus, base both of earth and heaven
    arranged in constellation. [emphasis mine]

Another Orphic fragment, 168 (123,43), reads:

Zeus became first; Zeus, the last, ruling the thunder; Zeus, Source
    [kephalē]; Zeus, Middle, and from Zeus all things have been
    produced . . .
Zeus, King; He is the first *author, origin* of all things.
                                                        [emphasis mine]

In a third version of this Orphic saying, 21 (33), the term *archē* ("beginning") appears in place of *kephalē* ("head"):

He says that God is plainly the creator in reference to the
Old Orphic saying which is this:

Zeus, beginning *[archē]; Zeus, Middle; and from Zeus* all things
have been made. Zeus [made the] base *[puthmen]*, both of the
earth and of the heaven arranged in constellations.

And this one [Zeus] is beginning *[archē]* as creative cause *[poietikon aition]*; And he [Zeus] is end *[teleute]* as final causality *[telikon]*; And he is middle as equally present to all things; and indeed since all things share him [Zeus] in a variety of ways.

Note that in the saying above, Zeus is considered the "creative cause" and the "final causality."

Another Orphic line about Zeus[6] comes to the question from another side. One writer addresses Zeus thus: "*All-generating* father, oh king, because of your head *[kephalē]*, the following things appeared:

Rhea Gaia [a goddess], and sea [personified son of goddess], and all things as many as heaven works within." Can anyone seriously question the meaning of "source" or "cause" for head *(kephalē)* in this quotation?

Onians explains further that Alcmaeon of Croton wrote explicitly that the seed came from the brain. A later sect, called the Templars, actually worshiped heads because the head was considered the source of wealth.[7] This concept became imbedded in European thought and is no doubt the reason we still speak of a "head" of corn (the source of seed). In Greek thought the head was also considered to be the source of strength and this lingered on in Roman thought.

The Greek writer Artemidorus yields numerous examples of head *(kephalē)* meaning "source." In Lib. I, Cap. 2, Paragraph 6, we read, "He [the father] was the cause *[aitios]* of the life and of the light for the dreamer [the son] just as the head *[kephalē]* is the cause *[aitios]* of the life and the light of all the body." In another section (Cap. 35, Paragraph 36) Artemidorus writes, "Indeed, the head is to be likened to parents because the head is the cause [or source] of life."

In many instances, the preconceived idea of the translator will determine the meaning assigned, but these are clear instances of the meaning of "source," "cause" or "beginning," as the meaning of *head.* All of these meanings—"beginning," "origin," "head," "author's creative cause," "final cause"—point to the wide range of meanings of which *kephalē* ("head") was a part.

The possible meanings of *kephalē* are important because this word in 1 Corinthians 11:3 and in Ephesians 5:23 has been consistently used as proof that since man is the "head" of the woman, he is in a God-ordained position of *authority* and leadership over her. If *kephalē* has other more probable meanings, these passages take on a quite different emphasis. In the Genesis narrative, man is the source or base of the woman, as mentioned in 1 Corinthians 11:8, 12. In Ephesians 5:23, the husband has Christ as a model. As Christ enables the church and brings it to completion (effective cause or agent) by giving his life for the church, so the husband is to be an enabler (or effective cause or agent) for his wife. By his self-giving love he helps her reach her full potential of all that God means her to be.

Paul and other early Christians clearly knew that the characteristic of Christian ministry and leadership was *service* rather than authority. They had heard clearly the words of Jesus, "You know how the rulers of the Gentiles lord it over them. . . . It shall not be so among you; but whoever would be great among you must be your servant (Mt 20:25-27 RSV).

In practice, servanthood has never been denied to women in the church! Women through the centuries have prayed for others, healed the sick, helped the poor, taught young and old to follow Christ, carried the gospel around the world—all the marks of servant leadership. Perhaps when we all stand before the judgment seat of Christ, we will learn that in the eyes of our Lord, women through the centuries have been the real leaders of the church.

Notes

[1]Wayne Grudem, "Does *[Kephalē]* Mean 'Source' or 'Authority Over' in Greek Literature?" Appendix to George W. Knight III, *The Role Relationship of Men and Women* (Chicago: Moody Press, 1985).

[2]Richard Broxton Onians, *The Origins of European Thought* (Cambridge: At the University Press, 1951).

[3]Ibid., p. 109; Onians refers this quotation to Aristotle on page 111, n.6.

[4]Ibid., p. 111, quoting Hesiod *Theog.* 924.

[5]Ibid., p. 111, quoting Aesch. Eum. 658-66.

[6]Ibid., p. 112; Fr. 2la, 2:21, I; cf. 168. 2 Kern.

[7]Ibid, p. 144.

4/AN EGALITARIAN VIEW:
THERE IS NEITHER MALE NOR FEMALE IN CHRIST

AN EGALITARIAN VIEW:
There Is Neither Male nor Female in Christ
Alvera Mickelsen

Does the Bible, properly interpreted, restrict women from serving God in ways that men are not restricted? Should some positions in the church have a "men only" sign on them? Are the spiritual gifts of God to women essentially different from the gifts that God gives men?

These are all forms of one basic question: Are restricted roles for men and women in church, family and society God-ordained, or are they the result of sin and/or cultural influences? Some writers in this book believe they are God-ordained; I believe they are the result of sin and/or cultural influences.

Most people who want to restrict the ways in which women can serve God build their cases on a few select verses of the Bible which they believe cancel out other teachings of Scripture. Those who believe there are no restrictions that apply exclusively to women point to other passages which they believe cancel out the apparent restrictions. Thus the basic issue centers on principles of interpreting the Bible. I say "appears" deliberately, for after years of studying, writing and speaking on this subject, I have come to believe that the issue has as much to do with the emotions and experiences of people as it has to do with interpretation of certain passages of Scripture.

For this reason, this chapter will consider the history and experiences of women in the church as well as principles of Bible interpretation and the oft-quoted "restrictive" passages.

God Has Called and Blessed Women as Leaders in His Work

Throughout the history of the church, God has called women to positions of leadership and blessed their work in the building of his church. Use of their gifts was often limited by the same mode of thinking that today keeps many women from full use of their spiritual gifts. But when and where women have been permitted to use more of their full potential, their influence has been profound. Many of their stories are little known, partly because most histories have been written by men who, because of their theological or cultural conditioning, tended to assume that women had no important leadership roles in the church.

One interesting example is found in 2 John, which begins, "the elder to the elect lady and her children, whom I love in the truth." Some commentators insist that this was addressed to a *church* rather than to a woman. Yet the simplest and most obvious reading is that the woman was leader of a "house church" and that the "children" mentioned in the letter refer to the Christians who met in her house. The apostle John often referred to believers as "children" (1 Jn 2:1; 3:18; 5:2, 21; 3 Jn 4). The phrase "the children of thy elect sister greet thee" (v. 13 KJV) could refer to another house church led by a woman. The elect lady is warned to keep her "house" (congregation) free from heresy and false teachers.

The example of Priscilla is well known. Priscilla and Aquila established a ministry in Ephesus and taught the brilliant Apollos more accurate Christian doctrine. John of Chrysostom (who was no champion of women) called Priscilla a "teacher of teachers." Priscilla is usually named first when the couple is mentioned in Scripture, implying that she was the more active of the two.

The history of Thecla is little known, despite the fact that she is mentioned by many of the church fathers, including Epiphanius, Ambrose and Augustine. In early noncanonical Christian literature, she is called an apostle. References seem to indicate she was a contemporary of Paul and traveled with him in proclaiming the gospel throughout Asia Minor, where such ministry of women was more acceptable culturally than it was in Palestine. Thecla, like Paul, was imprisoned for her faith. Some Greeks later wrote of her as "the first martyr and equal of the apostles." Basil declared that she not only won many to Christ, but that she also baptized them.

Catherine of Alexandria was considered the patron saint of philosophers. A gifted and brilliant woman, she vigorously defended her Christian faith in the learned society of Alexandria, and many of the pagan philosophers were won to Christ through her ministry. She was so successful that the emperor Maxentius, who was persecuting the Christian church, ordered her executed.

Another early woman leader was Marcella, who lived from 324 to 410 in Rome. She established in her home a center for Christian teaching, prayer, Bible study and community. She and some of the women whom she taught became so skilled in knowledge of Hebrew that they studied the Old Testament in the original language. Saint Jerome, the first translator of the Greek New Testament into Latin, once suggested that she settle a dispute about the interpretation of a certain Bible passage. Bishops and prelates came to her with problems of interpretation. Originally a very wealthy woman, she was killed by barbarians during the sack of Rome because she had given all her wealth to the poor and could not buy her freedom.

Catherine of Siena, who lived from 1347 to 1380, felt called at an early age to a life of evangelism and ministry. She won thousands to Christ, nursed countless sick and dying during the Black Plague, and was a great instrument for revival in the medieval church. She admonished the Pope and his cardinals to remember the church's mission of salvation, and she combatted ecclesiastical corruption.

In the nineteenth century in the United States, Phoebe Palmer was one of the most powerful evangelists, winning more than 25,000 people to Christ. One person strongly influenced by her was Catherine Booth, who later became cofounder of the Salvation Army. After hearing Mrs. Palmer preach, Catherine confessed that she, too, had heard the call of God to preach.

Frances Willard, most well known as founder of the Women's Christian Temperance Union and a leader in the campaign for gaining women the right to vote, began as an evangelist with Dwight L. Moody. She was among the first to object to common sexism in the language of preachers. She wrote, "Preachers almost never refer to the women of their audiences, but tell about 'men' and what 'a man' is to be." The story of women in world missions is fairly well known. Talented women have gone to many areas of the world and started churches, preached the gospel, taught, founded training schools for national Christians, and taught both men and women in those training schools. Women missionaries have supervised building projects, erected hospitals and directed them. Hundreds of thousands of men and women have been won to Christ through their ministries—even though most pagan cultures, like Western cultures, assign women second-class status. Yet the Spirit of God has used women in positions of tremendous leadership in the church in spite of their often being hindered by male religious leaders.

The same is true today. Naomi Dowdy was an evangelist when she arrived in Singapore in October 1975. She intended to make Singapore a base for her evangelistic efforts in Asia. But in February 1976 a small struggling Chinese church with a membership of 49 (mostly teenagers and college students) asked her to be their pastor. The church was torn with dissension and despair, and the previous pastor had left two months earlier. After much prayer, she agreed. Four years later (1980) the average attendance was 910. By early 1985 it had grown to about 2,000, with a multiple staff who had been trained and organized by Naomi Dowdy. She also is rallying the congregation to erect a building to house a theological center. The school is already in operation in rented buildings, with a student enrollment of 110.

Luz M. Dones de Reyes is a Puerto Rican woman who in 1971 was called to pastor a rural Baptist congregation of 12 people in Puerto Rico. It was assumed that she would simply preside over the burial of the little church. Ten years later she was still the pastor, but she had a congregation of 900—the largest rural church in the region. In 1981 four Puerto Rican Baptist churches were pastored by women. The quality of their work has made the concept of women in pastoral ministry well accepted among Puerto Rican Baptists.

The stories of Naomi Dowdy and Luz M. Dones de Reyes are uncommon only because women like them are so often hindered from fully using their God-given gifts in God's work.

While theologians debate whether God can and does call women to positions of leadership (with men as well as women), the Spirit of God is working through women whom he has gifted and called to leadership positions around the world.

Experience alone is not a test of what is biblical. But when experience through the centuries runs counter to our *interpretation* of the Bible, perhaps it is wise to reconsider whether our restrictive interpretations actually express the mind of God.

Principles of Bible Interpretation

Our principles of interpreting the Bible greatly influence the conclusions to which we come. The first question for the interpreter is: *What was the Bible saying through God's human servant to the first hearers or readers of that message?* What did they think was the meaning? This often demands some understanding of the history and culture of the time as well as the specific situation of the original readers. And it certainly demands careful examination of the *literary* context of a statement. The adage is true: A text without its context is only a pretext. The total flow of thought and the subject being addressed must be examined if we are to rightly understand what a particular verse, phrase or word means.

Another question follows naturally: *How should we understand and apply the passage* (if it should be applied) *to people today?* To answer this question we must take the second step.

We Must Identify Highest Norms and Standards

The second step for the interpreter is to identify the *highest norms or standards* taught in the Bible. These highest principles must take first place in our considerations and have top priority in all we do. In addition to highest norms or standards, the Bible also has many *regulations for people "where they were"* that were not necessarily meant to apply to all peoples under all circumstances. This distinction is not a way of getting rid of teachings we may not like. Rather, it gives a means of sorting through the many commands in the Bible that obviously are not intended to be universal for all times.

The Old Testament has scores of commands that most of us regularly ignore. Leviticus 19:19 states that there "shall not come upon you a garment of cloth made of two kinds of stuff." Nowhere in the Old or New Testaments is that law repealed, but most of us wear blends of polyester and cotton, or wool and silk. Apparently we do not believe this regulation to be universal and timeless. The New Testament, too, has commands given to all churches that most Christians ignore. Acts 15 tells of the controversy that arose in the early church when Jewish Christians insisted that gentile believers must keep Old Testament regulations. Paul and Barnabas, who had been preaching to the Gentiles, thought otherwise.

After long discussion, the disciples sent this message to the gentile churches: "It seemed good to the Holy Spirit and to us not to burden you with anything beyond the following requirements: You are to abstain from food sacrificed to idols, from blood, from the meat of strangled animals and from sexual immorality" (Acts 15:28-29 NIV). This message was sent to all the early churches (made up mostly of Gentiles). The New Testament never withdraws this regulation.

Most Christians today are also Gentiles. Yet these regulations are not a part of our statements of conduct or faith in our churches. Most of us do not feel guilty if we eat a rare steak. Why not? Because these commands (with the exception of the one regarding sexual immorality, which is reinforced elsewhere in the New Testament) had particular application for the time and place they were given. They were "regulations for people where they were."

In 1 Timothy 5 Paul gives instructions to the church for "enrolling widows" for special service. The same churches that use 1 Timothy 2:12 to restrict women, usually ignore the commands about widows in 1 Timothy 5.

What are the highest ideals or standards, and how can we recognize them? The process may be easier than we think.

1. Highest standards were emphasized by Jesus Christ (and sometimes by Paul) and were often plainly stated as the highest standard. For example, Jesus stated flatly that the Golden Rule was the highest standard: "So in everything, do to others what you would have them do to you, *for this sums up the Law and the Prophets*" (Mt 7:12 NIV—emphasis mine).

This same general statement appears in the discussion about the greatest commandment: " 'Love the Lord your God with all your heart and with all your soul and with all your mind.' This is the first and greatest commandment. And the second is like it: 'Love your neighbor as yourself.' *All the Law and the Prophets hang on these two command-ments"* (Mt 22:37-40 NIV—emphasis mine).

Paul says something similar in Romans 13:9-10: "The command-ments, 'Do not commit adultery,' 'Do not murder,' 'Do not steal,' 'Do not covet,' and whatever other commandment there may be, are summed up in this one rule: 'Love your neighbor as yourself.' Love does no harm to its neighbor. *Therefore love is the fulfillment of the law"* (emphasis mine).

Old Testament and New Testament commands that, if applied to-day, would be contrary to these basic "highest standards" so clearly taught by Jesus and by Paul, must be carefully examined to see wheth-er they are "regulations for people where they were" because of some local or temporary situation. For example, if men would not like to be restricted from being elders or ministers or teachers of mixed groups simply because they are males, then they had best examine whether their interpretation of passages by which they similarly re-strict women puts them in conflict with the command of Christ to treat others the way we want to be treated.

2. A second indication of highest standards is found in statements about the purpose of Christ's ministry and the purpose of the gospel. Jesus said he was proclaiming a *new order.* "Neither is new wine put into old wineskins; if it is, the skins burst, and the wine is spilled, and the skins are destroyed; but new wine is put into fresh wineskins, and so both are preserved" (Mt 9:17 RSV).

The gospel of Christ is "new wine" that must not be put into the old wineskins of Judaism, or of paganism, or materialism, or secular-ism, or any other questionable culture patterns. The Holy Spirit came to empower the young church to transcend barriers that divided rich and poor, slave and free, young and old, men and women.

3. Peter clearly enunciated a highest ideal at Pentecost when he quoted the prophet Joel: "And in the last days it shall be, God de-clares, that I will pour out my Spirit upon all flesh, and your sons and your daughters shall prophesy, and your young men shall see visions, and your old men shall dream dreams; yea, and on my menservants

and my maidservants in those days I will pour out my Spirit; and they shall prophesy" (Acts 2:17-18 RSV).

This message ran contrary to every custom of the Jews:

a. The Holy Spirit would come upon *all* flesh—not just Jews. Many kinds of people would prophesy—that is, be instruments of God to deliver his message.

b. Both men and women would prophesy, although women then played no part in synagogue worship.

c. Both young men and old men would see visions and dream dreams, although age always had priority in Judaism.

d. Even class structures would be ignored by the Holy Spirit—menservants and maidservants would prophesy.

Pentecost was exceedingly important. Joel foretold it in the Old Testament. The preaching of John the Baptist about the coming of the Holy Spirit is mentioned in each of the four Gospels: Matthew 3:11; Mark 1:8; Luke 3:16; John 1:33. The promise of the Holy Spirit was central in the teachings of Christ, both before and after his death, burial and resurrection (Lk 24:46-49; Jn 7:37-39; 20:19-23; Acts 1:4-8; 11:16).

Paul in Galatians 3:26-29 essentially restated Joel's prophecy about the coming of the Holy Spirit's power without regard to race, gender or economic status: "For ye are all the children of God by faith in Christ Jesus. For as many of you as have been baptized into Christ have put on Christ. There is neither Jew nor Greek, there is neither bond nor free, there is neither male nor female: for ye are all one in Christ Jesus. And if ye be Christ's, then are ye Abraham's seed, and heirs according to the promise" (KJV).

Although Peter preached that first message at Pentecost, his own lifestyle was not transformed. In fact, it took a special vision of God to convince him to go to the house of Cornelius (a Gentile) to preach. Peter had a hard time accepting in practice the highest norm that he preached at Pentecost—that God is no respecter of persons. Most of us have the same problem as Peter!

Relating highest norms and standards to the question of women in the church, society and family, we must ask whether our ideas come from our Lord and his often difficult teachings, or whether they are carryovers from pharisaical Judaism or from our cultural patterns or from the sinful desire for power over others.

Rarely do those who espouse hierarchy and male headship in the church and marriage discuss the teachings of Jesus regarding authority that are repeated in each of the four Gospels. "You know that the rulers of the Gentiles lord it over them, and their great men exercise authority over them. *It shall not be so among you;* but whoever would be great among you must be your servant, and whoever would be first among you must be your slave" (Mt 20:25-27 RSV—emphasis mine).[1]

Why do we ignore such teachings? Because they run counter to a power-culture that has been absorbed in many churches. The one kind of leadership that Jesus taught was the leadership of servanthood and self-giving—not a leadership of power and authority over others.

Several hermeneutical fallacies tempt all of us:

1. *Selective literalism* (selecting passages we like and ignoring those that seem to teach the opposite) has been used to make the Bible support causes far removed from the highest ideals taught by our Lord. These include the divine right of kings, slavery and many other unworthy causes—even by theologians as renowned as Charles Hodge, who wrote a book "proving" that slavery was the divine will.[2]

2. *Reading into the text meanings* that are not inherent in the text. This has been done extensively in the Genesis account as it relates to women. For example, because Eve was created after Adam in Genesis 2, some interpreters "read into the text" a subordination that is not present.

3. *Propositional exegesis* (asserting a proposition and then searching for support by selective literalism and "reading into the text") has used the Bible to prove almost anything the interpreter has chosen.

Only sound methods of Bible interpretation—including an understanding of the difference between highest norms and standards and regulations for people where they were, and careful attention to literary, historical and cultural contexts—will permit us to gain an overall sense of the teachings of the Bible and their applications to our own lives.

What Does the Creation Account Tell Us?

Interpretation of Genesis 1—3 forms a classic illustration of how faulty principles of interpretation may be used to support what we want the Scriptures to say.

These chapters give two rather separate accounts of creation. Those who espouse a male-dominated hierarchy largely ignore chapter 1 and emphasize the English translation of certain words in Genesis 2 and 3. Genesis 1:26-28 (RSV) states: "Let us make man [Hebrew: *'adam*] in our own image, after our likeness; and let them have dominion over the fish of the sea, and over the birds of the air, and over the cattle, and over all the earth, and over every creeping thing that creeps upon the earth. So God created man [*'adam*] in his own image, in the image of God he created him; *male and female* he created them. And God blessed them [male and female], and God said to them, 'Be fruitful and multiply, and fill the earth and subdue it; and have dominion over the fish of the sea and over the birds of the air and over every living thing that moves upon the earth' " (emphasis mine).

The Hebrew word *'adam* is sometimes used in the sense of *humankind,* as in these verses; sometimes as the name for an individual, as in Genesis 2; sometimes for Adam and Eve together, as in Genesis 5:3.

Genesis 1:26-28 clarifies several points:

1. Male and female are both equally made in the image of God— they bear the same divine imprint.

2. God gave to man and woman together identical responsibilities:

a. Be fruitful and multiply. (Neither can do this alone!)

b. Fill the earth and subdue it. (*Subdue* surely implies responsibility and leadership.)

c. Have dominion over every living thing. (*Dominion,* like *subdue,* implies authority.)

To see the shared and joint responsibility of men and women for the world in this passage is not dependent on "reading that meaning into the text." It could hardly be spelled out more explicitly. Both the man and the woman were created on the sixth "day" in Genesis 1—when God made animals and humans.

Genesis 2 gives another account of the creation of man and woman. Here the first man and the animals were made "of dust from the ground" (Gen 2:7, 19). God placed the man in the garden and told him to "till it and keep it." God told him to name the animals who came before him. As the man did this, his incompleteness became apparent. ("It is not good that the man should be alone.") He needed another person like himself to share the world and its responsibilities. So God said, "I will make him a helper fit for him" (Gen 2:18 RSV).

Instead of God's making the woman from the dust of the ground, as he had made the male and the animals, God caused a deep sleep to fall on the man and took some of the man's own body and from it "built" [Hebrew: *banah*] the woman. When the man awoke, he immediately recognized the significance of God's act. He said: "This at last is bone of my bones and flesh of my flesh; she shall be called Woman [Hebrew *'isshah*], because she was taken out of Man [Hebrew *'ish*]" (Gen 2:23 RSV).

Adam recognized that Eve was "made of the same stuff" as he and therefore could be the equal that God knew he needed to share responsibilities in the world. Some writers try to make the statement "I will make him a helper fit for him" imply that Eve was secondary to Adam—an assistant in a kind of divinely ordered hierarchy.

Examination of the Hebrew words here—*'ezer kenegdo* in Genesis 2:18, 20—shows the fallacy of this idea. The word *'ezer* (translated "helper") is *never* used of a subordinate in the Bible. It appears twenty-one times in the Old Testament. Seventeen times it refers to God as our "helper." God is hardly secondary or subordinate to us. The other three times (in addition to the Genesis reference) refer to a military ally. When God is spoken of as our "helper," we are really speaking of him as our strength or power. The Hebrew word *kenegdo* means "equal and corresponding to."[3] R. David Freedman, a biblical scholar at the University of California and a specialist in Semitic languages, examined all the uses of these two words in the Old Testament and concludes that the proper translation for Genesis 2:18 would be "I will make a power (or strength) equal to him."[4]

Genesis 2:24 reads, "Therefore a *man* leaves his father and his mother and cleaves to his wife" (RSV—emphasis mine). If that passage had read "Therefore a *woman* leaves her mother and father and cleaves unto her husband," some exegetes would surely have considered it absolute proof that a woman was to be under the authority of her parents until marriage, when she would be passed to the authority of her husband. Since it says the opposite, those who believe in male supremacy conveniently ignore it.

But it would be as wrong to read female supremacy into Genesis

2:24 as it is wrong to read male supremacy into Genesis 2:18—and for some of the same reasons. Neither interpretation squares with Jesus' own teaching about the nature of real leadership, nor with Jesus' other teachings about the way we are to treat each other.

Male dominance appears in Genesis 3:16 as part of the result of sin. Sin damaged all the good relationships that were present in Eden: (1) the relationship between God and people, (2) the relationship between people and nature, (3) the relationship between Adam and Eve. In all of these relationships, sin damaged the harmony.

Fellowship with God was damaged; Adam and Eve now were ashamed in God's presence and eventually were driven from the Garden. Harmony with nature was damaged. From now on weeds and thistles would grow. Tilling the ground would be hard toil. Toil would accompany childbirth. All people would die—men and women—although this punishment was addressed only to Adam. The oneness and equality between Adam and Eve was damaged. Instead of the previous harmony, the male would dominate the female, even though she still desired the old intimacy and harmony. Her desire (longing) would be for her husband, but he would rule over her (Gen 3:16). This ruling is the curse of sin.

Desire for power was the very essence of the first sin in the Garden of Eden. Eve and Adam (he participated freely and fully in the first sin, and God held them equally responsible) wanted to be like God— to know good and evil, since that seemed to represent power (Gen 3:5). History indicates that this sinful desire for dominance, power and control over others is the root of almost all moral evil—war, human bondage, murder, theft, cruelty of all sorts. Yet Christ came to free us from such bondage to sin and to create a new humanity who could be loving and compassionate rather than hungry for power. In this new humanity, servanthood would be the mark of true Christian leadership.

Many foreign ideas have been "read into" the account of Genesis 2. Some interpreters say, for example, that because Adam was created first, he was created to have some kind of supremacy, headship or authority over Eve. This "order of creation" argument has been used for hundreds of years. The Jewish preference for the firstborn is also often used to support this idea.

Yet the text never implies this—either in the Genesis account or in the rest of the Old Testament. In fact, *God's* acts in the Bible seem to point in the *opposite* direction. God rarely chose the elder child in the family for leadership. God chose Jacob (the younger twin) rather than Esau as the ancestor of the Hebrew people. When *God* chose a person to lead the Israelites out of slavery in Egypt, he chose Moses, the younger, rather than Aaron, the older brother. When Samuel was sent to anoint one of the sons of Jesse to be the new king of Israel, he assumed it would be the oldest son—in keeping with Jewish custom. God did not permit him to do so, but insisted on the youngest son instead—David. The list goes on and on.

In the New Testament, Jesus said that the one who would be great in his *kingdom* had to become as the *younger*—the less powerful. In light of God's own acts and Jesus' teaching, how can we read God-ordained authority into the fact that Adam was created earlier in the day than Eve?

Other strange things have been "read into" the Genesis account. Some have said that Adam's naming of Eve indicated his higher standing. Actually, Adam did not "name" Eve until after sin entered the world, and then he identified her as the "life source" of the human race—"the mother of all living." (Eve means "living".) In Genesis 2:23 Adam simply recognized the difference between male and female and made a play on words—*'ishshah* and *'ish.*

In the Bible it was usually the women who did the naming. Genesis does not say who named Cain and Abel, but Genesis 4:25 clearly states that Eve named Seth. All twelve sons who headed the tribes of Israel (except Benjamin) were named by Rachel and Leah. Rachel died at Benjamin's birth, and Jacob renamed him. In the New Testament, Mary was first told to name the baby Jesus. Instructions to Joseph came many weeks later.

Did this naming by the mothers mean that they had more leadership over their children than the fathers did or that they had some lifelong authority over them? Of course not. Yet some writers read this idea into Adam's recognition that the human race now had two halves—male and female (Gen 2:23).

The list of "read ins" to the Genesis account is almost unending. Some writers say that Eve's sin was not her disobedience to God's command not to eat the forbidden fruit—although that is what the Bible clearly states in Genesis 3:11. Instead they claim that her real sin was a "role reversal" in not looking to Adam for leadership when Satan tempted her. The Bible suggests nothing of the sort. How could it, since Genesis never indicates that Adam was "her leader" or that she was "his follower"?

Susan Foh states that when the Bible says, "Your [Eve's] desire shall be for your husband, and he shall rule over you," it really meant that Eve's desire was to dominate or control her husband.[5] The text never suggests this. The term *desire* comes in the context of childbearing. Childbirth does not usually result from a wife's desire to dominate her husband! The common-sense reading points to her longing for her pre-Fall intimate harmony with her husband.

Foh supports her reasoning by appealing to the use of the same word in Genesis 4:7 which speaks about Cain: "Sin is couching at the door; its desire is for you, but you must master it." Obviously, in this passage, sin is personified. The desire refers to the destructive drawing power of sin, while in Genesis 3:16, Eve's desire refers to the drawing power of love between the husband and wife to produce a godly posterity that will defeat Satan.

The Hebrew term used here for desire *(teshuqah)* appears only three times in the Old Testament—in these two passages in Genesis and in Song of Solomon 7:10. In Song 7:10 it appears in the passionate love poem where the woman celebrates her beloved's longing or desire for her. She says, "I am my beloved's, and his *desire* is for me." Is his desire to dominate or control her? Hardly.

Theologians in days past have "read into" the Genesis account many faulty ideas—that woman is less human than man; that all sin is due to woman and she must suffer without medical relief in childbirth as her punishment; that woman is the eternal temptress who keeps men from purity. Those ideas, like many that are put forth today, all come from reading preconceived ideas into the text, from faulty translations of words like *'ezer* ("helper"), and from propositional exegesis—starting with a preconceived proposition and then interpreting the Bible in light of the proposition.

The Genesis account shows that male and female are both created in the image of God. They were given identical responsibilities and "dominion" for the creation. They both sinned and bore God's punishment. They would wait together for the redemption that God promised through "the seed [posterity] of the woman."

Jesus' Purpose and Ministry to Men and Women

Much has already been written about how Jesus' treatment of women went contrary to Jewish custom—custom based on concepts of male superiority and authority over women. In Jewish life, women were considered the property of their husbands, along with household goods and slaves. While men could divorce their wives with relative ease, women could never divorce their husbands. How could something that is owned divorce its owner? Jesus did not go along with the customs regarding women. Jesus included women among the inner circle of his disciples and taught them the deepest truths of the gospel (Lk 24: 6-9)—even though most Jewish women were not then permitted to study the Old Testament. Jesus was not even embarrassed to accept the monetary support of women (Lk 8:1-3).

The first evangelist listed in the Gospels is a woman—the woman at the well. Jesus engaged her in profound conversation even though it was not customary for a rabbi to talk with any woman in public—not even his wife (Jn 4:7-42). Jesus commended Mary for taking her place at his feet as one of his disciples, even though it meant neglecting her "womanly" duties (Lk 10:38-42). In episodes of healing, Jesus treated women and men exactly alike—using the same teachings about the need for faith and repentance. He used both men and women as examples of spiritual truths in his parables. We look in vain for anything in the life or teachings of our Lord that point to "differences in function" for men and women in kingdom work.

Women were the first witnesses of Jesus' resurrection. Both the angel of God and Jesus himself instructed these women to take to the disciples the most important message that has ever come to human beings—the resurrection of Christ. In keeping with the Jewish attitude toward women, the disciples did not believe the women and considered their report "an idle tale." After his resurrection, Jesus deliberately chose to reveal himself first to a woman—Mary Magdalene—even though both Peter and John had come to the empty tomb to look.

Some who insist that men are to be leaders and women followers try to enlist Jesus by saying that Jesus only appointed men among the Twelve. This observation is meaningless so far as leadership approval for women is concerned. Jesus appointed only *Jewish* disciples—no Gentiles. Does that indicate that no Gentiles should be leaders in the church today?

Christ came to give us a whole new set of values—values so different from his world *and our world* as to be almost incomprehensible. For example, Jesus clearly condemns the desire of any believer to control or have power over others. The disciples had a very hard time with this teaching—even as we do. They all wanted to be "first" in the kingdom they thought Jesus would bring to this world. They wanted power over others. Jesus teaches that the only kind of power that counts in his kingdom is the power of servanthood. Every man and woman is asked to see themselves not on the "top rung" but on the "bottom rung"; to treat others the way they want to be treated themselves; to love God with the whole heart, mind and soul, and their neighbors as themselves.

These principles are contrary to the way we have been socialized to seek power and prestige. Men have been socialized to see themselves as the "heads" of their houses—the ones who always have the last word if they choose to do so. Wives have been culturized to find ways to manipulate husbands and to thus get power. Both are part of the sin syndrome that began in the Garden of Eden with disobedience to God. But Christ came to redeem us wholly from the power of sin. He came to bring us abundant life of rich fellowship with him and harmony and oneness with each other. He came to bring a New Covenant in his blood.

Much of what Jesus taught about relationships is contrary to our sinful culture. Tragically, Christians have often not recognized the difference between the culture of our world and the teachings of our Lord. Racism, sexism, elitism, oppression of the poor have often been upheld by the church which is his body because we have not permitted Christ to redeem our thought patterns, our emotional outlooks, our culture itself.

What Happened in the Early Church?

After the resurrection and ascension of Christ, the most important event in the life of the church was Pentecost—the coming of the Holy Spirit to empower believers to carry the good news of the gospel. At Pentecost, the "new way" of Jesus was experienced—power for service from the Holy Spirit—without regard to race, age, economic status or gender. Men and women would both prophesy—be instruments of God to carry his message.

This new power would take the good news of the gospel around the world. Careful reading of the Scriptures indicates that women were very active in the early church. In fact, every "house church" identified in the book of Acts meets in the home of a woman. The list includes Lydia, Chloe, the mother of Mark, Nympha, and Priscilla and Aquila (she is mentioned first).

The importance of women as leaders is seen in Acts 9:2. Saul determined to imprison those who were influencing others for the gospel. He asked for letters "so that if he found any belonging to the Way, *men or women,* he might bring them bound to Jerusalem" (emphasis mine).

A number of women leaders are specifically mentioned in the New Testament. In fact, in no instance is a man mentioned by name for a church office that does not also include women named for that same office. A careful study of this has been made by Peter Richardson of the University of Toronto.[6]

Romans 16 Pictures Women as Leaders

For example, Phoebe is mentioned by name as a deacon *(diakonos)* of the church at Cenchrea (Rom 16:1). She is the only one in the list of 27 people in Romans 16 of whom this term is used. The term *diakonos* is used of six specific men in other parts of the New Testament: Apollos (1 Cor 3:5); Tychichus (Eph 6:21; Col 4:7); Epaphras (Col 1:7); Timothy (1 Thess 3:2); Onesimus (Philem 13). Unfortunately, none of the English translations are true to the Greek in regard to Phoebe; they translate *diakonos* as "servant" or "deaconess" in regard to Phoebe, but "deacon" or "minister" when *diakonos* refers to a man. Some translators have tried to justify "deaconess" on the basis of its being the feminine form of "deacon." That may be grammatically correct, but not practically. In many churches today, deacons and deaconesses do *not* have the same responsibilities. Deacons are

often considered the spiritual leaders and decision makers, while deaconesses provide food for the sick.

Romans 16:2 also calls Phoebe *prostatis*. Phoebe is also the only one
in Romans 16 of whom *prostatis* is used. *Prostatis* is the feminine form
of the noun that means "leader, one who presides, stands before, a
patron."[7] This noun comes from the verbal root *proïstēmi* which means
"to rule and to care for" as we see in four passages in 1 Timothy: 3:4;
3:5; 3:12; 5:17. The use of the word in these passages is well discussed
by Bo Reicke in *TDNT*.[8] Reicke points out that in all these passages
the verb has the primary senses of *both* "to lead" and "to care for,"
rather than one or the other as Bauer's lexicon suggests. The concept
of the Christian leader as one who *both* leads and cares for is in full
keeping with Jesus' concept of leadership in the gospels. This description of Phoebe implies that she was a "ruling elder" as well as a
deacon.

Romans 16:2 is the only place where *prostatis* is used in the New
Testament. It is not common in secular Greek literature in the feminine. Since the masculine form so clearly indicates a leader, there
seems to be some sexist prejudice on the part of the translators who
choose to tone down this strong word to "helper" or "succorer." Further evidence of prejudiced translations is easily available.[9] Other
women mentioned in Romans 16 include Prisca (or Priscilla); she and
her husband, Aquila, are described as "fellow workers" to whom all
the churches owe a debt of gratitude because they risked death to save
Paul's life. The church in Rome met in their home.

Mary, Tryphaena and Tryphosa, and Persis are also described as
women who worked hard for the Lord. Junia (a woman's name) and
Andronicus are described as apostles. Unfortunately most translations
have made Junia into a male by adding the letter *s* to the name—
although there is no record in Greek or Latin literature of men being
called by that name. Almost all commentators on this text before the
thirteenth century regarded Junia as a female.[10] The change has been
justified on the grounds that since Paul calls this person an apostle, it
could not have been a woman![11] Andronicus and Junia may have
been a husband and wife or brother and sister. They are described
as fellow prisoners who became Christians before Paul. The RSV says
"they are men of note," but the Greek text does not say "men"—only

that *they* are notable. Such additions give the wrong impression to the reader of the English text.

The woman Persis, together with the men Ampliatus and Stachys, is described as "beloved." Apelles, a man, is called "genuine," and Rufus, a male, is described as "chosen." Richardson comments, "In six cases, the same or nearly the same terms are applied to both men and women (fellow-worker, apostle, first-fruit, fellow-countryman, fellow-prisoner, beloved); there are two cases of descriptive terms applied to men that are not applied to women (genuine, chosen); and there are five terms—including three of the more significant descriptions—that are applied only to women (deacon, protectress, hardworker, sister, mother). What this list shows is that in a single setting (Rom 16), and in a coherent list of greetings, women are honored more than men despite their fewer numbers, and are attributed more influential roles!"[12]

Romans 16 is not the only place that describes women in leadership roles. Philippians 4:2 and 3 describe Euodia and Syntyche as women who are fellow workers who "fought at my side in spreading the gospel" (literal translation). In 1 Corinthians 16:16, Paul urges Christians to "be subject to . . . every fellow worker and laborer." This is the terminology that Paul uses of Euodia, Syntyche, Priscilla, Phoebe and also of many men in positions of leadership in the early church. Paul himself, apparently, believed Christians were to submit themselves to both men and women who were their leaders.

Paul Shows No Differences in Spiritual Gifts

In Paul's lengthy discussions about spiritual gifts, he never indicates that some gifts are for men and other gifts for women. Instead, Paul teaches that the Holy Spirit gives gifts to every Christian without regard for racial background, economic status or gender, and strictly as the Holy Spirit chooses (1 Cor 12:11). All the gifts are given for "the common good"—to build up the body of Christ. All gifts are essential for the body to function and to grow as it should. In the passages about gifts that appear in four Pauline letters (1 Cor 12:4-31; 14:1-40; Romans 12:3-13; Ephesians 4:11-14; 5:15-20; Col 3:12-17), Paul never distinguishes between "male gifts" and "female gifts," nor does he suggest differences in the way the gifts should be exercised. He personally did not practice such differences.

Why, then, have some churches forbidden women to use their gifts except in limited ways and "under the authority of men"? Newer church histories indicate that women did use their spiritual gifts, including leadership gifts, with relative freedom during the early period of the Christian church.[13] The strictures against women grew in the second century and became more prominent in the third and fourth centuries. The radical change came with the reign of Constantine and his making Christianity the official religion of the Roman empire. That meant it had to fit into Roman culture patterns and Rome's pagan *patria potestas* concept. *Patria potestas* meant that fathers had absolute authority over everyone in their households—wives, children, slaves. Current "chain of command" teachings follow the same basic philosophy—philosophy far removed from the teachings of our Lord and of Paul's teaching of mutual submission among Christians (Eph 5:21).

How are such concepts justified by Christians? It comes by choosing a few verses from Paul's writings, often without full regard for literary or historical context, and setting them up as "highest ideals" in place of those highest standards of servant leadership and self-giving taught by Jesus.

In reality, most of the restrictions on women are based on the misuse or misinterpretation of two words in the writings of Paul—*head* and *authority*.

What Does Head Mean in Paul's Writings?
Didn't Paul designate the man as the head of the woman in 1 Corinthians 11:3 and in Ephesians 5:23? Yes, but we must ask what *head* means in these passages. In the English language, *head* usually means the one with authority over others, and it is natural for us to read that meaning into these contexts. Is that what Paul meant?

To answer that question, we must examine what the Greek word for head *(kephalē)* meant during the first century when Paul wrote these passages that used this Greek word.

The most comprehensive lexicon of the Greek language of that period now available in English is one compiled by Liddell, Scott, Jones and McKenzie that covers classical and Koine Greek from 1000

B.C. to about A.D. 600—a period of nearly 1600 years, including the Septuagint (Greek translation of the Old Testament) and the Greek of New Testament times. The lexicon lists nearly twenty-five possible figurative meanings of *kephalē* ("head") that were used in ancient Greek literature. Among them are "top," "brim," "apex," "origin," "source," "mouth," "starting point," "crown," "completion," "consummation," "sum," "total." The list does *not* include our common English usage of "authority over," "leader," "director," " superior rank" or anything similar as meanings.[14] There is an older Greek-Latin thesaurus published in 1851, but written primarily in the sixteenth century.[15] It also gives no meanings such as "authority over," or "supreme over."

Philip Barton Payne has also done extensive study of this issue. As part of his research, he consulted three secular specialists in ancient Greek literature.[16] They all verified that the idea of "authority" was not a recognized meaning of *kephalē* in classical Greek. Nor does *kephalē* appear as a synonym for leader, chief or authority. S. C. Woodhouse[17] lists many Greek equivalents for "chief" and for "authority" and for "leader," but *kephalē* is not listed as an equivalent for any of them. Apparently *kephalē* is considered to mean "authority over" primarily by those who are trying to find God-ordained male dominance in the Bible.

One small Greek lexicon used by many pastors and compiled by Walter Bauer does give as one meaning of *kephalē* "superior rank." As evidence for that meaning, Bauer lists five passages in the New Testament where he thinks "head" *(kephalē)* has that meaning. He also gives two references to the early Greek translation of the Old Testament (Septuagint) where *kephalē* has this meaning—Judges 11:11 and 2 Samuel 22:44.[18]

Those who, like Bauer, insist that *kephalē* indicates "superior rank" say that since *kephalē* is used with that meaning in the Septuagint, that meaning must have been familiar to Greek-speaking people in New Testament times. Careful examination of the Septuagint shows the error of that conclusion.

The Hebrew word *ro'sh* (meaning "head") was often used in the Old Testament the way we use *head* in English—to mean leader or authority over. *Ro'sh* appears about 600 times in the Hebrew Old

Testament. Nearly 400 of those times it refers to the physical head of a person or an animal. But 180 times the Hebrew *ro'sh* clearly refers to a chief something—a chief man, chief city, chief nation, chief priest—that is, the leader or authority figure in a group. Apparently this meaning for *ro'sh* ("head") was as common in ancient Hebrew as it is in English today.

But it was *not* a common meaning in the Greek language of New Testament times. This is confirmed when we examine the Greek words used by the translators of the Septuagint when the Hebrew *ro'sh* meant leader or chief.

In the 180 instances when *ro'sh* meant leader or chief, the Septuagint translators rarely used *kephalē*—although that surely would have been the simplest choice to make if the meaning of "head" in Greek were the same as in Hebrew. Instead, in 109 of the 180 times, they translated *ro'sh* with *archōn,* meaning "ruler," "commander" or "leader." Although *archōn* ("leader") was the most common choice, the Septuagint translators occasionally used one of 13 other Greek words, including *archēgos* 10 times (meaning "captain," "leader," "chief," "prince") or *archē* 9 times ("authority," "magistrate," "officer"), and other words fewer times. *Kephalē* appears 18 of the 180 times, but 4 of them are in head-tail metaphors where nothing else would make sense, and 6 of the other uses have variant readings, leaving only 8 of the 180.

Kephalē would have been the natural word to use in all 180 instances if the word had been commonly understood in Greek to mean leader or chief. Its rare usage indicates that translators knew that *kephalē* did *not* commonly carry this meaning. Most of the eight passages where it was used are in relatively obscure places in the Old Testament. Early Christians, most of whom knew no Hebrew, could have gone to church for years without ever hearing these eight verses scattered through the Old Testament where *kephalē* was used to mean something different from the usual Greek meanings.

The apostle Paul was a Greek-speaking Jew (he grew up in the Greek-speaking city of Tarsus) with Greek as his native language. He knew both Hebrew and Greek, but he wrote his epistles to Greek-speaking churches in areas where most of the converts (including Jews of the Dispersion) knew *only* Greek. A man of his superb intellectual ability and intense passion to spread the gospel would likely use Greek words with Greek meanings that his readers clearly understood.

Examination of the seven passages where Paul used *kephalē* in reference to Christ indicates that when they are read with common Greek meanings of *kephalē*, we see a more exalted Christ than when we read "head" primarily with the meaning of "authority over." When Christ is spoken of as the head of the church, it may refer to him as the church's source of life, as its top or crown, as its exalted originator and completer. These rich meanings are lost when "authority" or "superior rank" are the only meanings for head.

In Ephesians 5:28 Paul used *kephalē* in reference to Christ as the head of the church and man (or husband) as the head of the woman (or wife). ("Husband" and "man" are the same word in Greek—*anēr;* "woman" and "wife" are the same word—*gynē*. Meaning must be determined by context.) Most Christians have read all the passages in Paul's writings with the English meaning of *head* as authority rather than the Greek meanings of *head*. This misreading of the Greek word has been used to teach that male dominance is ordained of God, when Paul may have been saying something quite different. In each instance, the context must determine which of the common Greek meanings of *head* Paul intended.

In 1 Corinthians 11:3, Paul writes, "But I would have you know, that the head of every man is Christ; and the head of the woman is the man; and the head of Christ is God" (KJV). Almost every commentator agrees that this entire section of 1 Corinthians 11:2-16 is full of unknowns.

What does "head" mean? What is the prophesying to which the chapter refers? When does "head" mean the person's physical head and when does it refer to the "head" specified in verse 3? What is the woman supposed to have on her head and the man not supposed to have? Some translations read "veil," but the word *veil* is nowhere in the Greek text. The Greek simply says in verse 4, "Every man praying or prophesying 'having it down from the head' dishonors his head." The covering is never specified. Since so much of the passage (vv. 5-16) discusses long hair versus short hair or shaved heads, it is quite possible that the head covering refers to long hair rather than a veil.

Why Paul is so concerned about hair length is another question which is not answered in the text itself.

All commentators agree that this passage is full of unanswered questions that obviously are closely related to the specific problems at Corinth and involved with customs and culture of that city. No doubt the first readers of this letter understood exactly what Paul was writing about, but we are not so fortunate. Despite this, those who espouse male dominance point to this passage as one of their foundation stones.

A few things in the passage *are* clear:

1. Paul, with full appreciation of the changes wrought by Pentecost, *expected* women to pray and prophesy in the public gatherings of the church at Corinth. If he did not expect it, why would he tell them how they were to look when they did it?

2. Paul taught the interdependence of men and women. Verse 11 states, "In the Lord woman is not independent of man nor man of woman; for as woman was made from man, so man is now born of woman. And all things are from God" (RSV). That verse is clear—both in Corinthian culture and in twentieth-century Western culture.

Several things are not so clear and are open to several interpretations:

1. The meaning of *head*. 1 Corinthians 11:3 has often been read as a "chain of command." Yet all evidence indicates that "authority," "leader," "chief" were *not* common Greek meanings of *head* at the time Paul wrote this letter. The Greek meaning of *head* that fits best with the *context* here is "source" or "origin." Verses 8-12 are centered on origins—"Man was not made from woman, but woman from man" and "for as woman was made from man, so man is now born of woman. And all things are from God."

But in what sense is God the "origin" of Christ? Paul wrote in Galatians 4:4: "God sent forth his Son, born of woman" (RSV). One of the earliest doctrines enunciated by the early church was that the Son "proceeded from the Father." How is Christ the source or originator of man? Paul wrote earlier in this letter: "There is . . . one Lord, Jesus Christ, through whom are all things and through whom we exist" (1 Cor 8:6 RSV). This interpretation of 1 Corinthians 11:3 is found in some of the earliest commentaries by the church fathers.

Cyril of Alexandria wrote in the fifth century: "Thus we say that the head of every man is Christ, because he was excellently made through him. And the head of woman is man, because she was taken from his flesh. Likewise, the head of Christ is God, because he is from him according to nature."

2. What does 1 Corinthians 11:10 mean? The literal text says, "For this reason a woman ought to have authority on her head because of the angels." King James gives a literal translation. All the others add or change the text to mean something quite different from what it says. Phillips reads, "For this reason a woman ought to bear on her head an outward sign of man's authority for all the angels to see." The text says nothing about a sign or about men or husbands. This is another example of translators letting their personal beliefs get in the way of the text.

What authority is the woman to have? Probably the authority to pray and prophesy with the proper head covering or hair style. After all, that's what the whole discussion is about.

Jerome Murphy-O'Connor of École Biblique in Jerusalem is one of several scholars who believe the whole passage is talking about hair styles and Paul's wish not to eclipse the differences between the appearances of men and women.[19] Paul's point is the distinction between men and women—not the dominance of one over the other. Murphy-O'Connor believes that the instructions about hair styles were needed because of the prevalence of homosexuality and pederasty in early Corinth, and that male homosexuals often wore long ornately-arranged hair styles, and lesbians wore closely clipped hair—more like the usual cut of Greek men.

Some writers insist that the "prophecy" mentioned in I Corinthians 11 refers only to "testimonies." Such testimonies may be a part of prophecy but by no means all of it. Prophecy is defined in 1 Corinthians 14 (part of this same letter) as including upbuilding, encouragement, edification (vv. 3-4), evangelism (vv. 22-25), careful evaluation (v. 29), teaching (v. 31)—all the activities that make a church an organism of spiritual power. If women were to prophesy as indicated in 1 Corinthians 11, they would be participating in all these aspects. Since most early churches were small "house churches," it is hard to imagine dividing the congregation into separate groups of males and females for every service. Nowhere does Paul suggest that this be done.

Women were clearly prophesying, and some New Testament women apparently had the "office" of prophet (Acts 21:9). Paul wrote in Ephesians 2:20 that the "household of God" was "built upon the foundation of the apostles and prophets, Jesus Christ himself being the chief corner stone." Women as well as men were the prophets (and perhaps the apostles—Junia in Romans 16:7) upon whom the church was built. Paul does not say the church was built upon elders, or even pastors, but upon apostles and *prophets.*

Should Women Be Silent in Churches?

But doesn't Paul tell women in 1 Corinthians 14:34 not to speak at all? At first reading it seems so, but Paul had just expounded on how women *are* to pray and prophesy in public meetings. Therefore the passage must have another meaning.

There are at least two possibilities. Paul may be telling wives to stop interrupting the services by asking their husbands what everything means. Instead, they should ask at home. Or Paul may have been quoting false teachings of the Judaizers, who wanted women to be as silent in church as they had to be in synagogue. (There are no quotation marks in the Greek manuscript copies that have been handed down: all punctuation, capitalization, verses, chapter divisions, and so forth, have been inserted by translators who were not infallible, regardless of how devoted they were to their tasks.)

The argument of the Judaizers may well begin with "the women should keep silence" and end with "for it is shameful for a woman to speak in church." If such is the case, Paul's irate reply is easily understood: "What! Did the Word of God originate with you, or are you the only ones it has reached?"

One statement in this passage presents another problem: "They [women] are not permitted to speak, but should be subordinate, even as the law says" (1 Cor 14:34 RSV). Usually, when Paul speaks of "the law," he is referring to the Old Testament. But there is no passage in the Old Testament that says women should be subordinate or are not permitted to speak in public.

So what law does this passage refer to? It may refer to some of the numerous local laws against women speaking in public meetings. Or it may refer to the rabbinic interpretations of the Old Testament. If the passage is a quotation from the Judaizers, it probably refers to a rabbinic interpretation.

There are other possibilities, too, but no one can pronounce with authority the exact meaning of these verses, because we do not know the exact cultural-historical situation. Paul knew what it was; the Corinthians knew it. We do not. Even those who use "selective literalism" with these verses to rule out women teaching or preaching never choose to follow them exactly. If they did, women could not sing in choirs, or even in the congregation, or teach Sunday school or operate the church kitchens. What would actually happen if every woman "kept silent" in our churches?

Since these two verses seem to contradict what Paul said earlier in the letter, as well as Paul's own practice regarding Priscilla and his other "co-workers in the gospel," we dare not use them to nullify everything else that Paul wrote and practiced.

May Women Teach Men?
1 Timothy 2:11-12 is the favorite text of those who believe that male dominance in the church (and in the world) is ordained of God: "I permit no woman to teach or to have authority over men; she is to keep silent" (RSV). This passage, like all others, must be approached with the basic questions: (1) What did it mean to the first hearers or readers in their situation? (2) In light of that, what should it mean to us today? (3) How does this passage fit with the highest ideals and standards taught in other parts of the Bible? Careful examination of the literal and historical-cultural context for this passage indicates clearly that it was a "regulation for people where they were"—not a highest norm or standard in the Bible.

This letter of Paul was an intensely personal one to give Timothy advice on how to deal with difficult problems in the struggling church at Ephesus, a city with the largest pagan temple in Asia Minor—the temple to the goddess Artemis. Artemis was the most prominent and the oldest of the Asian goddesses of fertility, with a history that went back many centuries. Every Greek city had a shrine to Artemis, but Ephesus had the largest and earliest. Women played prominent roles in the worship of Artemis.

Reading this letter is like listening to one side of a telephone conversation. We don't know what Timothy had told Paul or what Paul had learned in his three years of living at Ephesus—we only know how Paul is answering Timothy. The letter does indicate, however, that false teaching was a serious problem. Paul discusses it immediately after his usual greetings. "As I urged you when I was going to Macedonia, remain at Ephesus that you may charge certain persons not to teach any different doctrine, nor to occupy themselves with myths and endless genealogies which promote speculations rather than the divine training that is in faith. . . . Certain persons by swerving from these [good conscience and sincere faith] have wandered away into vain discussion, desiring to be teachers of the law, without understanding either what they are saying or the things about which they make assertions" (1 Tim 1:3-4, 6-7 RSV).

Paul writes about false teaching again in 1 Timothy 1:10, 19, 20, and again in 1 Timothy 4:1-3, where he specifically points out the error of those who forbid marriage. He comes back to false teaching in 5:15 when he discusses widows who "have already strayed after Satan." The book ends on the same note: "Timothy, guard what has been entrusted to you. Avoid the godless chatter and contradictions of what is falsely called knowledge, for by professing it some have missed the mark as regards the faith" (1 Tim 6:20 RSV).

Although the heresy known as Gnosticism did not reach its full bloom until the second century, the seeds of its false beliefs no doubt appeared much earlier. Gnosticism and other heresies included many erroneous beliefs about sex and creation. Some Gnostics taught that truly spiritual women should not marry and have children. Others taught that, since matter is evil and spirit is good, what a person did with the body was irrelevant to what went on in the inner spirit. To these Gnostics, sexual immorality was acceptable and could even be pleasing to God. Some Gnostics said that Eve was created before Adam and that she enlightened him by her superior knowledge.

The full paragraph of 1 Timothy 2:9-15 is revealing. A literal translation might read: "Likewise I want women to pray in modest apparel, to adorn themselves in modesty and chastity, not in braiding of the hair or in gold and pearls or expensive clothing, but with good deeds, as befits women who profess godliness. Let a woman learn in silence with all submissiveness. I permit no woman to teach or to have authority over men; but [I am commanding her] to be [learning] in quietness. For Adam was formed earlier, then Eve; and Adam was not deceived, but the woman was deceived and became a transgressor. Yet woman will be saved through the child bearing, if they continue in faith and love and holiness with chastity."

Those who believe that verse 12 forever bars all women of all time from teaching or having authority over men usually ignore the commands in the other six verses in this section. This is a classic case of "selective literalism." If this passage is universal for all Christian women of all time, then no woman should ever wear pearls or gold (including wedding rings) or have braided hair or expensive clothing. Also, they should never participate in a Sunday-school class or any other church meeting.

The advocates of male dominance generally ignore verse 15 with the comment that it is difficult to understand. Susan Foh, who holds that 11 and 12 are forever normative, simply says, "The last verse in this section is a puzzle and a sort of non sequitur."[20]

However, if Paul is responding to the false teaching that women as Christians should not marry (which he mentions in 1 Tim 4:1-3), then verse 15 makes good sense. Paul is saying that women *are* acceptable to God within their childbearing function: "Yet woman shall be saved through bearing children, if she continues in faith and love and holiness with modesty." The full passage also stresses modesty in dress and decorum on the part of women. Who would need that kind of teaching? Most married Greek women wore a *catastola*, a loose garment that reached the feet and was worn with a belt. It was *very* modest. About whom was Paul writing?

Here we must consider the historical and cultural context as well as the literary context. In Ephesus with its huge temple to the goddess Artemis were hundreds of sacred priestesses who probably also served as sacred prostitutes. There were also hundreds of *hetaerae*, the most educated of Greek women who were the regular companions and often the extramarital sexual partners of upper-class Greek men. Possibly some of these women had been converted and were wearing their suggestive and expensive clothing to church. Since *hetaerae* were often respected teachers of men in Greece (many are named in Greek literature[21]), they would be more likely to become teachers after they became part of the church. Apparently lack of chastity and modesty were a real problem among some women in the church at Ephesus, for Paul twice mentions the need of chastity (Greek *sōphrosynē*) in this section (1 Tim 2:9, 15).

Syncretism (mixing pagan with Christian ideas) has been a problem throughout the history of the church, and there is clear evidence that the mixing of the gospel with teachings of Greek religions and Gnosticism *did* creep into the early church. Revelation 2:14 says that some people in the church at Pergamum taught that it was all right to commit fornication. A few miles from Ephesus in Thyatira (Rev 2:20-23), a woman *in the church* named Jezebel "beguiled my servants to practice immorality." It seems that newly converted women from Greek backgrounds of Artemis worship and pagan cultures were particularly vulnerable to the false teachers who came to Ephesus.

What Does Authority Mean in 1 Timothy 2:12?

The word *authentein*, translated "to have authority" in 1 Timothy 2:12, is *not* the usual Greek word for "authority." The word usually used in the New Testament is *exousia*. If Paul had meant authority in the usual sense, he surely would have used that word. *Authentein* is found *only this once* in the Bible. It is rare even in secular Greek literature. Essentially *authentein* means "to thrust oneself" and usually has a negative meaning. John Chrysostom (about A.D. 400) in his commentary on Timothy translated *authentein* as "sexual license."

Catherine Kroeger has done extensive research on this word in classical Greek literature.[22] Her research indicates that the earliest usage seemed to mean "murder." Another early concept was "to originate" something or "be responsible" for it. She has found some very early Latin-Greek and English-Greek dictionaries that include: "with the genitive 'to declare oneself the author or source of anything.' "[23] The verb appears with the genitive in 1 Timothy 2:12. Kroeger suggests that if this was the meaning Paul had in mind, he may have been prohibiting women in Ephesus (influenced by Artemis worship) from teaching a gnostic type of mythology in which woman (Eve) was originator and enlightener of man (Adam). If this is the case, the next verses contain Paul's refutation of that teaching: "For Adam was formed earlier, then Eve; and Adam was not deceived, but the woman was deceived and became a transgressor."

Some who use this verse to bar women from positions of leadership say that this text "is grounded in creation" (that Adam was created before Eve) and therefore is binding for all time. However, the Greek word *gar* (translated "for") is not necessarily causal. *Gar* can also be illustrative. In that case the meaning here would simply mean that Eve was being used as an illustration of a woman who was deceived by Satan—as other women at Ephesus were being deceived by Satan.

In light of the history of the church at Ephesus, it is nearly impossible to believe that Paul was laying down a universal law against women teaching men, or that Timothy would interpret Paul's words that way. After all, Timothy knew all about Priscilla and Aquila who together had taught Apollos at the very beginning of the Ephesian church. Paul never had anything but praise for this remarkable couple and their ministry.

Even those who want to forbid women to have leadership positions in the church on the basis of this verse (with its rare word *authentein*) do not usually apply it fully. They ignore the commands about pearls and gold and braided hair that are a part of the passage. And they equivocate in varying degrees on teaching, authority and silence.

Many say it is all right for women missionaries to teach the faith—despite the fact that the text says "[the woman] is to be silent." Some say it is all right for women to teach men if they are "under the authority of a man." The text does not say that. Some say that the only offices forbidden to women are those of elder or pastor. The text does not say that.

Few people would prohibit women from writing books that men read—although that is undoubtedly a powerful form of teaching. Hymns form one of the most lasting forms of teaching. If we removed all of Frances Havergal's hymns and all of Fanny Crosby's and other women hymn writers', our hymn books would be impoverished. Sound biblical interpretation, common sense and ordinary observation of how God has used hundreds of women in leadership and teaching positions in his church around the world indicate that this passage in Timothy is clearly a "regulation for people where they were"—not a highest norm or standard.

So how do we apply this passage? We apply it the same way we apply other "regulations for people where they were." If a present situation is similar to that in Ephesus—if a group of people are teaching heresy or are ill-prepared to meet the temptations of Satan—Christians show loving concern by helping them become *learners* before they become teachers. Actually the first emphasis in the verse is on *learning.* "Let a woman *learn* in silence" (the better translation is "quietness").

To make 1 Tim 2:11-12 a universal principle for all women for all time is clearly contrary to the principles taught by our Lord ("Treat others the way you want to be treated") and the norm laid down at Pentecost: "Your sons and your daughters shall prophesy." Prophesying involved evangelism, preaching, teaching, encouraging. Colossians 3:16 admonishes *all* Christians to "let the word of Christ dwell in you richly, *teach* and *admonish* one another in all wisdom, and sing psalms and hymns and spiritual songs, with thankfulness in your hearts to God" (RSV—emphasis mine). The picture in Colossians is of Christians freely using their God-given gifts to praise God and encourage each other. There are no gender restrictions.

Paul Urges the Galatians to Maintain Their Christian Freedom

Paul's letter to the Galatians zeroes in on this freedom so essential for Christian growth and service. The Galatians were reducing the gospel to a slightly expanded Judaism. They were observing days, months, seasons, years (Gal 4:10). They thought circumcision was essential (Gal 5:2-4).

Paul wrote to them his strongest message: Christ freed you for the freedom. Don't be entangled again with the yoke of bondage (Gal 5:1). The Judaism of Paul's day wanted women to be silent, submissive and submerged in certain prescribed routines and roles. Paul wrote to the Galatians: "For as many of you as were baptized into Christ have put on Christ. There is neither Jew nor Greek, there is neither slave nor free, there is neither male nor female; for you are all one in Christ Jesus" (Gal 3:27-28 RSV). The New Testament scholar F. F. Bruce has stated in his commentary on Galatians that in 3:28: "Paul states the basic principle here: if restrictions on it are found elsewhere in the Pauline corpus . . . they are to be understood in relation to Gal

3:28 and not *vice versa.* "[24]

Christian men and women are not to be entangled in a yoke of bondage. Men and women are to preach. Women and men are to make disciples. They are to minister with the gifts of the Spirit and the fruit of the Spirit. Christ freed men and women to serve, to love, to care for, to strengthen, to support. The Galatians had lost sight of this freedom. Have we?

The teachings of Genesis, the life and teachings of our Lord, the full scope of the writings and practice of Paul—all these point to the full dignity of women who are gifted and called *by God himself* to serve his church and the world. Restrictions placed upon the full exercise of those gifts have handicapped the church through the ages and kept the gospel from going forth in its full power. May God enable us to unleash his power in the lives of women and men alike to serve him fully.

Notes

See also Mark 10:42-45; Luke 22:25-27; Matthew 23:10-12; John 13:12-17.

[2]Charles Hodge, *Cotton Is King, and Pro-Slavery Arguments*, ed. E. H. Elliot (1860; reprint ed., Augusta: Prichard, Abbott and Loomis, 1968).

[3]Frances Brown, S. R. Driver, Charles A. Briggs, *A Hebrew and English Lexicon of the Old Testament* (Boston: Houghton Mifflin, 1907), p. 617.

[4]David Freedman, "Woman, a Power Equal to Man," *Biblical Archaeology Review*, January/February 1983, pp. 56-58.

[5]Susan T. Foh, *Women and the Word of God* (Phillipsburg, N.J.: Presbyterian and Reformed, 1980), pp. 67-69.

[6]Peter Richardson, "From Apostles to Virgins: Romans 16 and the Roles of Women in the Early Church" (paper delivered at the Evangelical Colloquium on Women and the Bible, October 9-11, 1984).

[7]Henry George Liddell and Robert Scott, *A Greek-English Lexicon*, rev. Henry Stuart Jones with the assistance of Roderick McKenzie, 2 vols. (Oxford: Oxford University Press, 1940), 1:1526-27.

[8]Bo Reicke, "προΐστημι," *Theological Dictionary of the New Testament*, 10 vols., ed. Gerhard Kittel and Gerhard Friedrich (Grand Rapids: Eerdmans, 1964-76), 6:702-3.

[9]Berkeley and Alvera Mickelsen, "Has Male Dominance Tarnished our Translations?" *Christianity Today*, Oct. 5, 1979, pp. 23-26, 29.

[10]Scott Bartchy, "Power, Submission, and Sexual Identity Among the Early Christians," in C. Robert Wetzel, *Essays on New Testament Christianity* (Cincinnati: Standard Publ. Co., 1978).

[11]E. Margaret Howe, *Women and Church Leadership* (Grand Rapids: Zondervan, 1982), p. 36.

[12]Richardson, "From Apostles to Virgins."

[13]Elise Boulding, *The Underside of History—A View of Women through Time* (Boulder, Col.:

Westview Press, 1976).

[14]Liddell and Scott, *A Greek-English Lexicon*, 1:944-45.

[15]Henrico Stephano, *Thesaurus Graece Linguae* (Post Editionen, ediderunt carolus Hase, Guilielmus Dindorfius et Ludovicus Dindorfius. Parisiis: Excuderbot Ambrosius Firmin Didot, 1985), pp. 1495-99.

[16]Philip Barton Payne, "Response," in *Women, Authority & the Bible*, ed. Alvera Mickelsen (Downers Grove, Ill.: InterVarsity Press, 1986), p. 118.

[17]*English-Greek Dictionary—A Vocabulary of the Attic Language* (London: Routledge & Kegan Paul, Ltd., 1932).

[18]Walter Bauer, *A Greek-English Lexicon of the New Testament and Other Early Christian Literature*, ed. William F. Arndt and F. Wilbur Gingrich, fourth/fifth revised and augmented editions (Chicago: The University of Chicago Press, 1957, 1979), p. 431.

[19]Jerome Murphy-O'Connor, "Sex and Logic in 1 Cor 11:2-16," *Catholic Biblical Quarterly* 42 (1980):482-500.

[20]Foh, *Women and the Word of God*, p. 128.

[21]Boulding, *The Underside of History*, pp. 262-63.

[22]Catherine Clark Kroeger, "1 Timothy 2:12—A Classicist's View," in *Women, Authority & the Bible*, pp. 225-44.

[23]One such dictionary was compiled by George Dunbar, *A Greek-English Lexicon*, 3rd ed. (Edinburgh: MacLachlan and Stewart, 1850).

[24]F. F. Bruce, *The Epistle to the Galatians: A Commentary on the Greek Text*, The New International Greek Testament Commentary (Grand Rapids: Eerdmans, 1982).

A TRADITIONALIST RESPONSE
Robert D. Culver

If I understand the argument of this essay correctly, Alvera Mickelsen wishes to convince us that, rightly interpreted, the Bible opens up all positions of leadership in the church to people of either sex, without any restriction whatsoever. The contrary view—that the position(s) or office(s) designated variously pastor, elder, bishop, overseer and the like should be restricted to adult men—has prevailed throughout the 75 or so generations since the beginning. It seems to be the majority view today.

Since Mrs. Mickelsen and her husband have been acquaintances of mine for about thirty years and have attended the same church with me and my family for some years, and since her husband was my colleague on the faculty of Wheaton College and Graduate School for about a decade, I almost wish now I had another task than to write this assessment, which will be designedly courteous but also I hope convincingly negative.

Her essay claims the Bible is plainly, not obscurely, on her side and that its clear message, admitting women as freely as men to every office and function of the church, has been hindered and blocked by invincible male opposition. This, by reason of what she seems to say, is due to a persistent quirk of original sin.

But lest I pervert or wrongly emphasize her assertions, I shall try to describe her theories in her own words. I quote: "Most people who want to restrict the ways in which women can serve God build their cases on a few select verses of the Bible which they believe cancel out other teachings of the Scripture." This implies that my part in the debate bypasses the true evidence. Traditionalists are said to consider only favorable prooftexts, though she does acknowledge that her position does some of this also.

Explaining why stories of women in positions of Christian leadership are little known, she says, it is "partly because most histories have been written by men who, because of their theological or cultural conditioning, tended to assume that women had no important leadership roles in the church." Presumably Eusebius and Schaff, both eminent church historians, were "conditioned" by theology and culture while feminist writers have been, shall we say, educated and liberated?

It may be true, I suppose, that many female servants of Christ have been neglected in the history books. Many of us, both men and women, might rightly feel neglected in this regard, but it is by no means plain that "sexism," to use that strange neologism, is the cause of it. The essayist concludes that good Christian female leadership is notable enough, in history rightly written, to show that "experience through the centuries runs counter to our [not her] interpretation of the Bible." Therefore, "perhaps it is wise to reconsider whether our restrictive interpretations [not hers] actually express the mind of God."

The essay gives important space to the idea that male advocates of restrictions on female leadership are disobeying Scripture in that they do not follow the Golden Rule: "If men would not like to be restricted from being elders or ministers or teachers of mixed groups simply because they are males, then they had best examine whether their interpretation of passages . . . puts them in conflict with the command of Christ to treat others the way we want to be treated."

On the basis of a simple pleasure-pain ethic, that might be an argument, but it is irrelevant in this debate where no one (we hope) wants anything to be done or not done to or for anybody except what God, the Lord, wills to be done. Who does not prefer pleasure to pain for himself and in good conscience for others also? But if God wants men to "love their wives as their own bodies" (Eph 5:28) and the wife to "reverence her husband" (Eph 5:33), then love will flow more in one direction and reverence in another, rather than the reverse. The Golden Rule does not direct us to mix things up. Mickelsen's argument is frivolous.

Later in her essay, Galatians 3:26-29 and Matthew 20:25-27 ("neither male nor female" and "servant of all" passages) are elevated to principles which render it necessary to interpret the passages from Paul and others which appear to teach some superior authority of men over women in church and home as meaning something else. She makes herself plain: "Why do we ignore such teachings? Because they run counter to a power-culture that has been absorbed even in many churches."

Now who is selecting her/his texts? And again, "The *one kind of leadership* [my emphasis] that Jesus taught was the leadership of servanthood and self-giving—not a leadership of power and authority over others." To answer such a slashing attack is hard to accomplish in a few words. I will leave it largely unanswered. I am sure godly writers of ages past and devoutly obedient Christians of today who try to follow a New Testament ideal of church leadership of the sort my essay defends are not swayed by a "power-culture." Nor are they lusting after "power and authority over others." Nor need they "ask" themselves whether their "ideas come from our Lord, . . . or whether they are carryovers from pharisaical Judaism or from our cultural patterns or from the sinful desire for power over others." We think we got the tradition (1 Cor 11:1-2) from Paul and other Bible writers.

There is much more of this depreciation of motives, methods of exegesis, hermeneutics and the like in the essay. We are said to "select passages we like . . . ignoring those that seem to teach the opposite." Some of her detractors are said to read "into the text" meanings not really there and read "preconceived ideas into the text, from faulty translations [her "faulty" ones are the standard versions] . . . and from . . . starting with a preconceived proposition and then interpreting the Bible in the light [darkness?] of the proposition."

This is only part of the list of errors the essay insists we "traditionalists" are guilty of. All these alleged horrid errors and perversities imputed to us are necessary to account for the things we and our 75 generations of predecessors have taught and acted on—part and parcel of us, it seems.

I cannot say exactly how the author came to possess the views of male and female leadership in the church that she has. I certainly do not think they came from the Bible in any standard version I read. I do know where I find her distinct ideas about Bible interpretation and absence of coherence in the biblical message on grammatical principles. They are not prevalent today in evangelical circles. They are prevalent in the literature of a rather special kind of so-called biblical theology which denies the basis in the Bible of a coherent system of theology or of ethics.

According to Mrs. Mickelsen, lower elements are to be suppressed in favor of higher, earlier for later. All had a progressive development within the Bible itself and have had a similar development in the church since the church began. This approach is not all wrong and has produced some positive results, but it has also led to widespread rejection of the idea of system in theology and coherence in biblical ethics. The proposed alternative is "biblical theology" in the very special sense of which I have just written. It has also led to a developmentalism in ethics which cannot help but tend toward the superseding of old standards by newer ones.

On the last point let me quote from a very highly respected Methodist writer on pastoral theology, Thomas C. Oden: "This hungry anxiety to accommodate to modernity is a major clue to the loss of clarity about ministry in our times."[1] The same author goes on to say that our ideas about pastoral ministry must by all means avoid what he calls "creativity" or innovation. He lays out what he calls a "central consensual tradition"[2] by consciously drawing from four sources: (1) *the Bible* ("Pastoral theology lives out of Scripture. . . . Scripture examines our prior understandings. . . . It puts them to the test"), (2) *tradition* ("at bottom . . . the history of exegesis"), (3) *"reason* as a criterion" and (4) *experience.*[3]

Oden applies these sources and finds, correctly, I think, that there is (contrary to Dr. Liefeld's essay) a distinct office of the Christian ministry as understood by nearly every Christian denomination. He holds (as I have argued in print elsewhere) that "very early in the pastoral tradition" there was an attempt "to develop something like a primitive theological education." He cites 2 Timothy 2:2: "You heard my teaching in the presence of many witnesses; put that teaching into the charge of persons you can trust . . . such as will be competent to teach others."[4] I have contended exactly this in lectures and articles for thirty years.

As I read the early Christian fathers, there was nothing which concerned leaders of the time more than orderly transfer of pastoral leadership (presbyters, overseers) through the vicissitudes of social change and over the generations. I find no evidence that an absence of official pastoral oversight ever existed. I find the presence of that oversight strongest among the earliest of the Apostolic Fathers, as the most cursory reading of Clement of Rome's *Epistle to the Corinthians* amply displays.

As for a woman in the pastoral office, I think Thomas C. Oden makes a better case for it than any other author I have read. He takes a calm, fair, objective point of view. I do not endorse it, but if one is intent on introducing women to the pastoral ministry, Oden's chapter 4, "Women in the Pastoral Office," is much more persuasive, I think, than the querulous advocacy the subject receives in this essay.

Notes

[1]Thomas C. Oden, *Pastoral Theology* (San Francisco: Harper & Row, 1983), p. 3.
[2]Ibid., p. 7.
[3]Ibid., pp. 11-12.
[4]Ibid., pp. 32-33.

A MALE LEADERSHIP RESPONSE
Susan T. Foh

Mickelsen begins by pointing out that part of interpreting the Bible is recognizing one's own biases—a well-taken observation, but one that is usually applied to interpreters other than one's self. We must remember that each interpreter thinks he or she is being true to the biblical text and that each, including Mickelsen, has his or her personal biases to recognize and take into account. Some personal biases are closer to the truth than others, and the only way to sort through them is to come back to the texts and the question of how to interpret them.

Mickelsen includes the history and experiences of women in the church; women's activity in the church and their influence on the Christian church throughout history are significant and indisputable. Yet experience cannot determine the meaning of the Scriptures, as Mickelsen acknowledges. Even considering the experiences of women in history, within orthodoxy, there is little, if anything, to support women as elders (those who teach authoritatively and exercise church discipline) until recent times. This fact does not undermine the importance of women to the church, nor does it make women second-class citizens of the kingdom.

Mickelsen distinguishes between the highest norms and those intended only for one time and place. In spite of the difficulties in making a precise case for not keeping the Old Testament ceremonial law (such as Lev 19:19) and in understanding why the Jerusalem council of Acts 15 singled out those particular items for the Gentiles to observe (incidentally, eating rare steak is not eating blood), it is still true that the context of the passage itself determines its applicability. For example, 1 Corinthians 14:33-35 indicates its applicability in all the congregations of the saints.

From the other side (a consideration of the cultural context), the existence of *hetaerae*, who may have worn expensive and suggestive clothing and who may have been accustomed to teaching men, does not automatically limit the applicability of 1 Timothy 2:9-15 to first-century Ephesus. It only enlightens us as to why Paul may have written those particular commands at that particular time. (If it was culturally acceptable for *hetaerae* to teach men, how can one argue that Paul was making a concession to a culture that could not tolerate women teaching men, as Liefeld suggests? It seems to be a problem to know exactly what the cultural context was.)

If the Golden Rule is used to justify women elders, it could be used to justify anything the interpreter decides is good, such as homosexuality or open marriage. Love does fulfill the law, but we, as finite sinners, need to have how to live spelled out for us; we do not know what is best apart from God's Word.

An appeal to the highest norm seems to me to be essentially the same as deculturizing the Bible. Mickelsen says, "We must ask whether our ideas come from our Lord and his often difficult teachings, or whether they are carryovers from pharisaical Judaism." Since the entire Bible is God-breathed, all of it, even Old Testament ceremonial law, is profitable to us; there is no contradiction or disharmony between a higher norm and the rest of the Bible.

Mickelsen's point concerning the servanthood of church leaders and the sin of being power-hungry is one that needs to be emphasized.

In her discussion of Genesis 1—2, Mickelsen, while arguing that the order of creation is unimportant, neglects the fact that Paul understands Adam's prior creation as significant.

There may be nothing in Jesus' teaching or life that expressly indicates a difference in function for men and women, but there is also nothing to indicate that women held leadership positions or taught in public. Jesus' treatment of women underlines our equality in being, our primary value to God as persons, but it does not countermand Paul's commands in 1 Timothy 2:11-12 or 1 Corinthians 14:34-35.

To suggest that *prostatis* in Romans 16:2 implies that Phoebe was a "ruling elder" is to put too much into the word. Could Phoebe have been a ruling elder of Paul?

Mickelsen's discussion of the meaning of *kephalē* ("head") is detailed, but it suffers from major flaws, which have been recounted in "Does *Kephalē* ('Head') Mean 'Source' or 'Authority over' in Greek Literature? A Survey of 2,336 Examples" by Wayne Grudem, an appendix in *The Role Relationship of Men and Women* by George W. Knight III (Grand Rapids: Baker, 1985). Grudem points out that the only evidence for understanding *kephalē* as "source" is two references cited in Liddell-Scott, a lexicon for classical, not specifically New Testament, Greek. (Bauer is the standard lexicon for New Testament Greek.) They are Herodotus 4.91 and *Orphic Fragments* 21a. Liddell-Scott places them under the general category "Of things, extremity." *Kephalē* means source (of a river) in Herodotus 4.91 (fifth century B.C.), but it is in the *plural*. In the singular, *kephalē* means "mouth" (of a river) in Callimachus, *Aetia* 2.46. Grudem writes:

> Those who cite Herodotus or the "head of a river" examples to show that *kephalē* could have meant "source" at the time of the New Testament have not been careful enough in their use of Herodotus or Liddell-Scott. First, it is improper to take a meaning from a category that is specifically stated to apply to "things" and then apply it to persons. Second, when Liddell-Scott specifies that the plural refers to a river's "source" whereas the singular applies to the river's "mouth," it is improper to use the meaning that applies only to the *plural* ("source") for the instances in the New Testament, all of which are *singular*. (p. 58)

In *Orphic Fragments* 21a (which cannot be dated later than fifth century B.C.), the sense of *kephalē* is closer to "beginning" or "first one" (Knight, p. 60). Grudem concludes that there is not one clear text in all of Greek literature to support the meaning of "source" for *kephalē*.

There is also no Septuagint support for translating *kephalē* as "source." The Hebrew word *ro'sh* (head) can be translated by *archē* or *kephalē* when it refers to "ruler" or "chief" (but more often it is translated by *archōn* or *archēgos,* more common words for ruler). Note also that *kephalē* could mean "ruler" in Greek, or the translators of the Septuagint would not have used it at all. Mickelsen undermines this evidence. *Kephalē* translates *ro'sh* in Judges 10:18; 11:8, 9, 11; 2 Samuel 22:44; 1 Kings 8:1; Psalm 18:43; Isaiah 7:8, 9; 9:14-16.

To see if *kephalē* could have the meaning "authority over," Grudem surveyed 2,336 instances from eighth century B.C. (Homer) to the first century A.D. (Philo, Josephus and the Apostolic Fathers) to the fourth century A.D. (Libanius). Most (87%) refer to a physical head. In 2.1% (49 instances), *kephalē* refers to a "person of superior authority or rank, or 'ruler,' 'ruling part' " (Knight, p. 87). Of the metaphorical usages, the percentage is 16.2. In this survey, *kephalē* was never used in the sense of "source."

In the New Testament, there are two passages that clearly use *kephalē* in the sense of "authority over": Ephesians 1:22 and Ephesians 5:22-23.

In defining *prophecy,* Mickelsen seems to be including its effects rather than its definition. 1 Corinthians 14 does not define *prophecy* per se; it discusses its effects as compared to the effects of speaking in tongues. The prophet is distinguished from teachers in 1 Corinthians 12:28 and evangelists and pastor-teachers in Ephesians 4:11. The prophet speaks the very words of God, not his or her own thoughts or formulations (2 Pet 1:20-21; Zech. 7:12; Eph 3:5; Deut 18:18, 20); what the prophet does is different from what a teacher or modern-day preacher does.

Concerning "selective literalism" in 1 Timothy 2:8-15, Mickelsen overstates the case. Paul does not forbid braided hair with gold (the two go together), pearls or expensive clothes; he says rather that Christian women should consider their adornment the qualities of reverence and sobriety (or sound judgment) and good deeds. It is a matter of focus (1 Pet 3:3-4). Also, I think Paul is forbidding only one role in verse 12—one that involves teaching and ruling, the office of elder. This view would allow women's participation in Sunday school (unless the teaching there was defined as authoritative teaching done only by elders) and church meetings.

Mickelsen makes a good point in relating 1 Timothy 2:15 to the teachings of Gnosticism. However, the presence of Gnostic teachings in Ephesus does not introduce the idea of false teaching into 1 Timothy 2:8-15. False teaching is not mentioned in this text. "Women" in verse 12 is not qualified in any way. All women should learn (v. 11); no woman (not just those who are false teachers) may teach or exercise authority over men (v. 12).

Concerning *authentein*, George Knight's study, referred to in my chapter, indicates that the primary meaning of *authentein* is "to exercise authority over." The word itself has no negative connotations.

If the conjunction *gar* (v. 13) is used in the sense of illustration, I have several questions. How does the prior creation of Adam fit in as an illustration? How would verses 13-14 be translated? Does Adam's not being deceived illustrate that the men of Ephesus were not being deceived (compare 1 Tim 1:3-4, 6, 19-20; 4:1-2)? In addition, I could not find this meaning listed in Bauer or Liddell-Scott.

Women are free to serve Christ, as are men, in the way prescribed for them in God's Word.

A PLURAL MINISTRY RESPONSE
Walter L. Liefeld

This is a positive and well-argued defense of unlimited ministry for women. The positive aspect is clear from the outset, as Mickelsen cites examples of women in leadership roles in the church. The example of the "elect lady" in 2 John is plausible and often neglected, that of Priscilla is often minimized. Thecla is indeed known in the early church, but the historicity of the apocryphal work about her is suspect. Mickelsen proceeds to provide a few of the many examples of women in church history. In doing this she comes close to Culver's methodology of citing tradition as proof. Nevertheless, having just worked on a history of women in the church, I am deeply impressed with the "untold story" of women who have not only served but led in Christian ministry and missions.

Mickelsen points out that experience in itself is not proof. It can, however, stimulate the thoughtful person to question seemingly obvious interpretations of Scripture that limit women. Like Foh, Mickelsen addresses the question of hermeneutics. It is not surprising that they emphasize opposite principles. The first principle cited actually includes several subsets. The reference to reader understanding in the original situation is important, although (since readers could misunderstand) that must be considered, as Mickelsen notes, in conjunction with the clear flow of thought in the passage itself. The distinction between norms and regulations is important. Perhaps a better example than the apostolic decree from Acts 15 could be cited, since that is in a third-person narrative and does not appear as a directive addressed to the reader of Scripture.

The insistence on "highest standards" is important. The example cited, the significance of Pentecost for women, is one that traditionalists seem constantly to overlook. In my judgment the treatment of creation and the Fall in this essay is more satisfactory than that by Foh, though both are concerned with exegetical detail. Nevertheless, when Mickelsen opposes the "order of creation" argument, she fails to deal with Paul's apparent use of that argument in 1 Timothy 2.

Overstatement is a hazard in this kind of discussion, one which Mickelsen fails to avoid when she says that women were included "among the inner circle" of Jesus' disciples. The fact that Jesus encouraged women to be his disciples does need emphasizing, and it is true that Mary "sat at the Lord's feet" in the posture of a disciple, "listening to what he had said" (Lk 10:39). And although Jewish rabbis generally did not have women disciples, it is commonly acknowledged that there were women who followed Jesus. But to say they were in the "inner circle" requires proof that they were on the "inside" in comparison with others. Were they as close as Peter, James and John, the true "inner circle," or even as close as the Twelve? It is more to the point to note that women were the first witnesses of the resurrection and also that Paul did not mention them in his list of credible witnesses.

It is also to the point to mention that every house church mentioned in Acts "meets in the home of a woman." Traditionalists have apparently not come to grips with that. Mickelsen's assessment of Phoebe corrects her downplaying at the hands of the traditionalists, but overstates matters in saying that the text "implies that she was a ruling elder." I have studied the evidence carefully and would have to say that while this assessment is not incompatible with the word *prostatis,* neither is it implied by it. Mickelsen may not be aware of the most recent papyrus evidence where *prostatis* refers to a widow in charge of her son's inheritance. The rest of the evidence in Romans 16 receives accurate treatment and needed emphasis.

One point that is made in connection with the topic of spiritual gifts is that "strictures against women grew in the second century." I have looked closely at the historical evidence to see if there is a pattern of women's freedom followed by restriction. While it may be debated whether this is a consistent "pattern," it is certainly often true. Especially in modern church history some women have begun movements or missions, only to be displaced by men as the work grew. Another aspect of this is the tendency to credit men with beginning works that were actually started or forwarded by women. In Foh's essay, for example, there is a reference to Robert Raikes as the founder of Sunday schools, overlooking women who were teaching and criticized for it.

The section on the Greek word for "head," *kephalē*, is full, but has its weaknesses. Perhaps a clue to the effort expended to prove the case is the reference to "one small Greek lexicon used by many pastors" that includes the meaning "superior rank." That "small" lexicon is the major lexical reference volume on the vocabulary of the New Testament and related works written by the German scholar Walter Bauer and edited by W. F. Arndt, F. W. Gingrich and F. W. Danker. It is used by scholars around the world. Of course, it is "small" in comparison with Liddell and Scott, which covers the larger body of classical Greek literature, but for detail on the New Testament period one consults Bauer before Liddell and Scott. Whether or not Bauer is correct, it does not "help the cause" to minimize its significance.

With regard to the use of *kephalē*, "head," it is interesting to note the way Mickelsen uses statistics in contrast to the approach of Grudem (cited in my essay, note 4).

Mickelsen claims that "in 109 out of 180 times" when the Old Testament Hebrew text used the word *ro'sh* to mean "leader" or "chief," the Septuagint translation used another Greek word *(archōn)* rather than *kephalē* to translate it. On his part, Grudem lists examples from among the remaining 71 instances to try to prove his point. He claims that in 2.1% of total uses in his sample, or 16.2% of metaphorical uses, *kephalē* means a "person of superior authority or rank" or "ruler," "ruling part." Thus each author cites the material in the way needed to strengthen his or her position, but the weight of the evidence seems to be on Mickelsen's side.

Someone needs to analyze the data and the various articles currently being written on the subject and come up with an objective, accurate conclusion. Mickelsen has properly warned against automatically assuming that the word meant "authority" or "headship" as we think of it. Too often that automatic assumption has been made with the consequence that wrong inferences and wrong conclusions have been drawn.

Mickelsen introduces Kroeger's interpretation of 1 Timothy 2:12, and especially of the troublesome verb *authentein*. The treatment here suffers from a weakness that appears in Kroeger's article as well. It assumes that the verb *authentein* is the object of the prohibition against teaching, as though Paul were saying they should not teach the myth that woman is the "originator" of man. But in fact the verb "teach" is used absolutely, with no object indicated, and *authentein* is a coordinate verb. Nevertheless, Kroeger's data should be weighed carefully.

In summary, Mickelsen brings out a number of facts about women in Scripture and in history that are often overlooked. Although some of the argumentation might have been improved, this should not cause out-of-hand rejection of the significant points that are made.

AFTERWORD
Bonnidell Clouse

The communion of saints that we call the church faced difficulties from its very inception. The early Christians met in each other's homes or went "underground" to escape detection and persecution. Sometimes they locked the door (Acts 12:14), admitting only those they recognized as fellow believers. They fled to other towns, followed by their oppressors (Acts 9:1-2), and there they spread the gospel of Jesus Christ. So great was their love for each other that they sold their possessions, giving to those who had less and having all things in common (Acts 2:45).

As their numbers increased through the teachings of Peter and the other disciples (Acts 2:47), so did the problems. There was deception by Ananias and Sapphira (Acts 5:1-3), murmurings as to the care of widows (Acts 6:1), the martyrdom of Stephen (Acts 7) and controversy concerning the place of Gentiles (Acts 10). This last concern, the acceptance of Gentiles as fellow believers, was especially difficult for the apostles. Jesus' example of talking to the Samaritan woman as he would have to a Jewish man seemed to have less impact upon the disciples than did the custom of the day in which a man would not talk publicly with a woman, nor a Jew with a Samaritan (Jn 4:9). It took Peter's vision of the unclean animals (Acts 10) and the conversion of the Ethiopian eunuch (Acts 8) and Cornelius (Acts 10) to bring an understanding that all peoples were to be included in the preaching of the gospel. The stated purpose of Saul's conversion was to bear Jesus' name before the Gentiles (Acts 9:15), and thus the way was paved for the missionary journeys of Paul, Silas and Barnabas.

The establishment of congregations in Antioch, Ephesus, Galatia, Corinth and Thessalonica brought great joy; yet, with the joy came difficulties not previously encountered by the church. To be sure, some problems were the same, being carryovers from Jewish custom. Circumcision (Rom 4), dietary restrictions (1 Cor 8), servants honoring their masters (1 Tim 6) and whether Jewish Christians had an advantage over Gentile Christians (Rom 3) were topics still debated. But many of the problems seemed to stem from the influence of non-Jewish cultures on the newly formed groups of believers, and, like all institutions, sacred or secular, the church was affected by the mores and customs of the times. It became important to sort out which practices were acceptable to God and which were not.

Some changes from Old Testament law were to be expected. Had Paul not written that believers are saved by grace not by works (Eph 2:8-9) and that justification comes by faith without the deeds of the law (Rom 3:28)? Was not the law only a schoolmaster to bring one to Christ so that after a commitment to faith one no longer was under the schoolmaster (Gal 3:24-25)? And did Paul not say that he had become all things to all men so that he might save some (1 Cor 9:22)? Yet, surely this did not mean that either Paul or the members of the newly formed congregations could do whatever they pleased. Some behaviors are desirable for those who bear the name of Christ; other behaviors are not to be tolerated. Whether in the home, the community or the church, Christians should live lives that are pleasing to God.

So questions were asked and answers were given on matters such as the proper relationship of husbands and wives (Eph 5:22-25), parents and children (Eph 6:1-4), young and old (1 Tim 5:1-2), slave owners and slaves (Eph 6:5-9; Philem), and on issues concerning how disputes should be settled within the church (1 Cor 6:7). Paul wrote on the practice of speaking in tongues (1 Cor 14), on the qualifications of a bishop (1 Tim 3:1-6) and deacons (1 Tim 3:7-13), and about how men and women should dress when they worship and pray (1 Cor 11). There was the need to discern whose teachings should be followed (1 Cor. 1:12; 2:4-8), what the proper format was for partaking of the Lord's Supper (1 Cor 11), and when divorce, separation and remarriage were permissible (1 Cor 7).

There were also the questions of whether some abilities or "gifts" are more prestigious than others and whether some members of the church are more important than others because of their abilities (Rom 12:3; 1 Cor 12). Sexual behavior was addressed as well, with homosexuality (Rom 1:27) and incest (1 Cor 5:1) strongly condemned. And, along with these, was the matter of the role of men and women in the church. Women, as well as men, were prominent figures in the early church, so it was important to know what their respective positions and responsibilities should be. Paul addressed this subject even as he had so many others.

Questions Today

Nineteen centuries have passed since the days of the apostles. Some of the concerns of the early church do not seem important to us now. Dietary restrictions based on whether the food has been offered to idols is not a part of our world. Nor do we own slaves or feel we should, and the "holy kiss" (1 Thess 5:26) has been replaced with a handshake. Nor do we struggle today with the question of whether Jewish Christians have more favor with God than do Christians of other backgrounds.

Other problems faced by the early church are important to some congregations but not to others. Some denominations today feel compelled to follow closely the qualifications for the bishop and deacons as outlined by the apostle Paul; others do not. Some settle any dispute within the church; others feel that given the laws of the land, they must go to court to keep the church property or settle other issues even though the opposing party may include fellow believers.

Some church groups mandate that all parishioners be in accord with Paul's teaching on divorce and remarriage; other church groups feel that the social climate of our Western world is such that these restrictions eliminate from Christian fellowship the very people who are most in need of a community in which love and understanding are shown. They point to Jesus' reception of the Samaritan woman and the woman taken in adultery as models for our own expression of care and acceptance. Some churches insist that men wear their hair short and women wear their hair long; other churches believe that hair length is a matter of personal taste and in no way detracts from living the Christian life or from worshiping God in spirit and in truth. Likewise, some denominations ordain only men to the Christian ministry; other denominations ordain both men and women.

None of us can separate ourself completely from our background. Even our approach to the Bible, as objective as we would like for it to be, is influenced by the groups to which we belong and by our orientation to many areas of our lives, some religious and some not. We may have come to adopt a conservative or traditional view of social and political issues which, in turn, affects our interpretation of religious matters; or we may accept a more liberal or progressive stance which also orients our thinking on religious concerns. But whatever direction we take and whatever our perceptions may be, the conclusions we come to always seem so right to us that we find it difficult to understand how others can see the same phenomena so differently.

It is tempting to set ourselves above others, to equate our position with being more spiritual or with having a greater desire to know and to do God's will than is true for those who are persuaded differently. But we are told in Scripture not to judge, for each of us is accountable to God alone (Rom 14:3-10). Apart from the two basic tenets of the Christian faith—namely, the deity of Jesus Christ and the inspiration of Scripture—there is room for opinion on a variety of topics, including the one specifically addressed in this volume on the ordination of women to the Christian ministry.

Believers who tend toward the conventional usually take a historical or traditional interpretation of Scripture, looking to the writings of the apostle Paul as their guide to faith and practice and following "the letter of the Law." They are often opposed to changes in society that result in greater freedom for the individual, for they feel this is contrary to nature and to God's foreordained plan. For example, if male-female differences are examined, the argument is made that men and women, by virtue of being created male or female, have different natures, purposes, personality characteristics, desires and interests. Deviation from this created order is not in keeping with the will of God and should be opposed—hence, the strong criticism of groups such as the National Organization of Women and Planned Parenthood. Many religious conservatives feel that Paul would have been solidly against the present-day women's liberation movement. Some even include feminism on their list of the great evils of the day.[1]

By contrast, believers who tend toward the unconventional are more apt to take an egalitarian interpretation of Scripture, looking to the life of Jesus as their example of godly behavior and following what they believe to be "the spirit of the law." Changes in society that make for greater individual autonomy are often welcomed as bringing us closer to a realization of the freedom we have in Christ. Again, if male-female differences are examined, the argument is made that dissimilarities between men and women, aside from obvious primary and secondary sex characteristics, are products of a culture that begins its influence on children as soon as they are born. The consequence is that many people, both male and female, are restricted from reaching their full potential, including their potential to serve God and to further his cause. Needed is a social milieu that encourages every person to be all he or she can be and does not distinguish on the basis of gender. According to those who are more liberal in their social and political views, Jesus did not treat men and women differently and neither should we.[2]

The Christian who takes a traditionalist position and the Christian who takes an egalitarian position both know that "all Scripture is given by inspiration of God, and is profitable for doctrine, for reproof, for correction, for instruction in righteousness" (2 Tim 3:16 KJV). No passage should be ignored. This presents a dilemma, however, when different passages are cited (depending on the orientation of the speaker or writer) and the passages do not appear to be in agreement. What does the listener or reader do when there are seeming contradictions between one Scripture and another?

Given our Western way of thinking, based on Aristotelian logic, contradictions or paradoxes make us decidedly uncomfortable. Were we trained in Oriental thought, we would have less difficulty. But this is not the case, so rather than accepting *all* Scripture (for examples, predestination and free will, God as a God of mercy *and* as a God of justice, "ye are saved through faith, not of works" *and* "faith without works is dead"), we tend to fasten on one or the other of the truths within each paradox.

The same reasoning occurs when we stress 1 Corinthians 11:2-16, which distinguishes between the sexes as to appearance and activity, or when we emphasize Galatians 3:28, which states that "there is neither . . . male nor female . . . in Christ." Both passages come from Holy Writ and both are valid, but it is hard for us to accept them as being equally important. We feel we must choose which text to emphasize and which text to give lesser consideration. Liefeld, in his essay, aptly refers to this as "theological scaffolding" in which a crucial passage "tends either to be cited as governing the interpretation of all other relevant texts or, on the other hand, to be minimized as to its implications."

Four Scaffolds

Each of the four contributors to this volume has grappled with this issue, and each has endeavored to create a "scaffolding" that comes closest to what he or she believes the Word of God teaches with regard to the role of women in the church. Robert Culver emphasizes the tradition "ordered by Scripture and apostolic regulation" which he believes takes precedence over "exceptions to a general rule," such as the "present-day eagerness of some [churches] to open up the 'clergy' to women."

Susan Foh states that "if there is nothing in the text to indicate that a command is limited to a special case or circumstance, we cannot presume to limit the text. . . . The New Testament gives no examples of female apostles, evangelists or elders. There are no examples of women teaching in public. . . . The more the church conforms to the biblical picture, the easier it will be to apply Scripture and to see what women can do in the church."

Walter Liefeld distinguishes "the principles of the Old Testament and the teachings of Paul" which are "universally true for all time" from the "particular application" which "may differ." Paul's principle of being "all things to all men, that I might by all means save some" (1 Cor 9:22 KJV) meant that in the pagan world of the first century, women were to wear veils and be silent. "Today it is just the reverse. A society that accepts women as corporation executives and university presidents will find it difficult to listen to a church that silences them."

Alvera Mickelsen differentiates between the "highest norms or standards taught in the Bible" from the "many regulations for people 'where they were.' " A standard such as the Golden Rule, "So in everything, do to others what you would have them do to you, for this sums up the Law and the Prophets" (Mt 7:12 NIV) coupled with "Love the Lord your God with all your heart and with all your soul and with all your mind" (Mt 22:37 NIV) are normative for all time; whereas "a woman should learn in quietness and full submission. I do not permit a woman to teach or to have authority over a man; she must be silent" (1 Tim 2:11-12 NIV) was a regulation for people where they were and does not necessarily apply to the church of today. "Highest standards were emphasized by Jesus Christ (and sometimes by Paul) and were often plainly stated as the highest standard." "Regulations for people where they were" came about "because of some local or temporary situation."

Each contributor, then, provides a rationale for the way the Bible should be interpreted. Each wishes to "rightly divide the Word" and make it applicable to our lives today. More specifically, each looks at what the Scripture says concerning the important issue of the woman's role in the church. It is for the reader to decide which position is best, keeping in mind that differences of opinion encourage us to search more deeply into God's Word and to examine our own understandings and beliefs. If we already *know* which view is right, we will find we are in good company and perhaps will acquire additional support for our way of thinking. But we also will be challenged by opposing arguments that should not be ignored. If we are not certain which position is best, we can ask God for wisdom, knowing that he is pleased to answer our request (Jas 1:5). Studying relevant passages of Scripture on a matter which directly or indirectly affects all of us should be given high priority.

Even as Jewish Christians in first-century Palestine questioned a number of practices in the newly formed churches within the Gentile world, and even as Jew and Gentile alike felt the need to sort out which of these practices were pleasing to God and which were not;

we as Christians today, living in the latter part of the twentieth century, often question innovative practices in today's churches that reflect the times in which we live. We, too, feel the need to determine which of these new ways of doing things are honoring to God and which are not, so that together with fellow believers we may worship our Lord in spirit and in truth.

There are new versions of the Bible, some faithful to the original text and some so loosely translated as to weaken the message of the gospel. How do we determine which version to use? There are new expressions of worship, new ways to dress, new types of songs. Does it matter how we pray or what we wear or what songs we sing as long as our hearts are right and we wish to glorify God? Can we worship the Lord in the dance or portray him in a stage play or serve him in a group therapy session?

Does it make a difference if we come to church in blue jeans and sit on the floor, attire ourselves in high fashion and sit on padded pews, or wear work clothes and stay in our car while the "drive in" service is piped to the church parking lot? Does it matter if the songs are the old hymns of the faith, a syncopated jazz rendition of these hymns, soul music or "Christian rock"? Is it important who leads the congregation in prayer or conducts the singing or takes up the offering or speaks from the pulpit? Can women do any or all of the activities traditionally assigned to men? Can children serve God in these ways?

Many of us have never attended a church pastored by a woman. It would take some getting used to before we could adjust. But we need to know if it is just a matter of "getting used to"—as we have gotten used to women physicians, women lawyers, women sports announcers and women astronauts—or if the issue is much deeper than this.

Would that like the Samaritan woman we could ask Jesus directly what we should do (Jn 4). Then we would have the answer. Or would that an apostle Paul with direct revelation would write to the churches today telling us whether the present trend toward female clergy is blessed of God or whether it is a sign of the "falling away" of the last days (2 Thess 2:3). Then we would know if the reticence some of us feel toward change is based on a natural inclination to resist the new or if it is rooted in a discerning conscience that alerts us when things are not going as they should.

But Jesus is no longer with us in the flesh and Paul is not here to respond to our queries. The Living Word has been taken from us (Acts 1:9) and the written Word is closed to new revelation (Rev 22:18), leaving us to search the Scriptures in an effort to discern the will of God.

That change within society affects the church cannot be disputed. It behooves us to sort out which departures from the traditional are desirable and which are not. All of us conform to a degree to the customs of the day because we feel more comfortable doing so. We go to church in suits and dresses; first-century believers (both men and women) wore robes. We arrive in cars or other motorized vehicles; they came on foot or on horseback. We bring our Bibles; they did not have Bibles, nor could they read. We have Sunday school for our youth; they did not appear to make special provisions for the teaching of small children. After the morning service we return to our homes for dinner or we go to a restaurant; they were more apt to share a meal together.

We do not consider these differences between ourselves and the early Christians to fall within the realm of the spiritual or moral. Rather, they are simply differences in style, a natural consequence of the passage of time in societies not isolated from the rest of the world.

So, we may ask ourselves why it is that we consider change that takes place over several centuries to be all right, whereas change that takes place within the space of a few years not to be all right. Where do we draw the line? Some congregations that would have frowned thirty years ago on a woman wearing slacks to church see nothing wrong with it now because wearing slacks has become customary attire for women. Other congregations hold that if it was wrong for our grandmothers, it is wrong for our mothers and will be wrong for our daughters in the years to come. Yet, these same congregations do not advocate a return to the robes (dresses) worn by men and women during the first century.

To bring up such matters as personal attire or order of worship may seem tangential to the question of whether a woman should be the preaching minister of the church, but it isn't really. Each of the contributors to this book has supported his or her answer with a statement about a woman's appearance during the worship service and what this appearance signifies in relation to the woman's role in the church.

Robert Culver states that "men are to exercise authority and take leadership in the church. Women should acknowledge that authority and support it in every Christian way, including how they dress and adorn themselves when they attend public worship."

Susan Foh writes that "possibly women should be covered during corporate prayer and Scripture reading, but without doubt, women should be covered when they pray and read Scripture individually." She further writes that when in doubt "it may be better for a denomination or a church to make a provisional decision, such as a standard for hair length or style."

Thus, for both Culver and Foh, a woman's attire in church should signify her subjection to her husband. This subjection, in turn, means she is not "to teach, nor to usurp authority over the man, but to be in silence" (1 Tim 2:12 KJV). It follows directly that if a woman is not to teach or even say anything during the church service, she cannot become the preaching minister or pastor of the church.

Walter Liefeld and Alvera Mickelsen, by contrast, hold that Paul's stipulation of how women should dress and what they could or could not do during the worship service applied to a unique situation at the time of Paul's writings. Liefeld says that "in the first century, loose hair signified a prostitute" and that "not only women's appearance, but even the very act of their speaking publicly had serious implications in first-century society. . . . In Paul's day a woman's speaking and teaching in the church could constitute a moral problem and bring shame on the church and on the Lord." Liefeld further states that "Paul's principle, then, is not the wearing of veils or the silence of women, but rather conforming to Jewish and moralistic pagan norms for the sake of the gospel."

In a similar vein, Mickelsen maintains that "the instructions about hair styles were needed because of the prevalence of homosexuality. . . . Male homosexuals often wore long ornately arranged hair styles, and lesbians wore closely clipped hair." Mickelsen firmly believes that in today's world "restricted roles for men and women in church, family and society . . . are the result of sin and/or cultural influences." She also believes that the spiritual gifts of God to women are not essentially different from the gifts that God gives to men.

We are given, then, varying interpretations by four scholars who have a keen desire to understand the Word of God and to apply it to the Christian church. Each contributor has carefully studied the Bible and has an understandable explanation for the position taken. Each believes his or her view to be Christ-honoring and faithful to the message of the gospel. That differences in interpretation exist shows that God has not chosen to reveal in detail answers to all the questions we face today. What is important is that Christ is honored. All of us are laborers together with God (1 Cor 3:9). The Corinthian church was divided between the followers of Paul, Apollos and Cephas (1 Cor 3:22). Let us not fall into the same trap. Differences of opinion are to be expected and at times help us to grow in faith, but they must never keep us from acknowledging our unity in Christ. We are one with Christ even as Christ is one with God (v. 23).

What's Happening in Churches Today

Whatever our personal feelings may be concerning women as ordained clergy, statistics show that more and more women are becoming pastors of churches. This is true in almost every Protestant denomination. No longer are women willing to confine their talents to the church nursery or the choir, or to the washing of communion cups. As important as these duties are, and *someone* must do them, an increasing number of women feel they have the same abilities as men and these abilities should not be hid under a bushel. In the past if a woman showed herself a capable leader and speaker, she could teach small children or other women, or she could become a missionary and teach indigenous peoples, both male and female, young and old. But she was not to preach from the pulpit in her home church, especially if men were present. If, on occasion, special permission were granted, usually by an all-male board, her presentation would be called a "talk" or a "story" but never a "sermon" or a "message from the Word of God."

But as society changes its ideas on the role of men and women, the church is being asked to take another look at its policies and practices in this matter. As has been mentioned, the church, like all institutions, is affected by the mores and customs of the times. Now, with over half

the women in the United States in the labor force and with many
households headed by a woman, the whole concept of what a woman
does and what a man does is changing. The idyllic picture of the
nuclear family—a working father, homemaking mother, and two or
more children—may persist in people's minds but constitutes less
than six per cent of households in the United States.[3]

Right or wrong, the feminist movement and economic necessity
have placed women in almost every job traditionally held by men. The
wonder is not that women are entering the ministry in increasing
numbers but that the trend toward women clergy has not kept pace
with the trend toward women entering other professions such as med-
icine, law and engineering. This clearly shows that the church, by and
large, is more traditional than other organizations. It also reflects the
fact that the church cannot be mandated by law, as are state and
federal institutions, to be an equal-opportunity employer. The separation of church and state remains intact. Nor would we want it any
other way. Nevertheless, the trend toward women occupying the highest positions in the church has begun. And there is reason to believe
it will continue, gaining momentum as more churches consider a
woman pastor as a viable option.

Many of the newer evangelical denominations such as the Evangelical Free Church, Church of the Nazarene, the Wesleyan Methodist
and various Pentecostal groups were ordaining women in large
numbers at the turn of the century. A few mainline denominations—
namely, the American Baptists, the United Church of Christ, the Congregationalists, and the Disciples of Christ—also were ordaining wom-
en to the Christian ministry in the 1800s. However, it was not until
the middle of this century that the movement picked up speed. The
United Methodist Church and United Presbyterian Church followed
in 1956, Southern Baptists and the Presbyterian Church US in 1964,
American Lutheran and Lutheran Church in America in 1970, and
the Episcopal Church in 1976.[4] Most Protestant denominations now
favor the ordination of women, although the Catholic church and the
more fundamentalist Protestant groups do not.[5]

This does not mean one can find a woman minister within the
approving churches as readily as one would find a man in this role.
It is estimated that currently only eight to ten per cent of ministers

in denominations that ordain women are female,[6] and the overall numbers in all Protestant churches may be closer to seven per cent.[7] Denominations, such as the United Methodist Church, that place their ministers have a higher number of women clergy than denominations in which each local church is free to "call" whomever it wishes.[8] The tradition of the male minister runs deep, and the idea of having a woman pastor is still so foreign as not to be entertained by some congregations, even though the practice may be approved and encouraged by the denomination.

Studies show that the initial resistance to women in the pulpit often gives way to acceptance once contact with a woman minister has taken place.[9] "The *experience* of having a woman pastor seems to prove less traumatic than the idea."[10] The "horror stories" of what will happen simply do not materialize.[11] The stereotypic image of female clergy fades with contact, even as most stereotypes wane when friendships are formed.

Even so, some congregations will never change their negative views, for they will never know what it is like to have a woman minister. The reasons are varied. They may fear a loss of membership or a loss of revenues or perhaps disfavor with the community. Or they may wonder how a woman can be an effective leader and make tough decisions when women are supposed to be tender, sensitive and caring.[12] Or they may adopt a hierarchical explanation of Scripture as it relates to male-female relationships. In many cases it never occurs to the congregation to consider a woman. Whatever the reason, such attitudes understandably are of grave concern to those women who feel called to the ministry but have not been able to obtain a position.

That more women will seek the pastorate as their chosen profession is reflected in the increase in female seminarians in the United States and Canada, an increase from 3,358—or ten per cent of the total—in 1972 to 14,572—or twenty-six per cent of the total—in 1985.[13] All women in seminary do not plan to enter the clergy even as all men in seminary do not plan on becoming clergymen; yet many women will seek a parish position, and this will create an even greater demand than in the past. The extent to which seminaries will respond by trying to place their female graduates remains to be seen, and the degree to which churches will respond by considering a woman pastor is difficult to predict. The leaders of the more fundamentalist denominations often discourage women from entering their seminaries for the purpose of ordination and may actively speak from the pulpit against women preachers.[14]

There are a number of ways a woman may enter the preaching ministry other than being called as a full-time pastor. One possibility is to be half of a husband-wife team known as the clergy-couple. The Salvation Army has been ordaining husbands and their wives since 1880, and the Pentecostal church has done the same since the early twentieth century. But it was not until the 1970s that other Protestant denominations visibly followed suit. The United Methodists, the United Church of Christ and the Disciples of Christ are now leading in the number of ministers married to each other. Most clergy-couples are young and serve the church equally, sharing the pulpit as well as other parish-related tasks. Depending on the needs and size of the congregation, the two may be hired as one full-time equivalent or as much as two full-time equivalents. They may serve one or more congregations.[15]

Another way is for a woman to serve as the interim pastor until a permanent replacement can be found. This may or may not lead to her being asked to become the regular minister but does appear to prepare a church to consider a woman when the final decision is made. Also, a small church with limited funds may ask a lay person to fill the pulpit. This may be a woman as well as a man, often without seminary training, but nevertheless a person who knows the English Bible and has served as Sunday-school teacher or missionary for a number of years. She or he may have a full-time job not related to the church but by speaking only on Sundays is able to do both well.

Other times the assistant minister or the director of Christian education will be asked to fill the pulpit for a period of time. Again, this may be a woman well known to the parishioners who is preferred to an "unknown" from outside the congregation.[16] Another "known" is the minister's wife who may be asked to preach if her husband is ill or on assignment. Some women have succeeded to the pulpit upon the death of their minister husbands. Whatever the arrangement, each time a woman speaks from the pulpit, the church will become less resistant to the idea of a woman minister. Such an outcome is applauded by those who believe that women as well as men are called by God to proclaim his Word to the church. Those who are against women clergy view this trend as contrary to Scripture and an evil that must be resisted.

As has been mentioned, most evangelical churches have not yet faced the question of a woman minister. Only men have served as pastors, and it does not occur to the laity that it will ever be otherwise. Even if women are enrolled in their denominational seminaries and even if the denomination at the national level favors the ordination of women, members of the local church do not see this as affecting them in any way. They may go to the ordination of the daughter of a friend or they may hear a woman preach on television, but they do not see this as having any bearing on their own congregation.

How long will it be this way? How long will it be someone else's church that has the woman minister but not our own? How long will the more fundamentalist churches remain firm in their resolve not to allow a woman to fill the pulpit?[17] Will there ever be a time when both women and men are considered equally qualified to preach the gospel? The answers are not known. We can only wait and see. We may know the answers in our lifetime or we may not. But for those of us whose lives are directly affected by the church and what happens to the church, we are more than a little curious as to the outcome.

What we do know is that change will come. The church, like all institutions, has changed in the past and will continue to change in the future. Sometimes the changes come slowly and perhaps laboriously, and sometimes they come quickly and perhaps without adequate preparation. But they do come. The church board may or may not approve of calling a woman to be the pastor of the congregation, but church boards come and go. The man who never would have considered the possibility of his wife being a preacher now proudly tells the world that his daughter is preparing for the Christian ministry. We want for our children what we may not have wanted for ourselves, and we commend in our children what we may not have commended in ourselves.

Women seminarians are praying for the opportunity to serve God as ordained ministers. At the same time their prayers rise to heaven, those against women clergy are praying that God will withstand the feminine forces of evil and roll back the tide of women preachers. Both the egalitarians and the traditionalists believe that God is on their side. Both feel they have the truth and that the truth will prevail. Furthermore, both are wary of the other believing that the opposing party has a larger agenda than just that of a woman becoming a minister or not becoming a minister. Both know that the answer to the question of women in Christian ministry has ramifications that extend beyond the church. As Krister Stendahl put it in an address at Harvard University, "The question about the ordination of women is not a question about offices but a question about the right relationship between man and woman in Christ, whether it applies to political office, civil service, career, home life, the ministry, or to the episcopate."[18] Is it any wonder that emotions run high when the question of women clergy is debated?

Whether the particular view we hold is correct or incorrect concerning women in Christian ministry, we are assured in Holy Scripture that God loves the church and will "present it to himself a glorious church, not having spot, or wrinkle, or any such thing; but that it should be holy and without blemish" (Eph 5:27 KJV). This should give us great comfort. God will take our strivings to please him, whether on course or misguided, and use them for his glory and for the edifying of the church. Even our prayers are edited so they are acceptable to God (Rom 8:26). Let us then share together in the joy that we are part of that great body of believers called the church. May the communion we have as heirs and joint-heirs with Christ overshadow our differences, and may our kinship within the family of God take precedence over our varying perceptions.

Notes

[1]There are several varieties of feminism, the major ones being *liberal feminism* that asks for equal educational and professional opportunities for women, *Marxist feminism* that believes women will only achieve equality when there is a classless society, *radical feminism* that opts for the abolition of the social institution of gender, and *social feminism* that incorporates Marxist and radical views calling for the elimination of both a class society and the institution of gender. Liberal feminists, which include both men and women, compose the largest group of feminists and are solidly for the passage of the Equal Rights Amendment. The use of the term "radical feminist" to apply to all feminists is inappropriate. For the application of the varieties of feminism to the home, the school and the workplace, see Elaine Storkey, *What's Right with*

Feminism (Grand Rapids: Eerdmans, 1985), and Alison Jaggar and Paula Struhl, *Feminist Frameworks* (New York: McGraw-Hill, 1978).

[2]Observation and research often support the view that both the society and the individual are better off if females are not restricted to traditional feminine roles and males are not restricted to traditional masculine roles. For example, had Corazon Aquino remained a housewife, the Philippine peoples would have missed the best thing that could have happened to them. Similarly, if children within the family have only *one* parent who is nurturing and warm, they, too, will miss the best thing that could happen to them. Men and women need to cultivate those traits, whether stereotypically male or female, that expand the range of behaviors open to them, permitting them to cope effectively in a wide variety of situations. In a study conducted by Sandra Bem ("Androgyny Vs. the Tight Little Lives of Fluffy Women and Chesty Men," *Psychology Today*, Sept. 1975, pp. 59-62) the "macho" type male not only was uncomfortable with a kitten or small baby and the "fluffy" type female not only felt helpless when asked to oil a hinge or pound nails into a board, but *both* suffered from lower self-esteem than did individuals who had personality characteristics typical of both males and females. Inge Broverman and four others ("Sex Role Stereotypes; A Current Appraisal," *Journal of Social Psychology* 28, no. 2 [1972]:59-78) asked mental health professionals, both men and women, to check the personality characteristics of the "mature, healthy, socially competent adult person." These clinicians had previously checked the personality characteristics of the "mature, healthy, socially competent adult man" and the "mature, healthy, socially competent adult woman." Interestingly, the characteristics of the healthy adult person were more apt to be the characteristics ascribed to men than the characteristics ascribed to women. This puts women in a double bind. If they have the characteristics of the mature, healthy, socially competent person, they are accused of being masculine. If they do not have these characteristics, they are considered not to be psychologically healthy. For additional research, see Richard Kahoe, "The Psychology and Theology of Sexism" in *Journal of Psychology and Theology* 2 (Fall 1974):284-90. Using college students as the subjects, Kahoe noted that "basic sexism was associated generally with maladaptive personality variables" (p. 284).

[3]Joseph Giovannini, "Nuclear family brings changes in housing" (New York Times News Service, Nov. 18, 1984) as reported in the *Terre Haute Tribune Star*, Sec. D, p. 10.

[4]Judith Weidman, "Introduction," *Women Ministers: How Women are Redefining Traditional Roles*, ed. Judith Weidman (New York: Harper & Row, 1985), pp. 1-11. See also Pamela Salazar, "Theological Education of Women for Ordination," *Religious Education* 82 (Winter 1987):67-79.

[5]Weidman, *Women Ministers*, p. 2. Also, Linda Watkins reports in "Women Ministers Face a Host of Obstacles in Chosen Profession," *Wall Street Journal*, Dec. 24, 1986, that "many members of the Southern Baptist Convention—in which women make up just 2% of the church's nearly 17,000 ordained ministers—are trying to stop ordaining women." Their objection is "based on biblical interpretations," p. 6. Velma Ferrell ("Called to Serve: Women in the Southern Baptist Convention," *Faith and Mission* 2 [Fall 1984]: 18-29) sees the resolution passed at the Southern Baptist Convention's 1984 meeting opposing the ordination of women as inconsistent with early Baptist practice and doctrine and states that even though women are excluded by many local churches, Southern Baptist women are being ordained in greater numbers today.

Derk Roelofsma, in "Besieging Church Barriers to Women in the Ministry" *(Insight, Washington Times,* April 6, 1987, pp. 12-13) writes that the Episcopal Church faces the threat of schism over the ordination of women. "A sizable number of Episcopalians have never accepted the changes made at the church's 1976 General Convention. One change was approving women as priests" (p. 12). The belief in "apostolic succession" seems to be the reason for the objection. Jesus chose only men, and Episcopal bishops are the successors to these apostles. The prediction that "very probably there will be at least one woman consecrated as a bishop in the next five years" (p. 12) is therefore very disconcerting to some Episcopalians. A woman bishop has since been elected in the Diocese of Massachusetts.

[6]Watkins, "Women Ministers Face a Host of Obstacles," p. 1.

[7]Weidman, *Women Ministers,* p. 3. Derk Roelofsma ("Women Making New Trip to Altar," *Insight, Washington Times,* April 6, 1987, pp. 8-11) puts the figure closer to five per cent. This is based on the following statistics: United Methodist Church with a membership of 9.2 million has 3,117 women clergy out of a total clergy of 37,500; United Church of Christ with 1.7 million members has 1,500 women clergy out of 10,000 total; Presbyterian U.S.A. with 3 million members has 1,421 women out of 19,450 total; Lutheran with 5.4 million has 821 women to 17,000 total; Episcopal with 2.7 million has 800 women priests to 13,000 total; and Southern Baptist with 14.6 million has 350 women clergy out of 60,000 total.

[8]One must keep in mind that not all men and women ordained to the ministry serve as pastors. Nor do all remain in the pastorate after a position is accepted. One drawback is that the candidate may feel he or she is not in the right church. For women, the United Methodist Church has the best record, having placed 2,262 women out of 3,117 ordained women. This is in contrast to 500 out of 1,500 ordained women for the United Church of Christ, 358 out of 1,421 for the Presbyterians, 230 out of 800 for the Episcopal Church, and 136 out of 821 for the Lutherans. See Roelofsma, "Women Making New Trip to Altar," p. 11, for this information. No comparison figures are given for men who are ordained.

[9]Marjorie Royle's review of the literature on this topic ("Women Pastors: What Happens After Placement?" *Review of Religious Research* 24 ([Dec. 1982]:116-26) shows that generally "women are accepted and supported by their parishioners once they are known" (p. 117). She matched 129 full-time clergywomen (14 from the Disciples of Christ, 21 from the Lutheran Church in America, 35 from the United Methodist Church and 59 from the United Presbyterian Church) with 129 full-time clergymen of the same denominations and found no significant differences in the size of church served, attendance or financial matters. Men and women ministers did differ, however, in marital status, the men being more apt to be married. In another study, Edward Lehman, Jr. *(Women Clergy: Breaking Through Gender Barriers* [New Brunswick, N.J.: Transaction Books, 1985]) also found that "contact with women in the role of pastor tends to be a positive experience for church members. The experience transforms resistance into acceptance" (p. 288). Lehman noticed, though, that acceptance in some churches centered on the particular woman who was the minister rather than on clergywomen in general.

[10]Weidman, *Women Ministers,* p. 6.

[11]Lehman, *Women Clergy,* p. 272.

[12]Katherine Flagg ("Psychological Androgyny and Self-Esteem in Clergywomen," *Journal of Psychology and Theology* 12 [1984]:222-29) studied 114 female ministers from ten

Protestant denominations in New England by using the Bem Sex-Role Inventory (BSRI) and the Texas Social Behavior Inventory. Thirty-two per cent were classified as Androgynous, scoring high on both Masculine and Feminine scales, 31% were Undifferentiated, 24% were Feminine, and 16% were Masculine. Androgynous and Masculine clergywomen scored significantly higher on self-esteem than did the other two groups, and Masculinity was also positively correlated with higher income. Better-educated, career-oriented women are more apt to have the personality characteristics of androgyny or masculinity than is true for women in general. This makes them successful in their professions. The majority of the ministers in this study were also wives and mothers.

In another study, this time with seminarians (W. Mack Goldsmith & Bonita Neville Ekhardt, "Personality Factors of Men and Women Pastoral Candidates, Part 2: Sex-Role Preferences," *Journal of Psychology and Theology* 12 [1984]:211-21), data was collected from 90 male and 114 female students in 11 Protestant seminaries. The BSRI was used with the result that males and females did not significantly differ in their responses. Both men and women seminarians are more androgynous than are males and females in the population at large. This should stand them in good stead for the large variety of tasks that ministers are to take care of within the church. In an earlier report ("Personality Factors of Men and Women Pastoral Candidates, Part 1: Motivational Profiles," *Journal of Psychology and Theology* 12 [1984]:109-18), Goldsmith and Ekhardt write: "As Christians, we may approve ordaining women or not on theological grounds. As psychologists, we should have no categorical objections to their adequacy as persons to serve" (p. 117).

[13]Watkins, "Women Ministers Face a Host of Obstacles," *USA Today,* June 17, 1987, p. 1, lists the percentage of women in theological schools as 25.8 in 1985 and 26.4 in 1986.

[14]An example is the moderator's address to the ninety-seventh annual conference of Brethren Churches delivered by John Mayes in Winona Lake, Indiana, on August 3, 1986. Dr. Mayes stated that the three great evils Christians must oppose are abortion, homosexuality and women clergy. The printed statement of Mayes's remarks ("Is Revival the Hope of the Grace Brethren Church?" *1987 Grace Brethren Annual* [Winona Lake: The Brethren Missionary Herald, 1987], pp. 5-12) omitted his negative comments on women ministers although "women in the clergy" was included in the final list of recommendations as to what the Social Concerns Committee should withstand. (See introduction to this book for the early practice of ordaining women in the Brethren Church.)

[15]For an interesting account of how one clergy couple, each hired three-quarters time, works together and divides the responsibilities, see Linda McKiernon-Allen and Ronald J. Allen's "Colleagues in Marriage and Ministry" in Weidman, *Women Ministers,* pp. 207-20.

[16]Career opportunities in Christian education have declined with decreased enrollments in Sunday school, vacation church schools and summer camps. Women seminarians who formerly would have opted to become the director of a Christian education program in a church now may consider becoming a pastor instead. For an example, see "Unboxing Christian Education" by Martha Rowlett in Weidman, *Women Ministers,* pp. 123-34.

[17]Some of us remember when the more conservative churches were solidly against television, and we as members of these churches vowed we would never own one.

But that era seems to have passed and gradually the television sets appeared in our homes, and with the passage of time the concern about the corrupting influence of this form of communication has lessened. This is not to say that television does not corrupt, for there is ample evidence that it does. Nor is it to imply that television is comparable to the question of women ministers. But it does serve as an example of how readily we can change our minds and behaviors concerning an issue, even though at one time we would not have thought it possible to do so.

[18]Krister Stendahl, *The Bible and the Role of Women: A Case Study in Hermeneutics,* trans. Emilie T. Sander (Philadelphia: Fortress Press, 1966), p. 43. Professor Stendahl, a clergyman of the Church of Sweden, was active in the 1950s in the debates over the ordination of women as priests in the Church of Sweden. (The question was officially settled in the affirmative in 1958.) Stendahl later became Dean of Harvard Divinity School and a member of the Executive Council of the Lutheran Church in America.

SELECTED BIBLIOGRAPHY

Bainton, Roland H. *Women of the Reformation in France and England.* Minneapolis: Augsburg, 1973.

_____ . *Women of the Reformation in Germany and Italy.* Minneapolis: Augsburg, 1971.

_____ . *Women of the Reformation in Spain to Scandinavia.* Minneapolis: Augsburg, 1977.

Bartchy, S. Scott. "Power, Submission, and Sexual Identity among the Early Christians." In *Essays on New Testament Christianity,* edited by C. Robert Wetzel. Cincinnati: Standard Publishing, 1978.

Beaver, R. Pierce. *American Protestant Women in World Mission: A History of the First Feminist Movement in North America.* Grand Rapids: Eerdmans, 1980.

Bilezikian, Gilbert. *Beyond Sex Roles.* Grand Rapids: Baker, 1985.

Boldney, Richard, and Boldney, Joyce. *Chauvinist or Feminist? Paul's View of Women.* Grand Rapids: Baker, 1976.

Booth, Catherine. *Female Ministry: Or, Woman's Right to Preach the Gospel.* New York: Salvation Army, 1975.

Boulding, Elise. *The Underside of History: A View of Women through Time.* Boulder: Westview Press, 1976.

Boyd, Lois A., and Douglas H. Brakenridge. *Presbyterian Women in*

America: Two Centuries of a Quest for Status. London: Greenwood, 1983.

Brown, Earl Kent. *Women in Mr. Wesley's Methodism.* New York: Mellen, 1983.

Bruce, Michael, and G. E. Duffield. *Why Not? Priesthood and the Ministry of Women.* Appleford, Abingdon: Marcham Books, 1976.

Brunner, Peter. *The Ministry and the Ministry of Women.* St. Louis: Concordia, 1971.

Carroll, Jackson W., Barbara Hargrove and Adair Lummls. *Women of the Cloth: A New Opportunity for the Churches.* San Francisco: Harper & Row, 1982.

Clark, Stephen B. *Man and Woman in Christ: An Examination of the Roles of Men & Women in Light of Scripture and Social Sciences.* Ann Arbor: Servant Books, 1980.

Culver, Elsie Thomas. *Women in the World of Religion.* Garden City, N.Y.: Doubleday, 1967.

Dayton, Donald. *Discovering an Evangelical Heritage.* New York: Harper & Row, 1976.

Dayton, Donald W., ed. *Holiness Tracts Defending the Ministry of Women.* New York: Garland, 1985.

Doohan, Helen. *Leadership in Paul.* Wilmington: Michael Glazier, 1984.

Elliot, Elisabeth. *Let Me Be a Woman.* Wheaton: Tyndale, 1976.

Evans, Mary J. *Woman in the Bible.* Downers Grove: InterVarsity, 1983.

Fell, Margaret. *Women's Speaking Justified.* Los Angeles: University of California Press, 1979.

Fiorenza, Elisabeth Schüssler. *In Memory of Her.* New York: Crossroad, 1983.

Fitzwater, P. B. *Women: Her Mission, Position, and Ministry.* Grand Rapids: Eerdmans, 1949.

Foh, Susan T. *Women and the Word of God: A Response to Biblical Feminism.* Phillipsburg, N.J.: Presbyterian and Reformed, 1980.

Gardiner, Anne Marie, ed. *Women and Catholic Priesthood: An Expanded Vision.* New York: Paulist Press, 1976.

Gibson, Elsie. *When the Minister Is a Woman.* New York: Holt, Rinehart, and Winston, 1970.

Giles, Kevin. *Women and Their Ministry: A Case for Equal Ministries in the Church Today*. Victoria, Australia: Dove Communications, 1977.

Greaves, Richard L., ed. *Triumph over Silence: Women in Protestant History*. Westport, Conn.: Greenwood Press, 1985.

Gundry, Patricia. *Woman Be Free*. Grand Rapids: Zondervan, 1977.

──────. *Heirs Together*. Grand Rapids: Zondervan, 1980.

──────. *Neither Slave nor Free: Helping Women Answer the Call to Church Leadership*. San Francisco: Harper & Row, 1987.

Hamilton, Michael P., and Nancy S. Montgomery. *The Ordination of Women Pro and Con*. New York: Morehouse-Barlow, 1975.

Hardesty, Nancy. *Great Women of the Christian Faith*. Grand Rapids: Baker, 1980.

Harkness, Georgia. *Women in Church and Society: A Historical and Theological Inquiry*. Nashville: Abingdon, 1972.

Hartman, Mary S., and Lois Banner, eds. *Clio's Consciousness Raised: New Perspectives on the History of Women*. New York: Harper & Row, 1974.

Hassey, Janette. *No Time for Silence: Evangelical Women in Public Ministry Around the Turn of the Century*. Grand Rapids: Zondervan, 1986.

Hearn, Virginia. *Our Struggle to Serve: The Stories of 15 Evangelical Women*. Waco, Tex.: Word, 1979.

Hestenes, Roberta, ed. *Women and Men in Ministry*. Philadelphia: Westminster, 1984.

Hill, Patricia R. *The World Their Household: The American Woman's Foreign Mission Movement and Cultural Transformation, 1870-1920*. Ann Arbor: University of Michigan Press, 1985.

Howe, E. Margaret. *Women and Church Leadership*. Grand Rapids: Zondervan, 1982.

Hull, Eleanor. *Women Who Carried the Good News: The History of the Woman's American Baptist Home Mission Society*. Valley Forge: Judson, 1975.

Hull, Gretchen Gaebelein. *Equal to Serve: Women and Men in the Church and Home*. Old Tappan, N.J.: Revell, 1987.

Hurley, James B. *Man and Woman in Biblical Perspective*. Grand Rapids: Zondervan, 1981.

Irwin, Joyce L. *Womanhood in Radical Protestantism, 1525-1675*. New York: Mellen, 1979.

Jewett, Paul K. *Man as Male and Female*. Grand Rapids: Eerdmans, 1975.

—————. *The Ordination of Women*. Grand Rapids: Eerdmans, 1980.

Johnson, Dale A. *Women in English Religion, 1700-1925*. New York: Mellen, 1983.

Knight, George W., III. *The Role Relationship of Men and Women: New Testament Teaching*. Chicago: Moody, 1985.

LaHaye, Beverly. *I Am a Woman by God's Design*. Old Tappan, N.J.: Revell, 1982.

Larsson, Flora. *My Best Men Are Women*. London: Hodder and Stoughton, 1974.

Lees, Shirley, ed. *The Role of Women*. Leicester, England: Inter-Varsity Press, 1984.

Lehman, Edward C., Jr. *Women Clergy: Breaking through Gender Barriers*. New Brunswick: Transaction Books, 1985.

Lindskoog, Kathryn. *Up from Eden*. Elgin: Cook, 1976.

MacHaffie, Barbara J. *HerStory: Women in Christian Tradition*. Philadelphia: Fortress, 1986.

Malcolm, Kari Torjesen. *Women at the Crossroads: A Path beyond Feminism and Traditionalism*. Downers Grove: InterVarsity, 1982.

McBeth, Leon. *Women in Baptist Life*. Nashville: Broadman, 1979.

Mercadante, Linda. *From Hierarchy to Equality: A Comparison of Past and Present Interpretations of I Corinthians 11:2-16 in Relation to the Changing Status of Women in Society*. Vancouver, B.C.: G.M.H. Books, 1978.

Mickelsen, Alvera, ed. *Women, Authority and the Bible*. Downers Grove: InterVarsity, 1986.

Micks, Marianne H., and Charles P. Price, eds. *Toward a New Theology of Ordination: Essays on the Ordination of Women*. Somerville, Mass.: Greeno, Hadden, 1976.

Mollenkott, Virginia Ramey. *Women, Men and the Bible*. Nashville: Abingdon, 1977.

—————. *The Divine Feminine*. New York: Crossroad, 1983.

Morris, Joan. *Against Nature and God*. London: Mowbrays, 1973.

—————. *Pope John VIII—an English Woman alias Pope Joan*. London: Vrai, 1985.

Otwell, John H. *And Sarah Laughed: The Status of Women in the Old Testament.* Philadelphia: Westminster, 1975.

Penn-Lewis, Jessie. *The Magna Charta of Woman.* 1919. Reprint. Minneapolis: Bethany House, 1975.

Porterfield, Amanda. *Feminine Spirituality in America: From Sarah Edwards to Martha Graham.* Philadelphia: Temple University Press, 1980.

Raming, Ida. *The Exclusion of Women from the Priesthood: Divine Law or Sex Discrimination?* Trans. Norman R. Adams. Metuchen, N.J.: Scarecrow Press, 1976.

Rice, John R. *Bobbed Hair, Bossy Wives, and Women Preachers.* Murfreesboro, Tenn.: Sword of the Lord Publishers, 1941.

Rich, Elaine S. *Mennonite Women: A Story of God's Faithfulness, 1683-1983.* Scottdale, Penn.: Herald, 1983.

Robbins, John W. *Scripture Twisting in the Seminaries, Part I: Feminism.* Jefferson, Md.: Trinity Foundation, 1985.

Ruether, Rosemary. *Womanguide: Readings toward a Feminist Theology.* Boston: Beacon, 1985.

Ruether, Rosemary, and Eleanor McLaughlin, eds. *Women of Spirit: Female Leadership in the Jewish and Christian Traditions.* New York: Simon and Schuster, 1979.

Ruether, Rosemary, and Rosemary Keller, eds. *Women and Religion in America: The Nineteenth Century.* Vol. 1. New York: Harper & Row, 1981.

——————. *Women and Religion in America: The Colonial and Revolutionary Period.* Vol. 2. New York: Harper & Row, 1983.

——————. *Women and Religion in America: 1900-1968.* Vol. 3. New York: Harper & Row, 1986.

Russell, Letty M., ed. *Feminist Interpretation of the Bible.* Philadelphia: Westminster, 1985.

Ryrie, Charles C. *The Place of Women in the Church.* New York: Macmillan, 1958.

Sannella, Lucia. *The Female Pentecost.* Port Washington, N.Y.: Ashley, 1976.

Sayers, Dorothy L. *Are Women Human?* Downers Grove: InterVarsity, 1975.

Scanzoni, Letha, and Nancy Hardesty. *All We're Meant to Be: Biblical*

Feminism for Today. Waco, Tex.: Word, 1974.

Schmidt, Elisabeth. *When God Calls a Woman: The Struggle of a Woman Pastor in France and Algeria.* Translated by Allen Hackett. New York: Pilgrim, 1981.

Smith, John W. *Heralds of a Brighter Day: Biographical Sketches of Early Leaders in the Church of God Reformation Movement.* Anderson, Ind.: Gospel Trumpet, 1955.

Spencer, Aida Besançon. *Beyond the Curse: Women Called to Ministry.* Nashville: Thomas Nelson, 1985.

Stagg, Frank, and Evelyn Stagg. *Woman in the World of Jesus.* Philadelphia: Westminster, 1978.

Stendahl, Krister. *The Bible and the Role of Women: A Case Study in Hermeneutics.* Translated by Emilie T. Sander. Philadelphia: Fortress Press, 1966.

Storkey, Elaine. *What's Right with Feminism.* Grand Rapids: Eerdmans, 1986.

Stuard, Susan M., ed. *Women in Medieval Society.* Philadelphia: University of Pennsylvania Press, 1976.

Stuhlmueller, Carroll, ed. *Women and Priesthood: Future Directions.* Collegeville, Minn.: Liturgical Press, 1978.

Swartley, Willard M. *Slavery, Sabbath, War, and Women: Case Issues in Biblical Interpretation.* Scottdale, Penn.: Herald, 1983.

Swidler, Leonard. *Biblical Affirmations of Woman.* Philadelphia: Westminster, 1979.

Swidler, Leonard, and Arlene Swidler, eds. *Women Priests: A Catholic Commentary on the Vatican Declaration.* New York: Paulist Press, 1977.

Tetlow, Elizabeth. *Women and Ministry in the New Testament.* Ramsey, N.J.: Paulist, 1980.

Theology News and Notes: Women in Ministry (1985). Published for the Fuller Theological Seminary Alumni/ae.

Troutt, Margaret. *The General Was a Lady: The Story of Evangeline Booth.* Nashville: Holman, 1980.

Tucker, Ruth A. *From Jerusalem to Irian Jaya: A Biographical History of Christian Missions.* Grand Rapids: Zondervan, 1983.

Tucker, Ruth A., and Walter L. Liefeld. *Daughters of the Church: Women and Ministry from New Testament Times to the Present.* Grand Rapids:

Zondervan, 1987.

van der Meer, Haye. *Women Priests in the Catholic Church? A Theological-Historical Investigation.* Philadelphia: Temple University Press, 1973.

Verdesi, Elizabeth Howell. *In But Still Out: Women in the Church.* Philadelphia: Westminster, 1975.

Warkentin, Marjorie. *Ordination: A Biblical-Historical View.* Grand Rapids: Eerdmans, 1982.

Weidman, Judith, ed. *Women Ministers: How Women are Redefining Traditional Roles.* San Francisco: Harper & Row, 1985.

Willard, Frances. *Women in the Pulpit.* 1889. Reprint. Originally printed in Chicago by the Woman's Temperance Publication Association in 1889. Reprinted in Washington D.C.: Zenger Publishing Company, 1978.

Willard, Frances E., and Mary A. Livermore, eds. *A Woman of the Century: Fourteen Hundred-Seventy Biographical Sketches of Leading American Women.* Chicago: Moulton, 1893.

Williams, Don. *The Apostle Paul and Women in the Church.* Van Nuys, Calif.: BIM, 1977.

Wyker, Mossie A. *Church Women in the Scheme of Things.* St. Louis: Bethany, 1953.

Zerbst, Fritz. *The Office of Woman in the Church: A Study of Practical Theology.* Translated by Albert G. Merkens. St. Louis: Concordia, 1955.

CONTRIBUTING AUTHORS

Bonnidell Clouse, professor of educational and school psychology at Indiana State University, was educated at Wheaton College (B.A.), Boston University (M.A.) and Indiana University (Ph.D.). Her publications include over two dozen articles in such periodicals as *Journal of Psychology and Theology, Christianity Today, The Reformed Journal* and *Journal of the American Scientific Affiliation.* Her major work is the book *Moral Development: Perspectives in Psychology and Christian Belief.*

Robert G. Clouse is a professor of history at Indiana State University, Terre Haute, and also is an ordained Brethren minister, having served churches in Iowa and Indiana. He graduated from Bryan College (B.A.), Grace Theological Seminary (B.D.) and the University of Iowa (M.A. and Ph.D.). As a student of the history of Christian thought, Clouse has edited *The Meaning of the Millennium: Four Views* and *The Cross and the Flag.* Other publications include *War: Four Christian Views* and *The Church in the Age of Orthodoxy and the Enlightenment.*

Robert D. Culver has taught at Grace Theological Seminary, Wheaton College, Trinity Evangelical Divinity School and Northwestern College. He has served as minister in the Fellowship of Grace Brethren churches and the Evangelical Free Church. He holds degrees from Heidelberg College (A.B.) and Grace Theological Seminary (B.D., Th.M., Th.D.). His published work includes numerous articles in books and learned periodicals as well as a major commentary, *Daniel and the Latter Days,* and a book on the Christian and the state entitled *Toward a Biblical View of Civil Government.*

Susan T. Foh is a graduate of Wellesley College (B.A.) and of Westminster Theological Seminary (M.A.). She has contributed articles and book reviews to various journals and the chapter "Abortion and Women's Lib" to the book *Thou Shalt Not Kill: The Christian Case Against Abortion.* She has written *Women and the Word of God: A Response to Biblical Feminism.*

Walter L. Liefeld has studied at Shelton College (Th.B.), Columbia University (M.A., Ph.D.), Union Theological Seminary and Tübingen University. He has been a minister to several Baptist churches, an InterVarsity staff member and a teacher at Shelton College. He currently serves as professor of New Testament at Trinity Evangelical Divinity School. In addition to numerous articles in publications such as *The Journal of the Evangelical Theological Society,* he has been a contributing translator to the New International Version of the Bible and has written the commentary on the Gospel of Luke in *The Expositor's Bible Commentary.* His most recent book (with Ruth Tucker) is *Daughters of the Church: Women and Ministry from New Testament Times to the Present.*

Alvera Mickelsen is a graduate of Wheaton College (B.S., M.A.) and Northwestern University (M.S. in Journalism). She has taught at Wheaton College and at Bethel College, and has served as editor for *Christian Life Magazine, The Conservative Baptist* and David C. Cook Publications. In addition to numerous articles, her publications include the following volumes: *Better Bible Study, Family Bible Encyclopedia, Understanding Scripture* and *Women, Authority and the Bible.*